Forrest "Forddy" Anderson is Head Basketball Coach at Michigan State University. He previously coached winning teams at Great Lakes Naval Station and at Drake University and Bradley University. He is also the author of *Basketball Techniques Illustrated* published by The Ronald Press Company.

Stan Albeck is Head Basketball Coach at Northern Michigan University. He previously coached at Michigan State University, where he received his M.A., and at Adrian College, and was Michigan Coach of the Year for the 1960-61 season.

COACHING BETTER BASKETBALL

FORREST ANDERSON

MICHIGAN STATE UNIVERSITY

STAN ALBECK

NORTHERN MICHIGAN UNIVERSITY

THE RONALD PRESS COMPANY • NEW YORK

Library of Congress Catalog Card Number: 64–22166

PRINTED IN THE UNITED STATES OF AMERICA

To

Dr. Edgar L. Harden
PRESIDENT, NORTHERN MICHIGAN UNIVERSITY

Dr. John Hannah
PRESIDENT, MICHIGAN STATE UNIVERSITY

and

Hank Fisher
sportscaster and friend extraordinary

Preface

The human and technical aspects of basketball and ways to build better basketball are the prime considerations of this book. In it we bring together our own philosophy, theories, and ideas concerning this great game. The materials and methods included here have been used successfully by ourselves or by our fellow coaches.

Some people believe the coach's job begins and ends on the court. This book rebuts this fallacy, and deals not only with the floor game, but also with the many incidental factors that make the basketball program a success. Several chapters are designed to acquaint the reader with the innumerable "after-practice" duties of a basketball coach.

Basketball has been good to us. It is our hope that this book, in turn, will be good for basketball and will prove of value to everyone interested in the game, whether coach, player, or spectator.

The completion of the book must be credited to many people. We wish to express our particular thanks and appreciation to: Jeanne Martel and Peggy White for their endless hours of typing with patience; James Jacobson for the line drawings; Bob Brumm, Paul Suomi, and Clair Hekhuis for their constructive criticisms of the manuscript; Charles Mangrum, Fred Stabley, and Nick Vista for the photography; and Gary Silc, Bob Armstead, Bob Pecotte, and Dave Cade for posing for the still pictures.

We are also most grateful to the young men who have worked and played so hard for us, and, finally, to our wives and families—the biggest inspiration of all.

FORREST ANDERSON
STAN ALBECK

Contents

COACHING
BETTER
BASKETBALL

1

Basketball Progress

As faculty instructors, and in teaching prospective coaches in theory classes, we find that many students have little knowledge of the game of basketball. This is due, in part, to their limited background in the sport and to the fact that not a great deal of time is allotted to the history of the game.

A good knowledge of the game can be gained by learning its rudiments, since, although the rule interpretations have changed quite frequently, the standards of equipment and dimensions remain basically the same as in the original rules.

The purpose of this chapter is to describe briefly for the student and coach the evolution of the game from its origin to the present. Among the highlights included are the original 13 rules for the game of basketball.

HISTORY

Basketball was originally planned to provide a game which could be played indoors throughout the winter months by groups of participants ranging in number from nine to 50 players. Actually, there was no real limit made to the number of men placed on the floor, since it was a game designed for mass participation in order to provide activity for as many students as possible.

Credited as the inventor of basketball is Dr. James A. Naismith, who, in 1891, organized the first game at Springfield College in Massachusetts. This game took place during a regular physical education class under the supervision of Dr. Naismith. Naismith's game had only thirteen rules, as contrasted to our present set of almost 500 different rule interpretations. Incidentally, the first rulebook was published in 1892 with these rules:

3

1. The ball may be thrown in any direction with one or both hands.
2. The ball may be batted in any direction with one or both hands (never with the fist).
3. A player cannot run with the ball. The player must throw it from the spot on which he catches it; allowance to be made for a man who catches the ball when running at a good speed.
4. The ball must be held in or between the hands; the arms or body must not be used for holding it.
5. No shouldering, holding, pushing, tripping, or striking, in any way, the person of an opponent shall be allowed; the first infringement of this rule shall disqualify the player until the next goal is made, or if there was evident intent to injure the person for the whole of the game, no substitute allowed.
6. A foul is striking at the ball with the fist, violation of rules 3, 4, and such as described in Rule 5.
7. If either side makes three consecutive fouls, it shall count a goal for the opponents. (Consecutive means without the opponents in the meantime making a foul.)
8. A goal shall be made when the ball is thrown or batted from the grounds into the basket and stays there, providing those defending the goal do not touch or disturb the goal. If the ball rests on the edge and the opponent moves the basket, it shall count as a goal.
9. When the ball goes out of bounds, it shall be thrown into the field and played by the person first touching it. In case of a dispute, the umpire shall throw it into the field. The thrower-in is allowed five seconds. If he holds it longer it shall go to the opponent. If any side persists in delaying the game, the umpire shall call a foul on them.
10. The umpire shall be judge of the men and shall note the fouls and notify the referee when three consecutive fouls have been made. He shall have power to disqualify men according to Rule 5.
11. The referee shall be judge of the ball and shall decide when the ball is in play, in bounds, to which side it belongs and shall keep the time. He shall decide when a goal has been made and keep account of the goals, with any other duties that are usually performed by a referee.
12. The time shall be two fifteen-minute halves, with five minutes rest between.
13. The side making the most goals in that time shall be declared the winners. In case of a draw, the game may, by agreement of the captains, be continued until another goal is made.

As you can see, many of these rules apply in our modern game, except that we have many more rule interpretations today.

In the original game, nine players appeared on each team. They were arranged in a circle with three centers, three forwards, and three guards. Later, in 1894, the number of players was determined by the area of the floor on which the game was played. If the floor was 1,800 feet or less in area, five men constituted a team; 3,600 square feet or less, seven; and over

3,600 feet, nine men. Shortly after this the team was permanently reduced to the present number of five.

SIGNIFICANT RULE CHANGES

It is not necessary to include all the rule changes that have transpired since the origin of the game, but we will list some of the highlights which have changed the game into one of the finest sports in the world.

The first college basketball squad in the United States appeared on the scene in 1892–93, when Yale organized a team. Both Cornell and the University of Chicago had teams in 1893–94. The first game, with only five players performing on a side, took place between Yale and the Bridgeport, Connecticut YMCA in 1896, with Yale winning the game 4–0. Quite a contrast from today's game! And speaking of firsts, Yale and Pennsylvania played the first intercollegiate game of basketball—with Yale winning 32–10 —in 1897.

Other highlights include the formation of the first intercollegiate conference in 1901–02, when Harvard, Yale, Princeton, Columbia, and Cornell were grouped in a basketball association. The University of Chicago acted as host for the first national high school tournament in 1917, which drew considerable interest throughout the country. With these two events basketball was on its way to prominence. Another important stride was made when a United States team participated in the 1936 Olympic Games, held in Berlin, Germany. Our country was one of 22 teams playing for the international basketball championship.

During the 1920's, one man was permitted to shoot all team foul shots, and, 10 years later, the elimination of the center jump after a field goal was made a part of the rules. The latter speeded up the game considerably, and was brought about to create spectator interest by eliminating the dullness of having to halt the play after each field goal. There is no question that it has increased play action.

A second innovation, in which the ball must be brought from the backcourt to the front court in 10 seconds, also initiated major changes in the game at this time. Thirdly, the three-second ruling was introduced to force the big pivot man out of the scoring area. A player could not remain within the free-throw lanes with or without the ball for more than three seconds when team possession occurred.

The fan-shaped backboard (Fig. 1–1) was adopted in 1941. At this time also the molded-type ball (Fig. 1–2) was recommended because of its superiority to other types with respect to shape, reaction, and durability. However, it was not decreed official until 1950.

The "bonus" free-throw rule, which completely changed the complexion of the game, was placed in effect in the 1954–55 season. This permitted

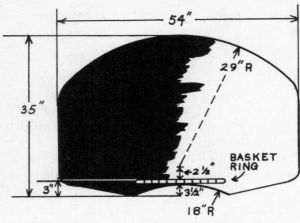

Fig. 1–1. The fan-shaped backboard, which appeared in 1941 is used in the majority of high schools.

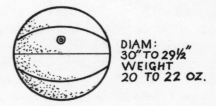

Fig. 1–2. The present molded-type basketball and its dimensions.

DIAM:
30" TO 29½"
WEIGHT
20 TO 22 OZ.

a player a second free throw if the first shot was successful following a personal foul, and led to a continuous parade to the free-throw line.

Opponents of the free thrower occupied the two spaces next to the end line on a free throw beginning in 1956, in order to give the defense better rebounding position on missed attempts, and eliminate the "cheap" offensive basket. This rule applies in our present game and is well-liked by everyone. The major change in 1957 was increasing the free-throw lane from six feet to 12 feet. This was to prevent the big "post" men from camping in close to the basket and scoring easy goals. Other rule changes today are primarily concerned with goal-tending and charging. The fantastic jumping ability and clever tactics of modern players have led to these changes in the current game.

EQUIPMENT AND DIMENSIONS

Under Naismith, peach baskets (Fig. 1–3) were utilized for goals in the first game. In those days a ladder was necessary to retrieve the ball from the basket after a successful attempt. In contrast to this, Figure 1–4 shows the rim which we have adopted for the modern game. The peach basket stopped being used before 1900, for it was inconvenient to retrieve the ball after every successful attempt.

Fig. 1–3. Peach basket used as
goal in 1892.

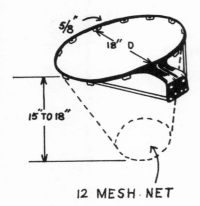

Fig. 1–4. The modern basketball
rim and its dimensions.

Naismith also deliberated over the selection of a ball. He thought
about using a spheroid football or a soccer ball, settling on the latter because, although it was considerably smaller than our regulation basketball,
it was close to what he was looking for. The players all wore full-length
trousers for uniforms plus a regular shirt.

COURT DIMENSIONS

Figure 1–5 gives the student and coach a complete listing of the court
markings of a basketball floor. This court specification can be used in
marking a floor or for the general knowledge of all concerned. It is thorough, up-to-date, and can be used in testing the players and as a general
review for the coach. Everyone connected with the game should familiarize himself with these dimensions and specifications.

A difference between the high school and college basketball backboard
is pointed up by comparing Figures 1–1 and 1–6. Figure 1–7 shows the
college gooseneck-type basket which is featured in many fieldhouses, with

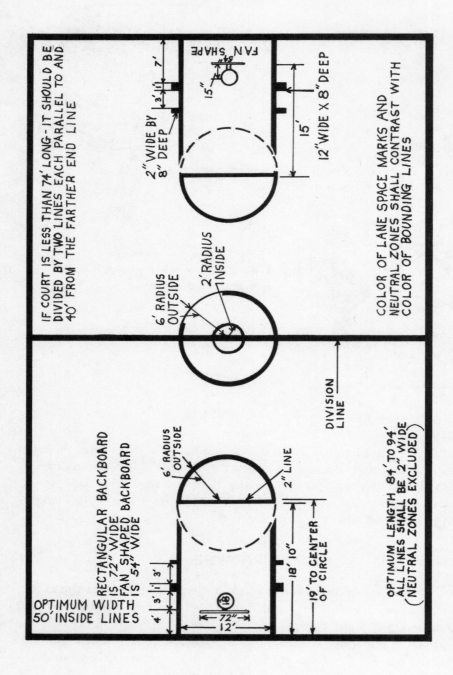

Fig. 1–5. The complete layout and markings of the basketball court.

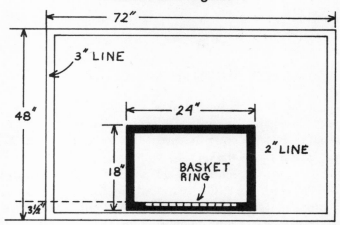

Fig. 1–6. The popular rectangular backboard used in many high schools and all colleges.

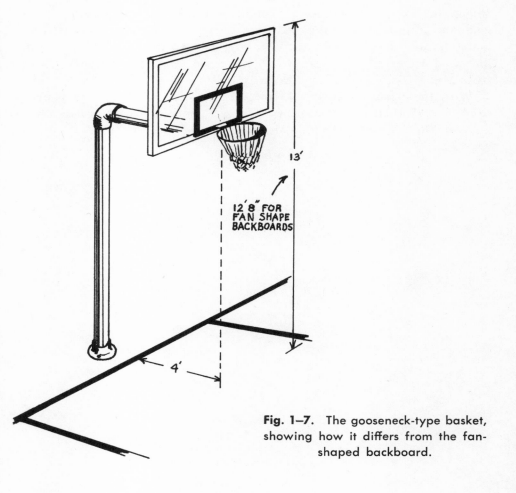

Fig. 1–7. The gooseneck-type basket, showing how it differs from the fan-shaped backboard.

specific dimensions. It is extremely popular, and recognized as a most suitable basket and preferred over any other type by college coaches.

PROJECTION INTO THE FUTURE

The game as it is now played has advanced beyond Dr. Naismith's greatest expectations and dreams. He would hardly recognize basketball today. The game has become the greatest spectator sport in the world. Almost every nation has a basketball team and is now competing in some form. In the U.S., grade schools, high schools, colleges, universities, the AAU, the NAIA, and the NCAA are all fielding teams for such events as the Pan-American Games, the World Basketball Tournament, and the Olympics. Certainly it is not uncommon to hear of crowds of 20,000 or more spectators at basketball games, as new arenas are being built to accommodate more and more fans.

One reason for the advancement of the modern game has been the change in players. Their improvement over the years has been phenomenal, and improved coaching aids and better techniques have been a great help. In addition, the number of boys participating in the game has increased tremendously throughout the years, and, consequently, better basketball players have been produced.

With these reasons in mind, we feel that the future of the game is bright. Basketball is a great sport, and will continue to be so if tradition holds in the future as it has in the past.

2

Developing a Sound
Basketball Philosophy

Many people do not understand the meaning of the word *philosophy*, and the authors would like to explain this term as it is related to basketball and to the coaching profession.

It is our belief that the definition of a sound basketball philosophy is best approached in the following manner. To have a sound basketball philosophy you must have a sound philosophy of life. In fact, a basketball philosophy is a way of life. First, you must understand your own physical and mental make-up and those factors which influence your thinking on relative subjects. Secondly, you must set up definite objectives along the way and expect to accomplish them. Finally, you must know the direction in which you are moving. The principles you stand for in your personal philosophy are most important. These are established early in life and shaped throughout your career with additions and limitations.

Basketball philosophy contains many philosophies within its framework. It is a series of ideas which underlies the sport. We want to make the young coach aware of what is expected of him from all aspects of the coaching profession. This chapter will deal with the various practical principles which will aid you as a coach in building your own philosophy.

COACHING PHILOSOPHY. Every coach will adopt or have a philosophy about basketball as he wants it played. This will be developed gradually and through actual experience. The foundation for such reasoning will be predetermined by many factors.

To begin with, there are many types of coaching philosophies. These are numerous and varied. Individual beliefs dictate this, as in our every-

11

day living. These range in scope from the "run-and-gun" method to the more disciplined or controlled offense. Each coach feels that the thinking behind his pattern of play is sound and will be successful. However, a word of caution is advisable. Never take it for granted that you have the best pattern in basketball and that nothing will cause you to change your mind. Changes come quickly and we will observe many more. Be flexible in your thinking and use your own initiative in adoptions which will be of assistance in your program.

Be completely sold on the merits of your philosophy. Believe in what you are doing and express confidence. If you do not have faith, then every phase will suffer. In order to sell anything to others, you yourself must be sold on the product.

ADOPTION OF A PHILOSOPHY. Since a great number of coaches have themselves played the game, they are probably employing a pattern of basketball similar to what they have been taught. It is our belief that "you teach what you know." You are not likely to gamble on anything you are unfamiliar with or not sold on. The knowledge you have of the game will be a strong motivating force in molding this philosophy. If you plan on making a change, it is suggested that you experiment with a freshman group for one year and then put it into your varsity program.

As a coach, you will go into this vocation with basic ideas as to what you hope to accomplish. You will want to survey the players returning and then proceed to analyze the type of pattern you believe will be successful. Few coaches attempt to build a new offense or defense without first knowing the minute details which make it function properly. Remember, details win ball games.

On the other hand, do not become stagnant in your thinking about this subject. If you see teams employing proficient tactics, do not be afraid to attempt to fit them into your system of play. There are few secrets in the game of basketball. If you can win games by utilizing another coach's pet play, and this maneuver fits into your organization, use it. It is the foolish coach who does not take advantage of a play which can be of help to his team. Simply because the plan originated with another colleague does not mean you cannot take advantage of it.

YOUR PHILOSOPHY. You have an obligation to put forth the best product on the floor which you know is possible. This goes beyond winning. You should avail yourself of a knowledgeable interpretation of the rules and regulations which exist in the game. These should be followed religiously. Respect the rules and encourage fair play.

The authors agree that the game should be taught for the average basketball player. You will encounter more players of this type than the exceptional one. Accordingly, you must gear your philosophy and thinking in this direction. There are cases where you have seen a coach, with average material, who molded his group into a well-knit unit and accomplished unbelievable feats. On the other hand, there have been coaches who have had the "horses" and still turned out mediocre clubs. The difference in the two teams is the man at the head of the organization.

It is imperative to throw your heart into coaching. Work diligently and patiently and it will rub off on your players. One of the great facts of life is the success which comes from hard work. Long hours are synonymous with this vocation. A coach must work far beyond the average schoolday and nearly every weekend.

Remember, you need not be embarrassed about being enthusiastic. Exude intense enthusiasm for the sport and you will never have to apologize to anyone for not doing the best job possible. You can never expect an easy route as a basketball coach. At the same time, do not be guilty of advocating a style of play that is too difficult to teach. Players are great imitators. The coach should be a model for his boys to impersonate. He will set the example for the squad to follow. Every detail the head man desires and demands from his players must first be exemplified by himself. You do not fool players. They are quick to spot "phonies" and will know before anyone else the true character of the coach. His conduct, social decorum, living habits, and sportsmanship will reflect in his players. If he does not display these qualities, then he cannot expect the group to possess them. In conclusion, the building of your philosophy on the ground level insures that it will always be on a solid basis. Coaching can best be summed up as service to players, schools, and communities; dedication of your life; and devotion before self.

PLAYER PHILOSOPHY. Players are products of their parents, coaches, and environments. These influences will be major determinants toward the attitude the player has established. Their ability to endure practice sessions, absorb instruction, practice self-discipline, and manifest desire for the game are traits which can be imminent from players.

Team members should anticipate work and know that the coach wants him to extend himself and operate at maximum efficiency. The squad can look for constructive criticism. We tell our players that the coach would not criticize them if he were not interested in their improvement. Once players are aware of this, they do not resent it but rather feel it is an assurance of their play developing to its fullest potential. They are interested in learning the game and will acknowledge your comments by realizing it is for their benefit.

The head mentor should count upon team members being coachable. Insist on open-mindedness, encourage attentiveness and freedom of play, and explain that you can improve their play only if you have their complete cooperation. Illustrate with a number of points what a "pet" move may mean to them during an entire season. Players accept this challenge before any other.

What can the players expect and how will this affect them? They can develop a wholesome attitude and outlook from their experiences in the sport. There is no better training ground in the world for learning situations than basketball. Every conceivable circumstance pertaining to life experiences will be shared by the individual player during his basketball tenure. These are garnered on and off the floor. Many times the outlook on life which players develop is directly attributed to basketball.

The ability of players to assume responsibility is given through the game, as are certain areas of accountability. Allowing them to carry their own basketball equipment, for example, encourages responsibility, dependability, and duty. Squad members learn quickly under this code.

Incorporation of knowledge and the absorbing of it are of extreme importance. If the players are unable to learn the intricacies of the game you employ, they should not expect to participate in it. On the other hand, it is up to the coach to present the philosophy which is best suited for the squad and which has the least amount of confusion. If this does not materialize, then a re-evaluation of your teaching methods and techniques is in order.

The individual can expect his coach to be his closest confidant. There are instances in every coach's life when he will be called upon to hear the personal stories and problems of his players. They often feel that they can converse with their coach with more freedom and understanding than would be possible with their parents or friends.

PLAYER DISCIPLINE. This training corrects, molds, and strengthens the individual player. Basketball teaches the obedience necessary to develop recognition for a set of rules to be observed. These rules are regulations to be carried out implicitly and without fail. Training rules as enacted are a requirement for all squad members. These are to be fulfilled.

Discipline begins and ends with the coach. He can influence his team more than any other force, and he can also anticipate being "tested" by his players. It will be up to the coach to communicate authoritatively in the event of a problem. In the handling of a situation he must exhibit consistency, fairness, and firmness. It is of prime importance to learn all the facts in any disciplinary problem before a decision is reached. There will be occasions in the profession when you will be tempted to extend the rules which have been set up. Never sacrifice what you believe in for an individual or for the winning of a game. Years of tradition can tumble with one instance and you will never regain the respect which was lost.

COMPLIMENT YOUR PLAYERS. In coaching, as in business, you will be faced with many personalities, temperaments, and abilities.

It has been our experience that more can be gained by praising a player than by being constantly derogatory. Everyone likes recognition for a job well done. When an opportunity appears, be quick to grant this recognition. A word of caution—seldom should an individual player be singled out for eulogy, lest the remainder of the team suffer. A number of coaches have adopted the policy of not speaking publicly about a player other than to acknowledge the team in its entirety. In this manner there is never any discrimination among team members as to heroes and unsung heroes. The coach will realize that there are exceptions and varying circumstances here which good common sense can command.

A device which calls for attention under this phase is "needling." There are times when a coach, using normal methods, cannot get a player to perform to his full potential. But if he knows the individual well enough, he can often "needle" him into top performance. Here the term "needling" means to arouse the emotions of the player and incite him to perform. Possibly it is just a matter of making him "angry," and the coach will therefore use a series of verbal blasts as sharp prods to stir the player. This is done only after the coach sees that the player is unable to get himself in the proper mental attitude in relation to the game or practice session. You may have to resort to this in your coaching career, and numerous coaches are past masters at it.

There is a distinct difference between complimenting your players and needling them, and you must know how far you can go with this psychological mechanism. To be effective you must be able to discern and recognize the strengths and limitations of each player.

COACH–FACULTY RELATIONSHIP. Here is the crux of any basketball program. Your administration's attitude toward the school's educational program will conclusively affect you. If it is in favor of a well-rounded program of scholarship and athletics, the majority of your problems will be solved. If, on the other hand, the administration is not in favor of athletics, then it will be up to you to present and defend the reasons for the existence of such a program.

You can enhance your relationship with the administration by appreciating its interests. This can be achieved in a number of ways. First, you should cultivate the interest of administrative personnel and faculty by regular attendance at school functions. Faculty meetings, PTA, teachers' institute days, and social gatherings of the staff members are examples in this category. Second, you should share in the interests of faculty members. Take a diligent concern in what they say and do. Learn to appreciate their problems as well as your own. Plan on having lunch at the faculty lounge. A good relationship can be developed by coaches who fraternized with the faculty and come to know them personally. These are the people who in many cases will "make or break" your squad at the academic level. Thus, close contact is a must for you as a coach.

It has been our experience in observing educational institutions that a particular pattern appears to be more and more prevalent. It is one in which a school has strong athletic teams in all sports; has an excellent academic program; and has equally competent music and forensic groups. This type of school has superior leadership in its administration because they have seen to it that all curriculums and extra-curricular opportunities have been made integral parts composing a great educational system.

PROFESSIONAL PREPARATION OF THE COACH. For many years coaches were hired on the basis of their reputation as players. This is not the situation today. Administrators are requiring advanced degrees in major fields. The trend is definitely toward stringent academic standards, and one must be better prepared than in the past.

The coach, in order to move up in his field, will find better coaching opportunities and teaching positions available if he has a master's degree. The additional asset of advanced education will enable him to gain added stature as a faculty member, better security, and additional salary raises.

A survey by C. V. Money,[1] Head of the Physical Education Department at Northern Michigan University, pointed out that presidents, superintendents, and principals, when hiring coaches, looked for those men who possessed the following:

1. Excellent moral character
2. A fine educational and strong academic background
3. Demonstrated ability in their field of athletics

These are rigorous, highly important criteria, of which every coach should be made aware. They indicate what is expected of not only prospective coaches but of the entire teaching profession.

Here is an area the importance of which many coaches fail to realize. Classroom responsibilities should not be neglected, since administrators will not tolerate such neglect on the part of an instructor. At present, many administrators will not hire basketball coaches and permit them to teach in the physical education department. They maintain that the coach will merely "roll out the basketball" for all gymnasium activity classes. The falseness of this theory should be demonstrated, and it is up to the coaches to do so not only by defending their ability to teach general physical education well, but by proving it in their teaching performance.

Normally, you will be hired as a teacher first and as a coach second. With this in mind, it is compulsory to perform your duties faithfully. Few coaches have difficulty in maintaining their positions if an excellent performance has been put forth in the classroom. This is attained by meeting classes regularly and promptly, asserting proper classroom procedures, being properly attired in an activity course, presenting a variety of physical education activities, and displaying absolute discretion in grading practices.

In the event that you are relieved of your coaching reins you can always

[1] By permission of C. V. Money, Head of the Physical Education Department, Northern Michigan University, 1962.

revert to demonstrated teaching ability in the classroom. By doing a good job, you will never have anxiety in securing a teaching position.

WINNING PHILOSOPHY. As a coach, you must stress winning. Nothing you can do promotes or insures interest more than winning basketball games. Never let it be said that your won-and-lost record will not predict your immediate position and future opportunities. This often is the only indicator many people use to evaluate a coach. At the same time, you must realize that coaches are in this profession to win and are expected to win their share of games. The consistent losing of games will bring sharp criticism of your basketball coaching and of your team.

In explanation of how to win, we can give no magic formula. Years of experience, however, have been an excellent guide in certain areas, and several factors are to be considered.

It is our basic belief in coaching that you must *want* to be a winner. If this attitude is conveyed to squad members by the coach then you have started as a winner. In every game there must be a loser. The number of times you minimize this factor the better off you will be. Losers never become state champions.

We are in complete agreement that you must believe you have an opportunity to win every game. Positive thinking is a great equalizer. On a given night in basketball any five men can triumph regardless of the odds and opposition. The mental approach your team has will help determine the number of victories you record during the year. If you have traditional winning seasons it is conceivable that this will help you continue to have outstanding clubs.

What makes a team successful? It is our basic thought that pride in not wanting to associate with a loser is the foremost ingredient. Rich basketball tradition definitely helps make a team successful. One only has to look at Bradley University and the University of Kentucky as excellent examples of rich tradition. Highly competitive schedules will make your clubs more successful. Concentrated over-all planning in pre-season practices by the coach will contribute to success. Advanced regular season plans will additionally prepare your club for any situation. Finally, goals of achievement must be established to avert losses.

The attitude your players assume toward winning is paramount. If they adopt your philosophy of positive thinking, then you have succeeded in breaking down all barriers. Along with this feeling, players know that winning comes from long hours of hard practice sessions, and if they can reduce their game mistakes they will be on the right side of the ledger.

Another phase which may seem irrelevant but is of great importance is the financial aspect of your basketball program. The amount of money you take in at the gate during a winning year is always greater than during a losing season. People will seldom follow a loser. The matter of money cannot be denied. If your basketball program can show a profit, then you augment and increase your standing. Without a profit it can be in jeopardy.

At present there is a clamoring for reduction, and in some cases removal, of athletics at the high school level. This is because of the great amounts of money often spent on the various sports. A curtailment here is not necessary if you run a solvent program. Basketball costs much less to operate than many other sports. Defend your program—and the best way to do this is to see that it produces winners and profits.

COACH–PARENT RELATIONSHIP. This phase of basketball will be of significance. To do a good coaching job you must have harmony and cooperation from the parents of your players. They will be instrumental in any team success or failure.

It is suggested that you keep in close contact with the player and his home. Visit the player and his parents, and learn the environmental circumstances of the home. This will be an asset in your understanding of the family.

You will be wise to have a "Parents' Night" before the actual season begins. At this time you can explain your philosophy toward the game and the reasons for your beliefs. Your offense and defense can be demonstrated along with fundamental drills. Discuss the joining of forces which is necessary for the basketball program to be successful. Let them know you seek their cooperation. It will involve the parents because of training rules to be observed, use of discipline, and the goals the coach and team have decided upon for the season.

Cap the evening with a full court scrimmage of 20 minutes' length. This gives parents an opportunity to observe their sons and at the same time will let the coach know who reacts well under pressure and who looks good in the pre-season training.

A small social gathering in the high school cafeteria following Parents' Night is recommended. Coffee and doughnuts could be served by cheerleaders and this would give the coach a chance to do some public relations work. He should be cordial and amicable and make it a point to visit with all parents.

Parental adversity is to be expected as a coach. No coach is without pressure of some type and this is the most common at the high school level. Every coach must withstand this pressure, as parents are vitally interested in their son's ambition to play. Most think he should be playing more than he is. This is a natural feeling on their behalf. In this event, the best procedure to follow is to invite the parents to a conference and intelligently explain why the boy is not playing more. You should present concrete facts. Testing results you employ should be on file in order to show the parents evidence of his performance. Statistics can be a major piece of argumentation when you have in black and white what he has accomplished. Comparisons with other members of the squad are a must to give them a better idea of what you desire.

Above all, be frank in your discussion. Parents will hold you in higher esteem for telling the truth, although they may not completely agree with your evaluation of their son. Their respect will grow out of this talk and the boy will express confidence in you for giving him equitable treatment both on and off the floor.

COMMUNITY PHILOSOPHY. In nearly every town or city with a high school, basketball is played. Keeping this in mind, we can make specific observations concerning the attitude of the community and what the coach can do to further better relations at this level.

The coach should become familiar with the background of the community where he is coaching. This will reveal the basketball traditions, standards, successes, and general outlook. He must bear in mind that these qualities are long established practices and thus will directly affect his philosophy. The coach should recognize the community philosophy, use it to his advantage, and hold it in high regard.

Fundamentally there is a close relationship between the school and the townspeople. The school has strong ties with the community and you will encounter strong allegiance and support. It is not uncommon in smaller places to "lock up the town" and journey to a neighboring city for a basketball game. If you have this situation you are fortunate and should be appreciative. Cultivate and encourage this action whenever possible.

The people of the community have a right to expect certain things of the coach. A most important factor is that they do not want a "commuter coach." This type of coach is usually unmarried and leaves the community at every opportunity. This is frowned upon by area people, as they want him to be a member of the town in which he coaches. They want and expect him to enter into community functions, affairs, and to be in good standing.

The coach should use his free hours visiting local merchants and business establishments. These people will enjoy your taking time out for a "cup of coffee" and talking about the basketball team or an upcoming game. The coach can offer to display the basketball equipment of the team, any pictures, and victory game balls in a store for advertising purposes.

Basketball equipment should be purchased locally. The sporting goods store is a community business which you should patronize rather than going outside of the area. This is not always possible because of the size of the town. If this situation occurs, you must go to a neighboring city. Whenever feasible, though, buy from your local merchants, since they in turn will support you. This will result in close cooperation and harmony between you and the local businessmen. Many beginning coaches make the mistake of ignoring this factor in their first positions, thus causing much ill-will.

There are several pitfalls within the community and the school about which every coach should be alerted. Keep in mind that you are the coach, and never become over-friendly with any one particular student. More coaches are lost in this manner than are fired for losing. This student-coach relationship can destroy your reputation and greatly affect your future.

In the choice of leisure-time activities, extreme discretion must be shown. A coach should never frequent drinking establishments. The result of players observing the entrance or departure of the coach will mean loss of all respect. You must practice your own training rules to a certain degree. Be a model example for your players.

Another way to advance within the community is by playing golf. It is a great game for meeting and making friends. We strongly advocate that you take up this sport and become proficient enough to play satisfactorily. Many problems and decisions have been arrived at and solved on the golf course.

POST-GRADUATION PHILOSOPHY.   On occasion, coaches sometimes fail to follow up on the careers of their players when in many instances they can be of major assistance. The support you can give them in securing better coaching positions or better business opportunities are two illustrations of how you can be of service to them beyond their playing days.

Coaching responsibilities include maintaining an interest in your players. Take pride in turning out fine gentlemen and citizens. Try and place your players in college and remain in touch with them. These boys will be direct reflections upon you and your ability as a leader of young men. Nothing gives a coach greater personal satisfaction than watching one of his former players become successful in his chosen field. This is a reward which is unmatched in the profession.

You can foster relations by letting your former squad members know you want their addresses and would like to hear from them. Send them the school newspaper or a program from one of the games. Keep them informed of what is happening back at the old school. Remind them to stop over at the office or your home when they visit.

It would be advantageous to make a card index of this group and to keep the mailing list up to date. This will take a little time and effort on the coach's part, but it is worth it for the follow-up benefits.

If you have boys at college, write to them and give them encouragement. Your reward will come when they return on vacations and ask to use the gymnasium to work out. They will be frequent visitors and you will have an opportunity to give them excellent counsel and guidance at these times.

3

Concentrated Pre-season Planning

The beginning coach has a Herculean task awaiting him in organizing for a basketball season. There are so many phases and areas which must be covered that it is impossible to do this in a short period of time. It is important to remember that what you do in this period will determine the success of your team during the regular season. Games are won during the pre-season session by proper preparation and concentrated planning on the coach's part. The manner in which you detail your plans and organize your season will indicate the sincerity and enthusiasm you have for the game.

In the hope that we will better prepare future coaches and be of assistance to others in the field, we have devoted this chapter to pre-season planning and to the duties a coach must complete before his schedule commences.

FIRST SQUAD MEETING. The first meeting of your squad should be publicized through your school paper. Notices should be posted on bulletin boards and other key areas where students congregate. It is advantageous to meet with your captain prior to the meeting and alert him to the proceedings and the contents so that he will pass the word along.

Frequent meetings with your squad are necessary throughout the entire season. You should have meetings to cover every possible detail which can help you win your next game.

Your first squad meeting should be considered the most important. If you are a new coach, it will be of added importance because you will want to make the proper impression upon the squad members. The best way is by being organized in every department. Leave no stone unturned.

21

MEETING SITE. Your gathering spot should be a location other than the gymnasium or the locker room. Our experience has been that merely getting away from these two locales has improved the atmosphere in our initial meeting. We attempt to hold them in the faculty lounge or a conference room where we have privacy, comfort, and pleasant surroundings.

Designate your manager to arrange the room in the fashion which you desire. You will need a blackboard with chalk and eraser. The arrangement of chairs should present unity rather than causing the players to be scattered throughout the room. If a table is available, have the group sit around it where it will be easy to address them.

MEETING PROCEDURES. The first item of business should be a short introduction by the coach. This can be in the form of a welcome to the returning lettermen, the squad members, and the new candidates.

You should have an information card which every candidate is to complete. This details their parents' names, occupations, street addresses, telephone numbers, years in school, and scholastic indexes. This information is necessary for a card file to which you can have immediate access in the event of an emergency or any type of routine matter. Background material on your players is always good to have, and it helps in familiarizing yourself with your squad members.

MEDICAL EXAMINATION. It is necessary for every prospective candidate for the basketball team to undergo a thorough medical examination before participation to determine whether he is physically fit. In high school and college the team physician usually administers such an examination. We advise all team members to have a flu shot at this examination, along with the coach and his staff. The biggest loss a team can suffer is when a player is unable to perform because of a cold or the flu. These illnesses are frequent and common to all basketball squads.

We favor a mid-year medical checkup as a precautionary move. Often, something can go wrong with the individual player during the season and be unnoticed. This mid-season type of action should prevent it and at the same time safeguard the health of the player. No one should be permitted to play or practice until he has a written statement from the doctor certifying his fitness.

ELIGIBILITY RULES. High-school academic standards throughout the country have risen, as have those on the college level. It is the duty of the coach to submit to the principal or the registrar a list of candidates who are out for the team.

The eligibility rules of your school, conference, state association, and national federation should be covered in the greatest detail with the squad.

In your meeting, pass out copies of the eligibility rules so that the entire group can go over them with you. Always regard these rules as law.

Since most high schools delegate eligibility requirements to the principal, he should record, file, and send out certified eligibility lists to all schools with whom his school competes. This is done every four to six weeks depending upon the school calendar year and the unit under which the schools operate. The wise coach will divorce himself from any role here other than that of a "watch-dog," as this is purely an administrative responsibility.

Your school will be affiliated with a group, and you should strive to maintain its eligibility standards. You are only asking for difficulty and problems if you violate any rules pertaining to this code. The rules concerning "all-star" contests and summer basketball regulations should be strictly adhered to and discussed with the group. This is the medium which needs and warrants special attention and you will have to acquire a thorough knowledge of the rules under this section.

ENFORCED STUDY.   Some coaches on the collegiate level have study halls to help insure eligibility. These are conducted five nights a week in the school library from 7:00 to 9:00 and are supervised by a member of the coaching staff. In this way the head coach knows that every player is thus assured of regular study habits. Usually, failure to show up for this study period means punishment of some sort ranging from not playing in the next game to the running of laps before practice the following day. Whether these study periods are feasible on the high school level is debatable but probably all colleges will hold similar sessions in some respect.

In the larger schools tutors are available for those players who are in need of special assistance. In the smaller colleges the coaches must depend on the faculty members, since they do not have the budget for this luxury. At Northern Michigan University and Michigan State we have found the faculty very willing to be of aid. On occasions, professors have taken time out from their busy schedules to counsel and help players with academic problems. We believe this happens many times on the college scene and the coach should be sympathetic and thankful for such action.

OBJECTIVES FOR THE SEASON.   The coach will set definite goals which he hopes to accomplish before the season starts. He should make his squad aware of what he wants achieved at this meeting. These objectives should be carefully planned and the coach should constantly insist that the squad aim for these goals.

Without objectives you cannot expect the players to perform with enthusiasm. They look forward to conference title races, post-season tournaments, and natural rivalries. Without these it would be difficult to play the game. Players thrive on competition. Basketball is competition, and objectives for the season are a necessary part of this competition.

SQUAD MEETINGS.   You will discuss these gatherings and impress the squad with their importance to the success of the team. They might range in time from 10 to 45 minutes. It will depend upon what is to be covered and whether movies are to be shown. Try and keep the meetings short but conclusive and light.

Drudgery can be evident and should be guarded against. You can quickly tell whether the squad is gathering the message. It is best to have a meeting immediately after you eat your pre-game meal if you are on the road. You have everyone assembled and it is easy to adjourn to a nearby meeting room.

Mimeographed scouting reports or other forms should be taken to the meeting and questions relative to strategy or other phases covered at this time. Any strategy you plan on using should be talked over to eliminate guesswork on the players' part.

Many times while traveling you will not have the facilities available to hold a meeting. In this case you should select the largest room in the motel or hotel where you are staying and conduct it there. The big disadvantage, of course, is that a blackboard and chalk are not convenient. All managers should anticipate such a situation and carry a portable play board or a replica of a basketball court on which the coach can administer his chalk talk.

When you play at home and find it necessary to have a meeting, you may decide upon your regular practice time after school as most suitable. Your players are free at this hour and it works out very well in most situations. The required materials to handle the meeting should be found readily in the locker room or on the floor, whichever you prefer.

It is understood that these meetings will commence on time and end on time, and no one is to be late. In the past we have locked the door once our meeting time has been reached and a player who misses this session is seldom late again. It also serves as a reminder to the rest of the group that this is serious business and should be conducted as such.

PRACTICE TIMES. You should discuss the time at which your practice sessions will begin and end, as well as any vacation practices to be held throughout the season. Most high schools begin their practicing sometime between 3:30 and 4:00 P.M. and conclude at 5:30 or 6:00, depending upon their facilities.

In numerous Illinois and Indiana high schools the coaches have a preschool practice which gets underway at 6:30 or 7:00 A.M. and runs until the first hour of school. Many of these same coaches will have their players shoot free throws during the noon lunch program and before the afternoon classes begin. After this the regular workout follows but it is normally shortened in length because of the previous sessions.

Command punctuality at all practice sessions. Insist that you be notified beforehand if a player finds it impossible to attend. A player who reports late for practice while the remainder of the squad is on time can quickly destroy team morale unless disciplinary action is taken. It will be up to the discretion of the coach in such a matter. Some players are slower in dressing than others, but if you have an established rule, stick to it and the players will be punctual. In regard to practice, a coach should schedule a minimum of two night drills before the opening game. This will familiarize the squad with actual playing conditions as they exist. They will notice many little things which will be different than the daytime sessions. This familiarization will be necessary as a confidence-builder, and, if more than two such practice drills are needed, hold them.

LENGTH OF PRACTICES.   The length of the sessions should be governed closely. As the season progresses, it will be necessary for the coach to be observant for signs of staleness and fatigue. If these are noticeable, check your practice schedule and make the necessary revisions. The authors have adopted a similar philosophy concerning practice sessions. In December our practice will normally run one hour and 45 minutes, and often two hours. In January this is reduced to one hour and a half (with special attention paid to final examination periods) and, in some instances, to an hour and 15 minutes. In February we hold our drills to one hour—and certainly no more than an hour and 20 minutes. By this time nearly five months of basketball have gone by the board and we want the players as fresh as possible. This has helped relieve the physical and mental strain appreciably and assisted us in having strong late-season finishes. This is also done in order to maintain a keen edge, which is vital during the late season. Most coaches have adopted this timetable. We believe it is essential to keep your club "up" rather than to work it into the ground and go backwards, which has happened to all of us.

"NO-PRACTICE" DAYS.   The squad reaction to practice will tell you many things. Enthusiasm and ardent interest should be conspicuous during early workouts. As the season progresses it can be expected to wane somewhat. You must be on the lookout for this and schedule a day with no practice. All the basketballs should be locked up and unavailable to team members.

We place a sign on our locker room door stating "No Practice Today— See You Tomorrow." You will have to insist that team members leave, as there will always be some who will want to work out. Do not let these players stay on, as this is the time when they are apt to get hurt. Unsupervised workouts are never to be encouraged, especially during the season.

This "no-practice" idea has helped break up the hard grind which all ball teams go through during the year. It improves morale, provides rest which is desirous, and gives the players extra study time to keep abreast.

Many college coaches will give their team a Monday off after consecutive weekend games. This will vary and depend upon your schedule but we heartily advocate one day a week devoid of drills during the second half of the season. This tends to keep your squad at its peak mentally and physically during this most important time. High school coaches normally give their team members Saturday off if it is a Friday-night game and the team will not play again until Tuesday.

EQUIPMENT

Before we get into basketball equipment it is important to give you a brief introduction as to what a young coach can expect in his first coaching position.

Yearling coaches have a definite weakness in this area. Few are able upon graduation, or even after accepting their first coaching assignment, to know how to properly buy equipment and understand what they are purchasing. This is a major problem in every coach's first year.

Since this is an area in which most novice coaches need assistance, the following suggestions are of value. First, the number of sporting goods companies which represent and sell athletic goods is multitudinous. However, do not buy from a firm which has anything less than a reputable name. It may cost more to deal with a well-known firm but you have assurance that you are obtaining established, quality goods. This is the cardinal principle in buying.

Your local sporting goods dealer will be happy to sit down with you and go over the various lines which he has available. You must develop a knowledge of the various products and find out the difference between items such as "skinners satin" and "tackle twill." It is difficult to find what you want, especially if all you know about what you are looking for is the color combination. Foster your relationship with the sporting goods representative, as he can be of invaluable aid. Another point of emphasis is: *Do not be afraid to recognize your weakness.* Counter this by asking former coaches and other people in coaching circles. You will find most of them very willing to assist you with this problem, as it is one which many have gone through themselves. Seek advice and learn what has been done in the past.

In buying equipment, your budget will dictate what you can spend. Some schools encounter few perplexities, while others barely have enough money for one basketball. Regardless of his resources, however, every coach should establish a budget. Along with this, an accurate accounting of the money spent must be made. It is recommended that a monthly statement be sent to the head coach from the principal's office or the business office. This will keep the coach informed of his expenditures.

Practice equipment should not be neglected. The players will spend more time in this uniform than in the actual game uniforms. Make your practice gear practical, inexpensive, and washable. This will aid you immeasurably during the season. Money used on practice equipment is always money well spent. In the past years, Northern Michigan University has bought less expensive game uniforms and concentrated on practice items which were felt to be more important. The game uniforms last approximately two years and then new ones are bought. This has proven profitable, and we suggest you investigate it as a possibility. This might be a point of controversy but it warrants your attention.

Your equipment supply should be such that you have enough for daily changes. Clean socks, liners, supporters, shirts, and trunks are necessities. If you work in a cool gymnasium or fieldhouse it will be to your advantage to have sweat shirts for the players to cut down on the possibility of catching cold once they sit down. The prevention of the cold can make or break your club, since, as we have pointed out, it can be costly to lose any man on the team.

EQUIPMENT CARD. This card clearly indicates the number of basketball items every player must have for the practice season. The player's shoe size and type-preference are recorded here. At present, there appears to be an interest expressed for the low-cut shoe over the regular shoe. It is our belief that this is a psychological matter with the individual and if he feels he can play better with one type or the other, this is what we buy. On our squads the player tells us what he likes and we try to arrange it. However, when schools are forced to put their shoe supply on bids it is not always possible to buy exactly what you want. We have used every brand of basketball shoe on the market and have observed them in every conceivable manner. In conclusion, we believe that whatever shoe is most comfortable and best fits the player is the right shoe for him.

His waist measurement, pants length, sock size, liner preference, uniform number (if he is a returning squad member), and game warm-up number should also be on the card. In this manner you will know the sizes and measurements of each squad member exactly, and when equipment is needed you can rely on this card file. It is kept in the equipment room and is easily accessible. At a glance, you get all the information you need in ordering equipment, and such a file will be of especial aid in case of an emergency.

INVENTORY. As equipment is worn out you will want to replace it. An inventory at the end of the season is advocated, as you will be able to recognize your particular needs immediately at this time. This inventory should include all basketball items, from shoe laces to game uniforms.

Should your budget prevent you from buying everything you desire, it is suggested that you purchase only the most important essentials and pick up the other particulars when you find it practical.

A second inventory can be made during the summer months after you have had an opportunity to check some of the new equipment on the market. It is wise to save a little of your budget for such an occasion since you will probably want to buy an item which you need during this time of the year and can take advantage of a sale.

Usually you can order equipment in the summer and receive it in time for your basketball practices in the fall. In order to be positive, however, you should order as quickly as possible and specifically alert the sporting goods company as to your starting time. A letter to the company a month before your equipment is due, stating your anticipation of such, is advised.

EQUIPMENT CHECK. Equipment given each squad member should be registered on a check-list and the list filed in the equipment room. The coach usually handles this matter in the smaller schools unless a full-time equipment manager is available, in which case his responsibility is lightened. Equipment is important, and equipment men have a big job in handling, storing, replacing, and caring for it. If you have a good man, he can save your basketball budget considerable money. The mishandling of hundreds of dollars' worth of equipment can be disastrous to your program. Impress your players with the importance of proper equipment care and explain to them how they can help in this matter.

When players desire a change of equipment, this can be handled in one of two ways. First, those wanting clean gear can present duplicates to the equipment man and receive their clean equipment. This is the most common method employed in schools today. The second method is where "rolls" are made up in advance by the manager or equipment man which include all practice items. The roll is then put into the player's locker prior to practice. At the same time the rolls of clean equipment are distributed, the soiled practice togs are picked up. This system practically eliminates loss of equipment.

On the collegiate level we have found the second method to be better. The big advantage is that the player has clean equipment when he arrives at his locker. Consequently he will report on the practice floor earlier than he normally might.

HANDLING OF EQUIPMENT. If an automobile is to last any length of time it must receive proper maintenance and care. Basketball equipment is the same. You will have to inform the team members what you expect from them and how to handle their own outfits.

From a health standpoint, encourage the players to care for their equipment as if it were their very own. Such a personal touch has helped many coaches along this line. It is important to look well dressed as a team, and this impression can be quickly dispelled by ragged uniforms which are wrinkled or soiled.

Make hangers available to your squad on which they may hang up their equipment. If a drying room is convenient, make use of it. By the following morning all gear should be dry.

If you are on a road trip and must stay overnight, insist that your players take their uniforms out of their traveling bags and hang them up once they return to their rooms after the practice session or played game.

PLAYER NOTEBOOKS.   We advise all coaches (novices and veterans alike) to present their basketball philosophy to the players through a player notebook. The notebook registers in detail the individualized ways to properly execute various basketball fundamentals. The total basketball program which you are running should be included. This will cause your players to perform in the same fashion throughout their years under your tutelage. The notebook will also provide you with a consistent method of coaching.

The player notebook will contain offensive and defensive patterns of plays to be employed, rule changes, jump-ball plays, out-of-bounds plays, training rules, and any material you deem important and needed. Recently, we have incorporated other articles such as eligibility rules, public relations details which players should carry out, squad meetings, the manager's position, and player attitude.

Long hours should be put in on this notebook and meticulous care should be given every phase you hope to cover. Do not put in writing anything you do not want carried out. If it is written and the players receive copies, then it should be treated as law. Your players should be made conscious of this.

The player handbook can be of value both academically and athletically. In its contents you can point out items of major consequence which in the past may have given you some difficulty. You can also emphasize to squad members other areas where you feel they might need special assistance.

The player notebook should be utilized by the players. They can study its contents and receive the full benefits of your entire philosophy. There should be no misunderstandings as to what you want when it is put in writing. They will be expected to carry out what you have given them in the notebook.

You will find it advantageous to have this type of written plan in your coaching program. It eliminates many problems and difficulties which you could encounter without a player notebook. You will discover that the most arduous job is putting together the notebook—especially finding the time to do it. However, once completed it should be a masterpiece of organization which you will never give up.

SELECTION OF SQUAD MEMBERS

This is without a doubt the most difficult task the coach will encounter. The beginning coach will find he is at a disadvantage, since it is nearly impossible to have the knack of picking the right players during his first year at coaching. He must choose those who he believes will develop, and yet there is no positive indicator that he will be correct in his judgment. All coaches have been guilty of mistakes in player selection. This will continue to be true because the make-up of no two players is alike, and individuals will not develop at the same pace physically, mentally, or emotionally.

The coaches who scan prospective players and have the ability to select the most promising are endowed with a sixth sense. Many veteran coaches may do this but it is seldom possible without years of observation as one's guide.

The coach must establish an exact rating whereby each candidate can be observed in every phase of basketball. This would include footwork, reaction time, shooting, jumping, passing, and dribbling. Each of these qualities is not to be overlooked in testing.

It is our belief that coaches are sometimes so engrossed in the abilities of a boy that they unwittingly overlook the boy himself. The player is salient. He must have the desire to play. He must be devoted and display loyalty to the program, the coaches, the school, and his teammates. Each player must discipline himself, recognize his weaknesses as well as his strengths, and work to develop into the complete basketball player. This means maximum effort in every session, whether it be practice or the game itself. There should be no room on the squad for anyone except the hustler, the aggressor, and the boy with a sincere desire to play basketball.

The scientific approach to basketball has taken over, and it has provided coaches with an objective way of rating their potential squad members. The number of tests which are available to coaches are innumerable. It is not our thought to cover this large field but rather to acquaint the coaches with the various testing devices which they can call upon to help them in player selection.

Testing devices can serve many functions, such as:

1. Determining the performance of a player in a certain skill, such as passing.
2. Providing a solid basis for keeping or cutting squad members.
3. Providing a stimulus for the player, since he will be aware of his being evaluated.
4. Cementing your own judgment, and increasing your self-assurance.

There are certain areas which coaches should be concerned with in player selection. We feel the following are among the most important.

SPEED. This not only implies speed afoot but with the hands and body. It is the most essential factor every coach looks for in players. Without it you can never expect to have a great club. Professional sports exemplify this characteristic and the better athletic teams all have this trait in common. The reaction time the player displays will tell you immediately if he is suited for the game.

SHOOTING. Every boy likes to shoot. It is universal that as you observe players coming onto the floor the first thing they do is shoot the ball. Seldom do you see them working defensively by themselves. There is little enjoyment in this phase but there is much satisfaction in seeing the basketball go through the net.

In order to win you must score; thus the emphasis you place on shooting with your players will determine the eventual outcome of your games.

Shooting is an individual matter. There are natural-born shooters with great "touch." They will employ sound fundamentals with unusual success. On the other hand, all of us have seen the player who violates every principle of shooting and yet is phenomenal. A fine illustration of this is Julius McCoy, who played for Coach Anderson at Michigan State. McCoy, who became an All-American, would shoot off the wrong foot on almost every field goal attempt and use excessive spin on the ball, yet was most effective in this manner. If Coach Anderson were to have tried to change his style he might have destroyed his abilities. If you have a player with this exceptional ability, do not minimize it by insisting he change to a "correct" style.

Players can develop touch through constant practice. We have talked with some of the country's best shooters, and they say that they know the moment they shoot whether the ball is going to go into the basket. Conversely, they also seem to know through this sense of touch when they will miss a shot.

In choosing your squad it is compulsory to have shooting drills from various parts of the gymnasium floor. This will distinguish the mere "shooters" from the scorers. There is a great difference, and the players will quickly identify themselves in these drills.

From our experience we can say that the key to shooting is relaxation, confidence, and touch. This is what you should look for in choosing candidates for your basketball team. Players displaying these qualities should be given prominent consideration in this shooting department.

HEIGHT. The tall man in basketball is here to stay. Every coach dreams of the day when he will encounter the good big man to bring him the championship. The changes the game has undergone in recent years have been mostly due to the big man. The ability of such a man to play offense, defense, and rebound is cause for worry on the part of all opposing coaches. The psychological advantage they enjoy over their opponents cannot be measured accurately. The case of Bill Russell, 6' 9" star center of the Boston Celtics, is an example. His defensive efforts in the professional ranks revolutionized the game, upsetting opposing players and causing coaches to completely overhaul their court tactics because of this one man.

Coaches must be willing to bend over backwards if they have a big boy to work with. You will find him to be normally uncoordinated and far from a polished player. You should never give up on the big boy, however, as he usually matures more slowly than the smaller boy. If you get one good season out of him, then your efforts will have been rewarded. In addition, you will have helped the boy to improve and develop not only in basketball but in other phases of life which are important—especially self-confidence.

You must be willing to work overtime with these individuals after practice and whenever the boy is agreeable to work. The height and weight he gives the team may be the necessary lift you are looking for. Every squad must have at least some semblance of height. As the tall boy develops, you will note how he loses the self-consciousness and awkwardness he possessed at the beginning.

BALL HANDLING. In order to perform acceptably in basketball every team must have good ball-handlers. The trademark of national and state tournament champions is that they are adept at handling and passing the ball. Unexcelled ball-handling and passing make for better basketball, and the crowds will applaud this phase as much as the scoring. Players who are able to handle the ball skillfully can play for you. You will find they can help in a number of ways but we think these are the most important:

1. They will present a confident, organized team which has the ability to make the offensive plan work against any type of defense.
2. They will set up scoring opportunities through this phase.
3. They will eliminate ball-control errors which prove costly in every contest.
4. They can control and dominate the tempo of the game.
5. They will combat the harassing type of defense, such as the zone press, man-to-man press, and other special defenses.

There are other game situations in which the ball handler will prove invaluable and it is fine to be able to call upon the clever and surehanded player in such a tactical situation. In your selection of the squad, remember to allow room for the good ball-handler.

MENTAL ATTITUDE. The squad members of the basketball team reveal themselves through their emotional makeup. Their ability to control their emotions in heated situations should influence your judgment as to whether they are potential basketball players.

In order to play the game of basketball, with its endless, changing sequels and instantaneous decisions, the player must be able to meet every conceivable situation with calmness, confidence, and stability.

The coach will set the example for the team. If he reveals a feeling such as anger under stress at an official's decision, he can expect the squad members to echo his emotion. More than likely he will have a bigger following sharing his sentiments in the home crowd. It is imperative that the coach conduct himself in a sensible manner.

Mental attitude encompasses the ability to withstand pressures. These may come in the form of practice pressure or in game results. A player may be an excellent practice shooter but once competition is added he never measures up to this practice performance. The same is true in actual contests. A player's preparedness for pressure cannot be rated until you observe him under game conditions. Once you have seen how he plays with a crowd on the sidelines, a time clock, officials, and a defense, you can then make a conclusive judgment.

DEFENSIVE ABILITY. This lost art has undergone a rebirth among basketball coaches. The coach has a conscientious duty to look for the boy who plays well on defense. As there is room for the good little man in the game, there is likewise opportunity for the good defensive player. Every team likes to have a "stopper." This is the player who is assigned to guard the star performer of the opposition, and he pits his defensive skill against the offensive-minded star.

According to statistics, 80 per cent of all high school teams are using a zone defense at the present time. It has been our theory that it is impossible to play an effective zone without a solid man-to-man foundation. Defensive principles must be learned through a man-to-man defense before becoming a unit zone.

Some players have a liking for defense, and they will be quickly discernible in practice sessions. Encourage this type of play and recognize such individuals immediately. A tough, hard-nosed defensive player is worth his weight in gold. The importance to Ohio State of John Havilcek's defensive efforts is a perfect example.

MANEUVERABILITY. A player must possess maneuverability. He must be flexible and have the knack of fooling his opponents. He can do this by constant jockeying, bobbing and ducking, and moving. The easiest man to guard in basketball is the one who is motionless. Those players who are in action and doing something without the ball are the boys you want playing for you. They are working to free themselves for every possible opportunity. They are the same athletes who will take advantage of the opposition by this clever manipulation. Those boys who run, jump, and shoot are the toughest to defend against and normally make the best basketball players. Change of direction and head fakes are paramount maneuvers you should be alert for in squad selection. Also, the speed at which the player operates is important.

MOBILITY. When we speak of mobility among players we mean easy dexterity of movement. High-school boys will normally not have this deftness of movement in the ninth and tenth grades but can be expected to display it as they mature. Mobility in basketball players includes quickness, nimbleness, and alertness. It is natural sureness and adaptability in the use of the hands and feet. The coach should look for these inherent standards when choosing his squad.

TRAVELING SQUAD. The regulation you set up as to the number of players making each trip will depend upon the coach and, in some instances, the size of his budget.

The high school coach will normally have 10 to 12 boys suit up for the varsity game. The junior varsity head man will have approximately 15 boys he wants in uniform for his game. The reason he has more is obvious. These boys develop more slowly and you will want to see what each boy can do in basketball situations. You will want each player to be given an opportunity to prove himself; thus, you can afford to wait for development at this early age.

Making the traveling squad is an honor and should be coveted. Players are reminded that their selection to the traveling squad will be dependent upon their practice and game performances. As a coach, there will be times when two players of equal ability are vying for a berth and you will have a difficult time deciding who should make the trip. If this is the case, you should get the opinion of your assistant coaches. They can be of great help, as they may see the players in a different light. If you have not reached a decision after this discussion you will be wise to call a conference of the boys and describe the situation to them. Suggest that one player make the first trip and the second player would make the next one. This democratic procedure has been of aid in some instances and usually satisfies all parties concerned.

You can dress more squad members at home if you wish and this is always an excellent idea. You may have the opportunity to insert your entire group into the game. The reserves look forward to this action with great anticipation. You will find your starters will cheer wildly for the reserves to do well just as the reserves have cheered for the starters. You as the coach will delight in seeing a substitute who has been out religiously for daily practice get into the game and score. Team unity is enhanced by this spirit and by admiration for one another.

4

Coaching Methods, Techniques, and Devices

There are more and better coaching aids available to coaches than ever before in the basketball field. The coach must utilize these in order to unite his team. The more teaching devices the coach can rely on, the easier it will make his job of communicating with the players. All of us know how important communication is on a basketball team.

It is impossible to bring you every coaching aid and method available. However, we do want to make you aware of as many as possible in order for you to become a better coach. The following coaching aids and methods are some of our favorites.

METHODS AND TECHNIQUES

A BASKETBALL PLEDGE. Many coaches on all basketball levels are requesting their squad members to sign a basketball pledge in which they give an assurance that they will perform in the best possible manner, not only on the basketball floor but in other capacities and respects as they represent their school.

The following is an example as used by Escanaba High School in Escanaba, Michigan:

I, Harvey Hook, promise to abide by all the rules and regulations set up by the school, the coaches and the Michigan High School Athletic Association during the coming year. I will observe all training rules and attend practice faithfully, working as hard as I am possibly able on the skills and fundamentals which make good players into championship players.

I will, at all times, conduct myself in a manner that will reflect credit on my family, my school, my community, and myself. I will endeavor to create interest in and help

35

those players younger than myself, encourage fair play at all times and respect the advice and judgment of all those connected with our team and school.

I am proud to be an American and a member of the basketball team of Escanaba High School. In order to show my appreciation, I will prove myself as a worthy athlete and citizen. My goal is to make our team one that we can all be proud of—a team of *champions and a championship team.*

BASKETBALL SCHEDULE CARDS. The publicity reaped from billfold-size cards with your basketball schedule adds stature to your high school, basketball program, and community. This is one of the better mediums of reaching your crowd. It is the duty of the head coach to designate what he wants in relation to the schedule card.

The card should be attractive, neat, and unique (Fig. 4–1). Some suggestions we might put forth would include a picture of your captain, coach,

Michigan State
BASKETBALL
1963 - 64   Home Games Capitalized

Nov. 30	(Sat.)	NORTHERN MICHIGAN
Dec.	4	(Wed.)	WESTERN MICHIGAN
	7	(Sat.)	BOWLING GREEN STATE
	14	(Sat.)	Pennsylvania
	18	(Wed.)	Tulsa
	20	{ Fri. }	Sun Devil Classic
	21	{ Sat. }	at Tempe, Arizona
	23	(Mon.)	Brigham Young
	28	(Sat.)	Butler
Jan.	4	(Sat.)	Illinois
	6	(Mon.)	WISCONSIN
	11	(Sat.)	INDIANA
	14	(Tue.)	Minnesota
	18	(Sat.)	NOTRE DAME
	25	(Sat.)	MICHIGAN
	27	(Mon.)	OHIO STATE
Feb.	1	(Sat.)	Michigan
	3	(Mon.)	Purdue
	8	(Sat.)	Northwestern
	15	(Sat.)	IOWA
	17	(Mon.)	ILLINOIS
	22	(Sat.)	Iowa
	29	(Sat.)	NORTHWESTERN
Mar.	7	(Sat.)	Ohio State

For ticket information, write or phone Ticket Manager, Jenison Field House, Michigan State University, East Lansing.
Phone: 355-1610 (Area Code: 517)

Fig. 4–1 (Views 1 and 2). Example of a basketball schedule card.

gymnasium, fieldhouse, or an action shot of the previous season. The card should tie in closely with your basketball program. The card should be changed yearly and can be made distinctly different each time. Some schools have a group photograph showing the faculty representative of the school, the coach, and the team captain. This idea has proven to be unique. Still another card which is being used more and more is the one which has games and dates superimposed on a map showing the location of cities in which your team will play.

Schedule cards in color are most attractive, but slightly more expensive. Regardless of the expense, they are eye-catching and this is what you seek in this type of venture. A coach can be of real service to his program through attention to this one phase of it.

A supply of schedule cards should be placed in strategic stores and business establishments for distribution within your city or community. This card should be included in all the coach's correspondence. This has been our practice for years and we have been the recipient of many favorable comments for this small but thoughtful act.

A schedule card, upon being printed, must be sent to all your opponents. This gives your fellow coaches a chance to set up scouting schedules in advance and they will express appreciation for this courtesy.

PERSONALIZED COACH'S CARD. This coaching aid has proven extremely popular during the past years and is fast becoming a standard procedure with nearly all college coaches.

The coach's card (Fig. 4–2) is similar to the businessman's card. It includes the name of the coach and school he represents. It lists his home and school telephone numbers. Other pertinent information might include recent honors the team has captured—such as winning a conference champion-

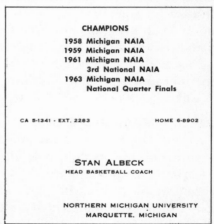

Fig. 4–2 (Views 1 and 2). Example of a personalized coach's card.

ship or winning a district, regional, or state tournament—as well as the school's home schedule. It might utilize the school seal or a picture of the school basketball mascot.

These, too, can be most advantageous in your correspondence. It is another area where coaches may enhance their positions and make favorable impressions. College coaches mail them to prospective athletes as a source of influence and recognition.

The cost of this type of card is not prohibitive. Colored cards range in expense from approximately two or three cents a card depending upon the quantity you desire. You will probably not have use for more than 200, although this will depend upon the coach.

COACH'S PERSONAL APPEARANCE. As soon as you accept your under-graduate degree and sign your first teaching and coaching contract you become a professional. Once you attain this status your whole life changes. Certain demands are made of you within the school system.

As a faculty member and a coach, you must always put your best foot forward in personal appearance. This includes being clean, smoothly-shaved, well-groomed, and neatly dressed with a conservative but up-to-date wardrobe. As previously stated, first impressions are important and you will be judged on the basis of your appearance by the administration, your associates, your students, and the community. Nothing kills a favorable impression more than seeing a coach who is slovenly. This creates a poor image of himself and what he represents.

As a coach you should expect to wear a white shirt and tie. It is almost an unwritten rule that teachers and coaches conform to this rule of society. There is no excuse for a coach's not adhering to this rule. If you are not used to this, you will learn to accept it as a normal routine after a short period of adjustment.

Since, as we have pointed out, many administrators frown upon the coach's teaching physical education classes, he will probably be given class-room duties in his minor teaching fields. If this is the case, then the white shirt and tie will be worn at all lecture periods. However, if you are teaching physical education activity courses then you will be wearing a regular gymnasium uniform. This uniform should be clean, pressed, and different from what the students are expected to wear.

COACH'S PRACTICE UNIFORM. Equally important as the coach's every-day personal appearance is his practice uniform. Coaches are recognizing this and have come up with some fine ideas. The most popular seems to be the wearing of bermuda shorts. These are practical for demonstrations and very comfortable to work in. To complete the uniform we would suggest a cotton T-shirt with your school insignia or name on the pocket. A light-weight jacket is also advisable for any short or quick trips you find it necessary to make around the school.

If you do not have the "knees" for bermuda shorts, a regular pair of khaki pants will be sufficient. Summer trousers are also recommended here because they are light; if you do any demonstrating, you will find that you will perspire less in this light-weight material. This would be our second choice for a practice outfit.

You will instill interest and good habits in your players if you *dress for all practice sessions*. Nothing will discourage players as quickly as their coach's failure to dress in the proper outfit for practice sessions. When they see the coach come to practice in a business suit rather than in conventional practice gear, players get the feeling that he is not really interested. Although this will often be inconvenient for a coach, he should remind himself that he must do it to instill confidence in his players. (On trips, however, they will realize the difference and will know that it is almost impossible for the coach to change into practice gear under these circumstances.)

The coach should be the first man dressed for practice sessions and, under normal circumstances, be the last man to leave the practice floor. By doing this, he can have the opportunity to work individually with certain members who need it, in addition to setting the kind of example which the players expect and will respect.

COACH'S USE OF THE WHISTLE. A group meeting at which you tell the squad what is expected of them once your whistle blows is essential for discipline and punctuality. You expect and demand that once the whistle is blown, their attention must be yours. Any rules you set up must be adhered to in this respect. Under no circumstances can you show any favoritism toward players or you will defeat your purpose. If you are beginning your warm-up you must not tolerate that "last shot" by any individual; the squad should respect your wishes and know that it is time to go to work.

The coach should double-check his whistle from year to year to see that it is in working order. We recommend the steel whistle, which outlasts the plastic type and resounds with much more authority when blown.

BULLETIN BOARD. In every basketball program you must have a communication center where you will be able to reach every player. The best such place is your locker room bulletin board.

It is important to place the bulletin board where the most traffic occurs. It should be convenient enough for your players to stop and read when both coming and going from practice. The best possibilities for a bulletin board are close to a drinking fountain, near a mirror, or in a hallway leading directly to the locker room. These three locations were chosen by us after watching players over the years and the habits which they followed. We found that they all drink water upon entering the locker room after practice. We also noticed them combing their hair after the shower. Finally, the hallway is often the only entrance and exit to the locker room.

The size of your bulletin board should not be neglected. Ideally, it should be about six feet by four feet. A cork base is an excellent bulletin board material, as it will stand up well against the constant punishment of thumb tacks and pens. It can be painted in your school colors and be made to look very attractive if need be. If it is feasible, have the bulletin board encased in glass. Your industrial arts department should be able to help you with this.

The bulletin board should be divided into two distinct sections. The first should be the "current" side, which will have such items as statistics of previous games, a scouting report on your next opponent, play diagrams, and any material which can be replaced during the week. Examples of such material are pictures of opponents, newspaper articles on opponents, cartoons, and conference news clippings.

Pertinent information such as the home telephone numbers and addresses of the coaches and the trainer should be a part of the second, or "permanent" section. The same information regarding the managers, players, and team physician should also be listed.

Training rules should be posted where every squad member can see them and know what is expected of him. Philosophy on diet for the basketball season is an eye-catcher for squad members.

Rule changes, which occur constantly, should be visible and clearly understood by all members of the squad and by the coaches. State regulations regarding eligibility should appear on the permanent side of the bulletin board, along with those of the conference with which the school is affiliated.

CONDUCT IN THE LOCKER ROOM. The basketball locker room is your second home for approximately five months and every effort should be made to see that it is kept clean and neat. Listed below are some disciplines that should be made into formal rules which all squad members can understand and follow.

1. There are containers in the locker room in which to place paper, tape, and other refuse—they should be used at all times.
2. For equipment to dry out properly, it must be hung up. It will only take about two or three minutes a day to properly hang up your equipment. (If a drying room is available, putting used practice equipment on hangers in this facility should be specified.)
3. Every boy should shower after a workout; he should wash with soap and dry himself thoroughly; boils, skin diseases, and other infections begin with uncleanliness.
4. Conduct in the locker room must mean, specifically, that no fooling around will be tolerated; violators should have a definite type of action taken against them to keep offenses at a minimum.
5. There have been too many cases on record of players who have lost weeks of practice and game competition because of injuries suffered while clowning around in slippery locker and shower rooms; this danger should be pointed out to the team members and such clowning around discouraged.
6. Under no circumstances should equipment be borrowed from other players; it should be sought through the equipment manager, the manager, or the coach.
7. You should make provisions for a "valuables" bag where players may deposit their billfolds, watches, or other costly possessions; the student manager should be placed in charge to prevent any misfortune.
8. After departing from the locker room provided by an opposing or a host team, the squad should make certain it is left in good order; pick up orange peelings, tape, and other items. If towels and other equipment have been provided, be positive you return the same number as were issued.

BASKETBALL EXAMINATIONS FOR THE PLAYER. There are occasions when coaches take too much for granted. They have especially taken for granted not only their team's understanding of the rules of the game but their own understanding of them as well. Since all of us are vulnerable to mistakes, we should acquire a thorough knowledge of the rules. This especially applies to your squad. A short quiz on the rules of basketball will show the coach which players know and understand them. This test can be expanded to include your own pattern of play, strategy, out-of-bounds plays, and basketball background. You will not be surprised when you notice that the academically better students will score well in this phase of your program. It is almost always certain to happen.

The coach should grade the tests and record the scores on the bulletin board. Making their grades public tends to stir those players who were deficient on the test into improving themselves. It likewise develops confidence among those members who scored well. It is amazing what you will "learn" from your players. For example, we were astonished to find out that a basketball weighs nine pounds! Needless to say, the boy giving this information was not a regular on our team. A basketball does not weigh nine pounds, but is inflated to nine pounds of air pressure.

If you plan on giving such tests, one suggestion we have would be to furnish uniform diagrams of a basketball court in order to eliminate much of the guesswork and many of the inconsistencies which occur in diagramming. It should be compulsory for the players to diagram the exact replica of the play called for in the test. Details must never be neglected and the players should be made aware of this before the test. Points should be deducted accordingly if this reproduction of the play is not complete and exacting to the minute detail with which you hope to have it run in the pattern.

PLAYER EVALUATIONS. An appraisal of players from a standpoint of weaknesses and strengths should be made by the coach not only during the season but immediately after the season closes. This permits the coach to sit down with the player for a personal conference. You will find it creates a relaxed atmosphere and affords both of them an honest appraisal of the player's ability.

During the conference, the player will usually talk more freely about his performances, likes and dislikes, study problems, and other critical barriers than at any other time during the season. This interview presents an opportunity for a definite insight into the player's personal make-up; thus, while the conference must be kept confidential, it should be recorded for your own reference.

A method of evaluation other than the coach's personal observation which can be used in a personal conference is motion pictures of the games. The coach should watch films of each game and determine any improvements or faults of the performer. He should advise the player honestly and not hold back anything concerning his ability and potential. It is up to the coach to establish goals for each individual and he should expect these to be realized in the coming season.

Attitude, desire, hustle, physical attributes, quickness, shooting, passing, and team play should be covered completely for the season in the coach-player conference. A look at your statistical sheet will tell you about both the player's shortcomings and his accomplishments.

You will find players appreciate this estimate of their basketball prowess. It should stimulate and improve them, and they will work harder to improve as a result of your interest.

TEACHING DEVICES

MOTION PICTURES. Movies are one of the better teaching aids which coaches employ. They can often be as important to the coach as a seeing-eye dog is to a blind person. Their importance can never be fully gauged because it is possible to do so many things with them.

Let us begin by conceding that movies are not feasible in every high-school and college situation. However, every endeavor should be made to obtain them for at least part of the games. Here is a promotion stunt for the coach to undertake if he does not have access to a camera and the other mandatory equipment. You will always find interested townspeople who will volunteer their services for such an undertaking. Survey faculty members as another outlet. Many times you will find ardent and skilled photographers in this group.

There are several determinants which must be considered before you film a basketball game. First of all is the cost of the film and the processing of it. Presently, you should figure about $8.00 to $10.00 per hundred feet processed for 16 mm. film. Eight mm. film will be somewhat cheaper if you care to use it. The price varies depending upon how good a salesman the coach is in finding a photo shop or studio where the work can be done for the price the coach is able to pay. Many times the local television station will process the film for a nominal fee and you will have no wait such as you encounter when you send the film out of town to be processed. It is worth investigating. You can save film by not taking crowd shots, warm-ups, or cheers led by the cheerleaders. Another way of saving footage is not to film jump-ball situations or free throws unless they are in the critical period of a game and will decide its outcome.

It is the cameraman who does the shooting, however, and he must be briefed as to what to film. Tell him exactly what you want in the film so he will not waste it. A couple of hints include not moving the camera too fast, but yet attempting to keep ahead of the play to prevent having to move the camera as quickly as possible in the event the ball changes hands. The coach should relate game plans and strategy to the cameraman so he will be ready to film certain items such as a press. It is many a disappointed coach who has not informed his cameraman that he was going to press his opponent, and has had his strategy work beautifully only to find it was not in the film. The most ideal position for the cameraman is at one of the free-throw lines, rather than in the middle of the court. The perception is much better, as is the angle on the play. If it is possible, the camera should be on a permanent platform and not directly on the bleachers, to avoid unnecessary movement caused by the crowd's jarring the boards. Once again, you can consult your industrial arts staff for assistance if it is needed.

If your budget permits, take 800 feet of film, as this will almost cover an entire game for you on any level. Many of your colleges shoot as much as 1,200 feet, but this includes many extras which you need not have. In using the 800 feet, try to break it down to two 400-foot halves if the camera permits this operation. If you are able to take only 400 feet, our advice is to shoot it entirely in the second half of the game. You should never attempt to jump around, but rather, take continuous action.

With regard to inadequate lighting—and it is a problem in many gymnasiums—it is our suggestion that you take the films at "sound speed" of 16 frames per second. Look for a faster lens such as a F–15 and use a faster film (Tri–X). This will solve your filming troubles in a darker gymnasium.

There is a wide difference of opinion as to what lens to use. The one-inch lens is most ideal, as it picks up the over-all picture and has met with considerable success among photographers. A wide-angle lens can be used to cover a wider area of the floor. A two-inch lens is used for closeups, but at best you can usually get only two people in the picture and this is not practical for basketball. However, if you have one on the camera this lens is good for a change of pace in the film. A new cinemascope lens is now being experimented with. This lens covers the entire floor and enables you to see what each individual on it is doing. For all practical purposes this lens would appear to have the best potential for basketball coaches and players.

GAME FILMS. Game films have numerous uses and should not be stored away once the season is completed. This will deny to the public—and most of all, the player—the analysis and stimulation they provide. They should especially be used by the coach to allow each player to evaluate himself by seeing his own weaknesses and the mistakes he makes. There is no better way of correcting these errors than with the visual aid of the motion picture.

A training film of your pattern can be made from parts of films taken over several seasons. This can be shown to your current squad to illustrate what you expect offensively and defensively. In this type of demonstration, the players can see past squad members making your phases operable. Such a film encourages fine play and adds prestige to your program.

Studying game films can help a coach decide whether he has an applicable offensive or defensive pattern. He also should look at the opposition's offense for some idea he might fit into his own pattern while still maintaining his basic philosophy. Should he have a poor season, a look at the films will tell him many things.

LOOP FILMS. Loop films are excellent motion-picture teaching aids. They are nothing more than small clips of film in which a performer illustrates the proper way to execute a fundamental or phase of basketball technique. One commercial company has a number of renowned All-American basketball players demonstrating their pet moves on film, and these are very well done. You can obtain them for a small fee, show them to your squad members as visual education, and trust that they will be able to imitate them.

Coaches have been known to edit game films of their star players who have fine individual moves and make their own loop films. This provides added incentive and has more meaning for players, since they can see their former friends and teammates actually undergoing these phases. You can also film the player during a game separately for such a loop; this can prove very satisfactory and highly informative.

In defensing a "super-star" of the opposing team, coaches have cut up old game films of that star and spliced them together for scouting purposes. When enough footage is accumulated, the coach and the man assigned to defense the star can study the loop religiously to find some way of stopping or slowing down this star.

SLIDES. These are a relatively new innovation which can be used successfully in teaching your players proper fundamentals, play patterns, and identification of defenses. It is yet another advisable technique of testing players and their knowledge of the system, and it is easily adoptable.

James Curry of Norwalk, Ohio has been a pioneer leader in this field and has the simplest and most effective slide system devised. A coach can have his entire offense and defense put on slides for a nominal fee through Mr. Curry, and we sincerely believe it is well worth it. A second area where slides have proven popular is at coaching clinics. Here, instead of diagramming and then erasing, you merely have to flip to the next slide. By doing this you have uniform and correct images on every situation. This also eliminates any guesswork. It assures you of organization, which is a highly desirable trait in any coach.

COACHING CLINICS. The best refresher course a coach can take is to attend a coaching clinic. He should make an effort to get to at least one a year, if not as many as possible. By attending such a clinic he can reaffirm his faith in and thoughts toward certain aspects of the game. All of us need this kind of reassurance at one time or another.

The coach should use discretion and pick a basketball clinic where he can expect to learn about a particular aspect of his philosophy or the use of a successful maneuver he employs. (Fig. 4–3) He should never go without the definite purpose of improving some phase of his game. The latest methods and techniques are discussed at these clinics, and keeping abreast of the field is of prime importance. You are a lazy coach if you do not attend clinics and strive to improve not only your own knowledge of the game, but also to help your boys become better basketball players.

It is strongly recommended that coaches organize clinics in their own communities, to bring about a closer relationship between the school and community. The head coach should invite to this clinic parents, faculty, administration, friends, and members of the community, along with representatives of the press, radio, and television.

The program should be effectively organized so that it does not drag. A demonstration of offensive and defensive moves, fundamental drills, and philosophy should be included. You would also be wise to have your players put on a twenty-minute scrimmage, not only as added entertainment but so that people can get a preview of your squad.

Organization of your own basketball clinic is also highly encouraged. The fall one-day clinic has proven to have great merit. Most coaches who cannot get away for two or three days during the school year will attend a one-day session. It gives them an opportunity to return home on the same day and thus avoid missing practice sessions, which are so essential at that time of the year. Everyone we have talked with over the years seems to favor this type of clinic over the longer session.

Speakers for such clinics are in abundance. However, you should search your own area for key speakers and invite them to appear on your program. If this is your first clinic you should work that much harder to see that it is a success. If you are a high school coach and desire a college coach for the program, most of them will be more than willing to accommodate you. A number of these affairs feature both high school and college coaches to satisfy everyone in attendance. It is understood in this profession that high school coaches do some of the finest coaching jobs in the country and without these indispensable men the college ranks and their basketball programs would suffer. This is the reason we find many of the outstanding high school coaches in demand for clinics throughout the year.

TAPE RECORDERS. Basketball coaches have found an additional coaching aid in the recorder. More and more coaches are making use of this device with success. It makes a number of valuable contributions which we will mention.

If the tape recorder is to be used properly, we suggest you start in your practice sessions, where you can place the recorder in a convenient spot near you, the coach. You can then merely pick up the microphone and record mistakes which you have just witnessed, made either by an individual or by the entire team. A reminder here: do not wait any length of time before recording a mistake, as you might forget it. Once the session is completed, you will have a complete record of individual and team mistakes through this simple technique.

You should follow up your initial analysis by replaying the tape before you leave the office and jotting down the mistakes you recorded. If you have

CLINIC INFORMATION

WELCOME to Michigan State University and the 10th Annual Basketball Coaches Clinic. The program has been carefully designed to fit your special coaching needs. It is hoped that the discussions and demonstrations will be both stimulating and profitable.

HEADQUARTERS for the Clinic will be in the Kellogg Center for Continuing Education located at the corner of Harrison Road and Michigan Avenue on the campus.

REGISTRATION for the Clinic will begin at 9:00 a.m., Friday, November 16, in the Kellogg Center Lobby. An identification badge will be provided to registrants and *admission to all sessions will be by badge only.*

ONLY A LIMITED NUMBER OF TICKETS ARE AVAILABLE FOR THE MEALS OVER THE PRE-REGISTRATION NUMBER. TO BE ASSURED OF A PLACE, YOU MUST RETURN THE PRE-REGISTRATION FORM. RESERVED MEAL TICKETS ARE RELEASED FOR GENERAL SALE FIFTEEN MINUTES BEFORE SERVING.

RESERVATIONS FOR THE MEALS MAY BE MADE BY CHECKING THE APPROPRIATE COLUMNS ON THE ADVANCE REGISTRATION FORM AND RETURNING IT AT YOUR EARLIEST CONVENIENCE.

Conference Costs

Service fee to share Clinic expenses including syllabus, materials, coffee hour, complimentary ticket to Intra-squad game and coaches party _____$7.00

Luncheon at Kellogg Center November 16, Big Ten Room _____$1.85

Dinner at Kellogg Center November 16, Big Ten Room _____$2.60

Breakfast available in Kellogg Center State Room and Cafe.

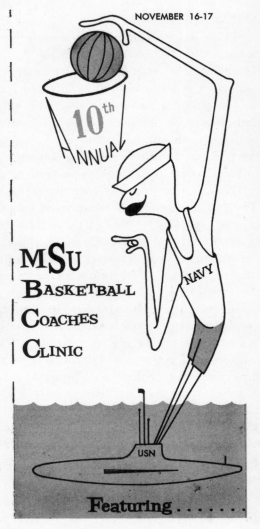

Fig. 4–3 (View 1). Example of a basketball clinic brochure.

a secretary, she can replay the tape the following morning and put down on paper every error as you announced it. This can be placed on file for the coach's use or put on the bulletin board to remind the squad of its mistakes. We also have found it a fine way to make your post-practice sheet of the day's activity.

A second method valuable to the coach is having his assistant coach tape-record an entire game from an observation point or scouting deck. The assistant observes play during the game and acts as a scout. He dictates both good and bad moves made by both teams. This method is normally used in post-game analysis, but it sometimes is helpful at half-time. It provides

Ben Carnevale, Head Basketball Coach, U.S. Naval Academy . . .

Ben is in his 17th season as coach of the Midshipmen, during which time the Navy has never had a losing basketball team. With his two years at the University of North Carolina, his overall record is 272 wins, 126 losses. Carnevale has led Navy to five N.C.A.A. tournament appearances and one in the N.I.T. In the last four seasons, his teams have qualified for three post-season tournaments.

Forddy Anderson, Head Basketball Coach of Michigan State University . . .

One of the best known and respected of modern day mentors. Under Forddy's direction, basketball at STATE attained all-time prestige peaks in the late 1950's. Before coming to MSU, Anderson coached at Great Lakes, Drake and Bradley. His 17 year coaching record shows 308 wins as against 164 losses.

Bruce Fossum, Assistant Basketball Coach of Michigan State University . . .

Formerly a highly successful coach at Green Bay West High School, Bruce is begining his fourth year at MSU. His 1959 team became the first Green Bay team to ever qualify for the state tourney. As an undergraduate at the University of Wisconsin he played guard on some highly touted Big Ten Teams. After college, Fossum coached the Wisconsin freshmen for one year and then became head coach of West Bend High School before moving to Green Bay.

PROGRAM

sponsored by:
Department of Intercollegiate Athletics
A Continuing Education Program of
MICHIGAN STATE UNIVERSITY

November 16
FRIDAY MORNING

9:00   Registration — Kellogg Center Conference Desk
      Coffee and doughnuts — Big Ten Room

10:00   Opening Session — Kellogg Center Auditorium
      WELCOME — C. L. "Biggie" Munn, Director of Athletics, MSU

10:10   NAVY OFFENSE — Ben Carnevale, U.S. Naval Academy

11:00   SPECIAL SITUATIONS — Forddy Anderson and Staff

12:00   LUNCHEON—Big Ten Room, Kellogg Center

1:30   Second Session—Men's Intramural Building
      BREAKING THE PRESS — Ben Carnevale

2:30   COMBINING DEFENSES — Forddy Anderson and Staff

3:30   DEFENSIVE DRILLS — Ben Carnevale

4:30   DEMONSTRATIONS AND DRILLS

6:00   DINNER — Big Ten Room, Kellogg Center

8:00   INTRA-SQUAD GAME — Men's Intramural Building
      (Featuring the experimental use of 12 foot baskets)

November 17
SATURDAY MORNING

Kellogg Center Auditorium

10:00   SPECIAL SITUATIONS — Ben Carnevale

11:00   PANEL DISCUSSION AND REVIEW — Ben Carnevale, Fordy Anderson & Staff

Fig. 4–3 (View 2). Example of a basketball clinic brochure.

a record of practically every game situation as it happened, and is the most accurate analytical mechanism available to the coach for recording and studying game occurrences.

Still another use calls for the coach to station a tape recorder directly under the bench during a game. When an error is made he merely snaps the machine on and dictates the mistake. One major drawback here is that the crowd background noise sometimes drowns out the coach's voice, especially since the machine is sensitive and picks up nearly every sound.

High school coaches in the Midwest have found the tape recorder to be a great help in scouting opponents. They chart opponents' plays and then dictate their individual characteristics to the recorder. Any general suggestions, comments or items of interest are also placed on the tape.

There are many kinds of tape recorders. We advocate the compact, battery-operated type for scouting purposes. It is easily accessible and takes up a minimum amount of space. For floor purposes—either in practice or in regular games—we believe the conventional tape recorder can be used most effectively.

The tape recorder certainly merits every coach's attention, as it makes scouting easier than ever before. The degree of emphasis placed on this machine will depend upon the individual coach, but we are excited about what it has done for our programs. Most schools have equipment such as a tape recorder available and are willing to let you use it. Remember, it might help you win a game.

STATISTICS. The ultimate in basketball statistics can be summed up in three words, "The Basketball Profile." The profile (Fig. 4–4) was the original idea of Coach Anderson, which he conceived after noticing—while at Bradley University—the dire need for an improved evaluation device in basketball. It is the best type of statistics sheet in basketball.

This is the most valuable chart you can have as a coach. In order to give you the very best story of the game, statistics must be kept accurately. This can best be achieved by using your assistant coach as your official chart man. He can classify this material readily, and his conclusive charting will add much more meaning to this profile sheet. In addition, it places greater importance on the basketball profile. However, if for some reason the assistant coach is unavailable for this duty, most schools will rely on student assistants. If this is the situation in your school, a thorough briefing of the boys by the head coach should take place. The coach should explain the entire chart and stress exactly what he desires to be charted. After this briefing, he should invite them to a special scrimmage session, and also let them practice charting during a regular scrimmage. Here we wish to emphasize the use of practice statistics. More enthusiasm for the practice session can be realized with the keeping of statistics. We have found that they make the scrimmages much more meaningful and game-like.

In using student assistants, better chart coverage will result if you back up a recorder with an observor. This insures that nothing will be missed. One hint to the charter: write as small as possible, but still quite legibly. This takes consummate skill which must be acquired in order for the charts to be thoroughly kept.

One slight difference in the basketball profile which we use at Michigan State and Northern Michigan is that we do not count a bat of the ball as a shot attempt by the individual player. Our recorders are notified of this beforehand so that the only time they do count a bat of the ball is when it goes into the basket. We give these instructions to our players so that instead of being penalized, they will be encouraged to continue tipping.

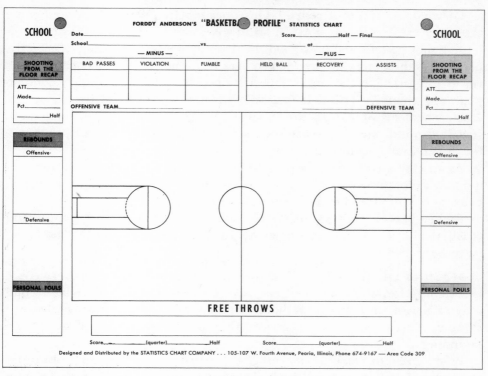

Fig. 4–4 (Views 1 and 2). "Basketball Profile" Statistics Chart.

Of what use is a shot chart? This question frequently arises and there are many valid answers. First of all, it gives the coach a picture of the offensive shot pattern and how good the defense is that he is using. Secondly, he receives the exact shooting percentages from the charts. All of this material is important to the coach, especially at halftime when he may contemplate any change. Third, it can be used as a scouting aid by telling the coach where his opponents are shooting from when they are scoring well. It will also indicate "hot spots" by individual players which can prove useful in defending against them.

As an easy identification system of charting, we recommend the use of a different-colored pencil for each of the two halves. It breaks up the normal black and white trend and is easier to read.

Remember—if statistics are to be true and worthwhile for players and coach, the key is a reliable statistician. Insist on accuracy and that no favoritism be shown.

REBOUND CHARTS. Rebounds are wins. Victories are what every coach is searching for, and continued emphasis upon rebounding is today second only to that upon scoring. Rebounding is a knack which must be learned through doing. Thus all practices should include some phase of rebounding.

Board strength means many things for the coach and his team. In order to fast break you must have the ball, and the only way you can get it is by beating the other team off the boards. Most winning teams usually manage to gain extra shot attempts at the basket through aggressive offensive rebounding. The second and third shot attempts raise the percentages in your favor.

In charting rebounds, we indicate a tip as an offensive rebound because it gets you possession of the ball. Some coaches' philosophies differ in this respect, but this points up the fact that you and the statistician should be in complete agreement on what you desire.

Your two recorders can keep track of both offensive and defensive rebounds very easily on the basketball profile. These statistics can be profitable if used to make a graph consisting of all team members and their rebounding performances for each game. This can be made advantageous by posting them on your bulletin board. Of course, a tip is a rebound unless it goes in; then it's a successful shot.

OTHER CHARTS. Individual reactions, offensively and defensively, good and bad, are recorded for all games the same as the shots and rebounds. Adequate and concise space is available on the sheet for all of these. Bad passes, violations, and fumbles are all charted against the player. With this information it is helpful in order to arrive at the type of game the boy played. This is employed to help improve his over-all game and his other abilities through Coach Anderson's plus-and-minus system of grading.

Held balls can receive either a credit or a loss depending upon whether you gain or lose possession of the ball. Recoveries and assists should be tallied throughout the game. An assist is defined by the authors as a direct act causing the automatic basket to be made. It is given only when a basket is scored to complete the play.

DEFENSIVE SCOREBOOK. The "Defensive Scorebook" was originated by Coach Albeck in 1959 after he noted a need for an effective device to help evaluate the defense. It is a standardized scorebook which flashes a clear and unmistakable warning of sloppy defense, blows the whistle on the player who tends to relax or rest on defense, and reflects credit upon the player who hustles on defense as well as on offense.

The book serves three major purposes. It gives a complete team record on defense, with detailed information on areas which are noticeably weak. It provides an individual statistical comparison of players, revealing who is doing the best job defensively and pointing up each player's strengths and weaknesses. Finally, the material can be given to sports writers and sportscasters, directing proper attention to the important role of good defensive players who too often are overlooked or underrated.

It was especially the tendency to ignore defensive ability while praising the more obvious accomplishments on offense that prompted Coach Albeck to develop the defensive scorebook. A basketball player still must go both ways. It's better to have this in mind before and during a game than after the final buzzer, when it's too late to matter.

The defensive scorebook is divided into two sections (Fig. 4–5). One side contains a listing of the 20 most common defensive errors. The other side lists 20 defensive credits or defensive maneuvers which are extremely important but which are too often neglected from a coaching standpoint. When a player commits a defensive error, such as "failing to protect the baseline," his number is listed opposite the fault. Thus, the coach knows that this particular player neglected a fundamental and the blunder can be pointed out. On the defensive side, a player receives recognition for such defensive skills as "deflections." Incidentally, credit for deflections is given regardless of whether our team gains possession of the ball.

The book also divides the game into halves and contains columns for overtime, error total, credit total, and game total. Another column indicates defensive assignments for each player for every game. The separate column for overtime periods provides a clear and distinct record of overtime action. In the conventional statistic chart, overtime statistics are simply part of the second-half figures and are difficult, if not impossible, to isolate.

A statistician and spotter who are reliable can handle this scorebook in the same manner as the offensive statistics.

The defensive scorebook can be a valuable coaching aid. It provides a sound basis for half-time analysis and adjustment. It contains a summary

DATE: _____   DEFENSIVE SCOREBOOK

Team: _____ vs. _____ at _____

PLAYER'S NAME	No.	DEFENSIVE ERRORS	FIRST HALF	SECOND HALF	OV'T.	ERROR TOTAL	MAN ASSIGNED
		Left shooter unmolested					
		Left feet on fake shot					
		Unnecessary foul					
		Did not protect baseline					
		Did not screen out man					
		Did not protect against quick cut					
		Did not hustle back on defense					
		Did not talk on screen					
		Unnecessary slapping at ball					
		Did not help teammate					
		Did not keep hand up on shot					
		Went behind screen					
		Made a poor scissor					
		Did not fight through screen					
		Poor defensive footwork					
		Did not sag to help out					
		Improper shuffling					
		Improper approach to man					
		Has poor vision on play					
		Did not point out offensive man					
		TEAM TOTALS					

REMARKS:

DATE: _____   DEFENSIVE SCOREBOOK

Team: _____ vs. _____ at _____   Game No._____

PLAYER'S NAME	No.	DEFENSIVE CREDITS	FIRST HALF	SECOND HALF	OV'T.	CREDIT TOTAL	GAME TOTAL
		Stealing the ball					
		Blocked shot					
		Interception					
		Deflection					
		Recovery					
		Secured Held Ball					
		Did protect baseline					
		Hurried Shot Off					
		Screened off offensive man					
		Did keep hands up on shooter					
		Made an effective switch					
		Did sag properly to help out					
		Did fight through screen					
		Prevention of point by hustle					
		Slowed man on fast break					
		Tipped ball out of trouble					
		Made a good two time					
		Made a good outlet pass					
		Pressured rebounder					
		Did talk on a screen					
		TEAM TOTALS					

REMARKS:

Fig. 4–5. Defensive errors page (top) and defensive credits page (bottom) from the "Defensive Scorebook."

for the season, is useful in improving your defense and preparing for the opposing team's offense, and it stimulates player reaction to liking defensive play.

WHAT CHARTS DO FOR YOU. If used properly, the basketball profile which we have described will provide you with a precise as well as completely unbiased written story of what has happened in each game. You will find it valuable for the following reasons:

1. It screens the players and their individual performances.
2. It makes for an objective method of evaluating team members.
3. It gives a certain amount of incentive to the players.
4. It can be used as a double-check against the players as the coach sees them on the floor.
5. It will aid the coach in diagnosing where he can improve a player.
6. It is useful when you are furnishing statistics to the press and other public information people.

SCOUTING REPORTS. This part of basketball has assumed greater prominence than ever before. It should not be passed off lightly since it will be a strong influence upon whether or not you win your share of basketball games. It is not uncommon for college scouts to fly from the East Coast to California and vice versa to scout a basketball opponent. In certain areas in high school, we have heard of prep team coaches scouting an opponent as many as 15 or 20 times in a season. This gives some idea of the degree of emphasis which is placed on scouting by certain coaches.

A thorough scouting report is to be valued beyond estimation. It relates detailed items which enable you to properly identify and prepare your team for the opposition. The degree of emphasis placed on reports will vary, and once again this decision will rest with the head coach. However, we strongly advocate that you scout every opponent at least once. There is nothing which disturbs a coach more than to go into a game without a knowledge of his opponent.

The following is a suggested plan for the scout to observe, whether he is a beginner or a veteran.

PROCEDURE

1. Secure a good seat and have your materials ready for use and organized in advance. You should sit as high as possible so that you can look down on the action.
2. Arrive for the preliminary game so that you can watch the reserves play. They sometimes may show you more than the varsity group.
3. Do most of your scouting in the first half, especially the first 10 minutes. This is the time when teams run their patterns best.
    (a) Diagram and explain team moves and patterns.
    (b) Record individual notes at all times.
    (c) Take down all special plays such as jump-ball plays, out-of-bounds plays, and last-second plays.

4. Use the half-time intermission to make mental notes and register specifically all individual and team moves you have observed.

5. Use the second half to pick up what you missed in the first, along with any change in operation from the first.

   (a) Include any variations which might be used.

   (b) List particular pet plays the team employs as well as individual moves.

   (c) Note the first substitutes and characteristics of each.

   (d) Register any strategy employed by the team, including any stall or delay game. The pressing game should also be written down as well as the zone press offense.

6. You should attempt to complete your report with statistics of the game. Many times these are made available by the host team upon request. If you have a second scout he can chart and record the necessary statistics you desire.

ANALYSIS

1. It is the duty of the scout to attempt to think out the other coach's basic philosophy in a general way:

   (a) Is he a fast break exponent?

   (b) Does he believe in a single or a double post?

   (c) Does he have a hard-cutting team using many screens?

2. The scout should analyze the opponents and see if their actions were dictated by the play of the opposition.

   (a) How did their opponent defend against them?

   (b) What will they do if we do this, or even *this?*

   (c) What strengths do they have which we must take away?

   (d) What sacrifice will we have to make to counteract their strength?

EMPHASIS

1. Be careful not to key the team for each game in the same way.

2. Do not overscout. It is easily done and you can expect grief if this happens. Overscouting refers to supplying your team with so much material that they become confused and do not perform well on defense. The offense also usually suffers as a result of this overpreparedness.

3. The importance of the scouting report depends upon the team using it and the tradition of recognition given the report.

NO-BOUNCE TRAINING BALL. Recently a manufacturer in the basketball sporting goods line produced a "no-bounce" basketball. One of the first men to realize the need for such a training device was Coach Anderson. He has always maintained that there is excessive dribbling on the part of most players and he has a slogan which pretty well sums up his feeling for the dribble-happy player. It is, "Excessive dribbling by a player is like too much candy—it makes you sick." The no-bounce ball, as it is designed, helps eliminate this untimely habit by the individual player. It is used exclusively in passing drills, especially during the early season practices, but can also be used in some of your fast-break drills where you stress the passing game.

The ball is regulation size in circumference and weight and has the "feel" of a regular basketball, although the cover is made of rubber. You can fire a normal shot at the basket with it and it will react the same as a regular ball until it hits the floor. As it hits the floor, you then become aware of the fact that you are not going to get anywhere with it by trying to dribble. We firmly believe it is one of the better coaching aids in the field.

SHARPSHOOTER RIMS. This coaching idea received great acclaim when Loyola University of Chicago won the NCAA basketball championship in 1963. Much of the Ramblers' shooting success was attributed to the fact that the team practiced on a smaller 15-inch goal for the greater portion of the season. It was felt by the players that their shooting percentage was improved by spending a long period of time practicing on this smaller goal.

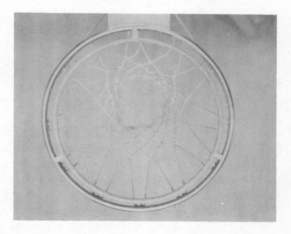

Fig. 4–6. The 16-inch "sharpshooter rim" inside the regular rim.

There have been other rims similar to this. One such shooting rim is a 16-inch removable rim which fits into your regular basketball goal and is held tightly in place by a single set screw. (Fig. 4–6) It has been proven that players become better shooters after continued use of this device. Whether part of the answer lies in the psychology of the rim we may never know. However, all the players we have encountered who were using these sharpshooter rims were sold on their value and believed it was making them more accurate shooters.

TRIP ORGANIZATION

One of the major tasks a coach undertakes in this field is the organization of out-of-town travel for basketball contests. There are many factors to be considered. In the organization of any trip, the distance to be traveled is important, along with the mode of transportation. Things to be noted are the number of players making the trip and the amount of supervision that will be adequate. School administrations insist on proper supervision, and rightly so, because there is nothing as important as the student under these circumstances.

Foresight on the coach's part is necessary in planning trips. Random planning and hoping for the best is haphazard. All plans for trips should be organized in advance of the upcoming game. This insures elimination of all carelessly-planned projects and travel.

A list of items, such as school insurance for your players, acquisition of bus or station wagons, and the use of cars should be completely double-checked early in the fall before the season starts. Of paramount importance is whether the trip will be overnight. Hotel accommodations, meals, and other arrangements have to be taken care of at the earliest convenient time.

PLAYER RESPONSIBILITY. The coach should delegate a number of responsibilities to each individual team member making the trip. These include the following:

1. *Promptness and Punctuality*

   It is obligatory that each player be ready to leave 10 minutes before the scheduled time of departure. The players should familiarize themselves with the complete agenda of the trip, noting all times of meals, squad meetings and departure times.

2. *Itinerary*

   On overnight trips, an itinerary should be posted on the bulletin board and copies handed to each squad member. They are expected to have the itinerary with them, and to use it. Copies will also be given to the superintendent, the athletic director, and every parent. The itinerary is to be followed rigorously and yet must be flexible enough to allow for changes or emergencies. It should be prepared one week in advance.

3. *Proper Dress*

   Players should wear suits and ties if possible. A buttoned collar on a sport shirt with coat is advised secondly. Shined shoes, a clean shave, and a haircut are ingredients which cannot be overlooked. Letter jackets or sweaters are discouraged as is any other inappropriate apparel. If the trip is overnight, players are expected to be in a sport coat or suitcoat at all times, especially when they are in the hotel lobby or motel entrance. You may receive a test here and you should make any player return to his room for the correct attire if he is not outfitted respectably and in the manner you require.

4. *Social Decorum*

   The coach can do a real job here since many boys have not been subjected to conformities which they will face on trips. You must remind each player that he is representing his high school, community, parents, and himself on all trips. He is constantly being judged on his actions, conduct, and manners by various people. It is imperative that he perform admirably, or be replaced. Here are items which should be brought to the players' attention:

(a) Players must conduct themselves as gentlemen at all times.

(b) While in any public place (hotel lobby, hotel, restaurant, etc.), players should speak softly and practice their best manners.

(c) The assignment of roommates will be delegated by the head coach. Do not forget your bus driver. He should have a private room of his own to provide him adequate rest and comfort.

(d) Table etiquette should be discussed with the players as a group and the proper etiquette brought to their attention. This can save you later embarrassment, and it will take only a few minutes of your time.

(e) The need for chivalry should be explained to the group, as well as the need for exercising general courtesy whenever the opportunity arises.

5. *Bus Conduct*

This can become a trouble spot if the coach does not step in immediately and establish certain rules for the players to abide by while they are enroute to a game.

Players may be assigned seats on the vehicle, although it is not necessary. Should you have a junior varsity squad with you, have them sit together on one side of the bus and the varsity members on the other side. Both teams should be concentrating on the upcoming game and should avoid any horseplay whatsoever.

The opening of any windows is discouraged completely. This eliminates yelling at girls when you go through other cities. It might seem trivial at the moment, but do not forget the image which you are presenting to the public. Shouting out of windows does not enhance it.

Card playing is frowned upon, but each coach will have his own philosophy concerning this. Finally, obscene language should never be tolerated on the bus. The earlier you make the squad aware of this rule the quicker you will have command of the situation. With most teams it is a minor problem, but you may encounter it some day and will want to know what course of action to take.

Finally, the golden rule for all athletic trips should be: *Every member on the bus is expected to return in the same manner, and there will be no exceptions.* Conduct must be the same going and coming.

BENCH DISCIPLINE AND PROCEDURE.   There is nothing more important for a coach to maintain than proper bench control. Unless your players are instructed as to what you expect, you may have problems. The coach can prevent any difficulties by imparting his rules in a syllabus or at a squad meeting prior to the opening game.

Many coaches like all of their players to gather around the team when a time-out is called and before a ball game commences. This is up to the individual coach, but we believe it is an excellent coaching aid. It gives the starting five confidence, promotes squad spirit, and creates the psychological effect of allied association and unity upon all members.

Players on the bench should be instructed to sit down. Under no circumstances should they be allowed to converse with an official. They should be permitted to shout words of encouragement to their fellow teammates, but never be allowed to make a disparaging remark to either an official or an opposing player.

The coach's conduct is of paramount importance in these situations. He is a leader and the home crowd, players, and fans will look to him for his reaction. They will quickly follow the pattern of behavior he pursues. If he is a so-called "wild man" on the bench and constantly berating officials' decisions, you can expect his players and fans to be influenced by this conduct. They will follow a similar pattern. On the other hand, if he can remain calm on the bench and accept the official's decisions, the fans will follow suit. This is one of the major points of emphasis at yearly basketball conventions. The improper conduct of coaches is a real menace to the game.

It should be pointed out, however, that the coach should fight for his players, or at least discuss with the officials any question there might be concerning one of their decisions. The opportune time is at a time-out, where he can instruct his team captain to ask for an interpretation of the decision. The coach can query the official himself if the play concerns a technicality. By doing this at a time-out, he will show fairness and respect to the team, fans, and himself. In most cases, the officials will be glad to explain the situation. An established pattern which has been useful to us in planning and organizing this phase is as follows:

1. As the team first appears on the floor they should go immediately into their lay-up drill or three-man weave. These combine running, passing, and shooting in a snappy drill. After approximately eight minutes, or ten turns (whichever occurs first), by each member, have them go into their pattern shooting. The free-throw line during your free-shooting period should be occupied by every player, each of whom should attempt a minimum of 10 free throws.

2. Most squads will return to the locker room for a last-minute briefing. This is a good time during which to have the national anthem played. Many schools are using this time rather than delay the game at the outset. It also seems to take the "edge" off the players.

3. If you are introducing both teams prior to the opening tip-off, be sure you advise the opposing coach and relay specific instructions in order that he can tell his squad where they are supposed to be for the pre-game ceremonies.

4. Organize your pre-game huddle so that all members either group around you and the starters or remain seated. The time-outs should be duly organized in the same manner, although this will depend upon the coach and what he wants to do.

5. The coach must also explain to the number one, two, and three substitutes that they are to sit next to him so that he can keep them informed at all times as to what is happening on and off the floor. At this time you should also make sweat-suit arrangements with all substitutes. Their jackets and pants should be unzipped or unbuttoned, ready for immediate entry into the game without any loss of time.

PUBLIC RELATIONS COMMUNICATIONS

Public relations is not a new field. It began when the first pupil faced the first teacher in the first classroom. Coaches have public relations simply by the very nature of their work. They have contact with students, parents, and people in the community. The coach's public relations consist of what people think about his basketball program, how they value it, and what he is attempting to do with it. Their thoughts and attitudes about your program will be vital and respected. For this reason, you must put your best foot forward.

Every coach in basketball inescapably is a public relations agent. A coach must develop the desire and ability to have good relations with all people. He must reveal the right attitude and know-how at all times. If he is not blessed with these qualities then he must work harder to develop a better public image.

One Big Ten Conference basketball coach has repeatedly stated that his first job is to have the ability to recruit excellent basketball players. His second task is to establish and maintain excellent public relations. Finally, he is a coach. This is a rather strange order of criteria for a basketball coach, but one which should not come as a surprise since it is absolutely valid. Never in the history of the game has so much emphasis been placed on public relations.

Since so much is demanded of the coach, he must be aware of the "big three" of public relations. The following are some suggestions as to how to handle these three important areas.

RADIO

1. Provide available space for the broadcasting team in your gymnasium and make them as comfortable as possible.
2. The radio station should be notified of all your scores when the games are played out of town and not being broadcast.
3. Regular news releases should be prepared and sent to the radio station for use on their sports programs.

4. Visits by the coach and players to the radio station, for interviews, should be encouraged.
5. Your complimentary season pass list should include the radio stations.
6. Your conference can promote interest via this media by arranging a weekly coach's interview or by having a special basketball show.
7. If you are to appear on a radio station, be organized and prepared.
8. Help the sports director recognize possible programming ideas.

TELEVISION. The impact of television can be seen by the number of television sets now in use in America. Well over 85 per cent of our population either owns or has access to a T.V. set.

Where radio relies on sound to communicate, television employs visual images as well. Every object and motion visible to the viewing audience influences them in some manner. The coach should thus be properly aware of this factor.

This communication medium reaches right into the living room of thousands of people in a way that no other medium can, and it makes the school, the coach, and the players visible to these and countless others. The impression made on this audience can do much for your image and that of the school.

Do not forget that your appearance on camera, mannerisms, ability to communicate, and speech will make profound imprints upon the television audience. We have listed other relevant ideas which can be of aid to all coaches, when they come in contact with television:

1. The sports director and coach should agree upon what is to be discussed before appearing, in order to insure complete coordination of program subject matter.
2. The proper attire for a television appearance must include a suit (or sport coat) and tie.
3. Brief your players, if they are to be on the program. At the same time, *encourage them to speak up when they are asked questions.*
4. When you are on camera, speak distinctly and take your time. Look at the camera or the interviewer rather than away from both.
5. Arrive at least 15 minutes ahead of time for a briefing period, so that you won't be caught off guard by any questions.
6. Make as many appearances as possible and cooperate genuinely with these people.
7. Suggest that the sports director or announcer come to one of your practice sessions and film a short interview with you for a change of pace. This on-the-spot interview is a favorite of television sports announcers.
8. Try to arrange a half-hour sports show during the basketball season to promote your sport. See the station's director and arrange this part of the program.

NEWSPAPERS. Of these three media of communication, the oldest is the newspaper. It is also the most important to the basketball coach. Supporters of radio and television will challenge this statement, but the press can give better and more thorough coverage to basketball than the other two media. It is usually easier for a newspaper to run a daily basketball story than it is for the other two media. Both radio and television are somewhat hampered in that they must condense their material and are unable to devote the great deal of time and space to a subject that a newspaper can.

Whether the newspaper writer is from a small town or a large city, most are avid basketball fans. Their write-up of the game has a bearing on the coach and the team. If the coach is cooperative in these matters, he will find his position with the press to be much richer and more worthwhile. Remember, these writers are in a position to praise or criticize. Be patient and cooperative with them.

To be successful in this area, you should:

1. Always submit all statistical information to them.
2. Send every basketball release to them, as well as all early season notices and a "thank-you" letter at the end.
3. Be honest and try to answer their questions.
4. Never ask for or expect favoritism from any newspaper.
5. Never try to "use" a newspaper in any way.
6. Encourage the sports writer to attend practice sessions, and be courteous to him when he is in your school.
7. Be certain the sports writer has proper seating, parking, etc., at all home basketball games.
8. Make all release dates on publicity available to all newspaper people at the same time—do not show favoritism.
9. There will be times when you will take the newspaperman into your confidence and tell him what you are doing. The sportswriter should respect your judgment and keep this confidence.

In conclusion, a final rule which makes a great deal of sense spells out what procedure must be followed in public relations communication: *Whatever is done in public relations must be done well.* Poor public relations efforts are worse than none at all.

COACHES AND PUBLIC SPEAKING. The coach is constantly before the public, being called upon to deliver innumerable speeches in front of various groups. On the podium, he must reflect a keen interest in the group to which he is speaking. He must be proficient in all speech situations. These will include school assemblies, pep rallies, service club, luncheons and banquets.

This area can be one of the coach's strongest assets, if he is willing to give time and attention to its strengthening. You can never spend too much time as a coach on the study of speech organization and presentation.

Speech organization demands rich resources, materials, and interest in the subject. These can be drawn from the coach's personal and professional interests and experiences, current affairs, and his reading. Every coach should develop a number of types of speeches and attempt to have one ready for each occasion at which he may be requested to speak. Here again you are presenting the inevitable "image," and you will want it to be a good one.

THE HIGH SCHOOL AND COLLEGE ALL-SPORTS BANQUET. This ceremony is what your athletes have been waiting for all during the year. The recognition and awarding of letters is traditionally the highlight of any sports year. It is at this time that the boys are rewarded for the many sacrifices made on the hardwood during the long winter months. They look forward to this night and you should not detract from its importance. Besides, not only the players are involved but, in many cases, the parents and community are invited to the banquet. Since we are called upon to make many speeches to groups of this kind, it has been our experience to observe the following about high school and college all-sports banquets:

1. *Organization*
    (a) Set a date as close to the end of the sports year as possible. Do not forget the time of the banquet.
    (b) Secure a speaker four weeks in advance.
    (c) Contact your toastmaster well in advance.
    (d) Have the necessary awards on hand, since this is the primary function of the banquet.
    (e) Send your speaker a reminder note three days prior to the banquet.
    (f) Make the necessary arrangements for obtaining the gymnasium, church, or other facility you will be using. Make certain it will be large enough to handle all of the people.
    (g) Arrangements for the cooking staff must be made early. The menu should be arranged by these people. We recommend cafeteria-style serving as it is the easiest and quickest for high school banquets where a larger group of community people may be involved.
    (h) If tickets are to be sold for the banquet, they should be printed and circulated early in order that all who desire to attend can obtain tickets.
    (i) Publicity should be released to news outlets periodically, to remind the public of this event.
    (j) Make available a movie projector, reel, extension cord, and screen for any showing of movies by the speaker. If movies are to be shown, this should be done upon the completion of the regular program and on a voluntary basis. Often you will find people who do not wish to stay for the film and this gives them an opportunity to leave.
    (k) Letters expressing your appreciation should be sent out to all key individuals who helped in putting on the banquet.
    (l) Seating for the teams and players must be provided.
    (m) Programs must be provided. They can be printed outside or mimeographed by school personnel, whichever is more desirable.
    (n) Any musical group presentation should be arranged for through the music director of the school.

2. *Program*

   (a) Start the banquet on time. People want events to begin promptly and delays cause considerable inconvenience.

   (b) Minimize talks by other people. Honored guests should be recognized, but not heard from.

   (c) A toastmaster should "move" the program and keep it from dragging out.

   (d) The coach, in his presentation, should be as interesting as possible. Loose organization here will be most evident. Be sincere and hold your talk to a minimum. Talk about a review of your season and some of the highlights for the team. If you are going to introduce your team members do it by classes, with your seniors last.

   (e) The banquet should be as pleasing as possible. This is the culmination of the year's work and the players want it to be the best.

   (f) The main speaker should be the first man on the program. This eliminates his waiting until last, when the entire group's attention begins to wander.

   (g) Cheerleaders should be recognized at the banquet, for their efforts during the year.

   (h) Pictures should be taken of the most valuable players and coaches, along with photos of any persons receiving special awards.

3. *Team Members*

   (a) All members of the team should be in attendance for this function. No excuses can be accepted. Their parents, too, should be invited. This is not always necessary on the college level.

   (b) All members should wear a suit and tie or, as a minimum requirement, a sport coat with a sport shirt that is buttoned at the collar. In high school, the coach might have to be of help in this. Perhaps not all individuals will have the proper attire, and you should be willing to help secure it for players who do not.

   (c) Encourage players to be neat and clean in appearance.

   (d) Name cards for each player should be made, and should be as decorative as possible, to encourage the players to keep them as souvenirs of the program.

   (e) Senior members should sit together as a unit. Proper acknowledgment should be accorded them, as it is actually their evening. If it is possible, have the senior table elevated on risers so they can be seen.

LETTERMEN CLUBS AND THEIR ACTIVITIES. Any consideration of basketball programs would be incomplete without mention of the lettermen clubs and their activities. Since over 90 per cent of our high schools and 85 per cent of our colleges sponsor a basketball team, this organization can be of service in supplementing the athletic budget. Many schools do not have sufficient income or athletic budget, and this club can go a long way toward helping obtain things for the sports program which their teams ordinarily would not be able to have. A lettermen's club may be used as an athletic promotional organization whereby all members are urged to participate actively.

Many of our high schools make use of different promotions for the purchase of items not provided for in the regular athletic budget. Among the ideas which we have come across are:

1. Purchase of blazers for the teams.
2. Color motion picture film, to be used for a basketball highlights movie.
3. Pre-season dance and party for lettermen's club.
4. A trip to the state tournament, a college game, or professional game.
5. Purchase of photographs, to be displayed in local high school or business establishments in your community.
6. Record board of all-conference and all-state players, to be placed in lobby of gymnasium or fieldhouse.
7. Flags of conference schools or non-conference opponents, to be hung in the gymnasium.
8. Purchase of other recreational needs for the school, such as a table for table tennis.

Money-Making Projects. The purpose of a lettermen's club, in most schools, is that of a fund-raiser. The group will attempt to organize various promotions to raise money. Some of the most successful we have observed are as follows:

1. Members selling pencils, candy, booster buttons and advertising for basketball programs.
2. Bake sales have been popular as a fund raiser.
3. School dances, car washes, and the selling of sweatshirts with the name of the school are other means of making money.
4. A club-sponsored carnival in the gymnasium may be attractive and worthwhile.
5. The running of concessions at all athletic events during the school year.
6. The sponsorship of professional entertainment as an attraction.
7. A cookbook to be sold. The players' mothers may give their favorite recipes.
8. An edition of the school newspaper which can be sold to the community. This edition should be something "special" for this money-maker.

LEADERSHIP DEVELOPMENT. First of all, the successful basketball teams we have seen through the years seem to have leadership. This leadership comes either through respect of team members for such a leader causing them to win or as a team with that intangible spirit that cannot be beaten. Nothing great is ever achieved on the basketball floor without leadership. Every coach is looking for the player who will "take charge" on the floor and off, directing the team's activity. These individuals are rare in the field in comparison with the number of boys playing the game. It is the responsibility of the coach to be constantly on the lookout for a boy with this ability and quality. Sometimes it is a factor that is difficult to determine, especially by the younger coaches.

1. *How to Develop Leaders*

   (a) When looking for an individual with possibilities as a leader, the following criteria should be established: In what manner can he be rated as a player? In what regard does the squad hold him? Is he bright enough and interested enough to hold their respect? Will he show maturity and cooperativeness with the coaching staff? Is he dependable?

   (b) Leadership can be developed only when individuals are given responsibility. The captain of the squad should meet with the coach and discuss openly what is expected of him as a leader.

   (c) The captain should be instructed to hold informal meetings with the squad during the year to air any problems. The captain will then carry the results of the meeting back to the coach.

   (d) The captain and senior members of the squad will be expected to enforce training rules on both varsity and junior varsity squads.

   (e) The captain and players should work up the training rules subject to the approval of the coach.

   (f) The captain should be encouraged to use his initiative in handling minor problems without first running to the coach.

   (g) The coach must show his confidence and give complete backing to his captain and players whenever possible.

2. *Examples of Leadership*

   (a) The coaching staff must set the example before any players can be expected to follow.

   (b) Floor poise by the coaching staff will be reflected in the players.

   (c) In the event of a head coach's absence, the assistant coach and captain should be placed in charge of the practice session.

   (d) Coaches should help players with special problems.

   (e) The captain should report any player absent and the reason for this absence, if he knows it, beforehand.

   (f) The coaching staff should be kept informed of what is going on.

SQUAD SPIRIT AND MORALE. Every successful activity is structured upon an ideal, and the contingency of such an activity is greatly determined by the sincerity with which this ideal is nurtured. Great teams are built around both discipline and tradition. Schools want coaches who can get the best results out of the player personnel and inspire the players with ideals of sportsmanship.

The maintenance and promotion of squad spirit and morale is a major contribution which the coach must make. It is a significant aspect of coaching, since any basketball team operates as a family. In doing this, they learn to sacrifice their own desires for the sake of the team. Your team should recognize the fact they act for the *whole* team and not just one part.

The coach must learn how to handle each player as a personality. This is a difficult task at best. There is no set of rules on how to inspire fine basketball performance. What is good for one player cannot always be used effectively on another. Some players need to be driven into performances, while others will rebel at the same type of tactics. There are those who, when handled silently but persuasively, blossom into better basketball players.

Some of the greatest basketball victories in history have been achieved during the pre-game talks given by the coaches. Teams who have been out-manned in every respect have pulled off remarkable upsets. If you look behind the scenes of each game, you will find it was more than luck that enabled the underdog to win. More than likely, you will uncover the answer in some form of inspiration or leadership which was engineered to give the team momentum for this crucial contest.

The coach should have the ability to strike fear from the players' hearts. He must make the boys show utter disregard for the opponent's power. They must display a fighting spirit, which means the building of team morale to create this spirit. This inspiration increases strength, and strength when tied to a fundamentally sound team can cause an upset.

The authors have been asked how they handle such situations. This is a difficult question to answer, but the following will serve as a guide for you.

1. *Player Treatment*
   (a) The coach will have a written policy which will inform the players of what is expected of them. In this way, players know where they stand.
   (b) The coach must be close to his players and yet far enough away to maintain respect. Players may attempt to take advantage of you and the coach must bear down immediately to retain his position. Any decision you make must be final.
   (c) The coach will use, whenever possible, a positive approach on all matters pertaining to player personnel.
   (d) Criticism will always be constructive.
   (e) A player will be "chewed out" in private, never in front of the squad. This should be done immediately after an occurrence or practice session.
   (f) Those players who are not playing hard enough and who insist on not making an attempt to improve their attitude will be asked to leave the squad.

2. *What Is Expected of the Coach*
   (a) The coach is expected to show ardent zeal and enthusiasm for his sport. This is contagious and will be picked up by team members.
   (b) The coach must be punctual. Players will not respond if you are habitually late for practices, meetings, and other affairs. This might be interpreted as a token of your interest.

(c) The coach *must* keep all promises to players regardless of what they might be. Players feel it is your obligation, and you are duty-bound to carry it out.

(d) The players expect fair treatment. Be tough when you have to be, and yet by all means fair.

(e) You should endeavor to see that the best schedule available is arranged. Your team would rather play against better teams than to continually beat weaker opposition.

(f) The coach should be persistent in seeing that players travel, eat, and sleep first class. It cannot always be this way, but your budget will allow for a few indulgences which the players will appreciate.

(g) Good equipment is of great consequence to players. It lifts their morale and spirit. A coach can elevate himself in the team's eyes with this psychological weapon.

(h) Finally, the coach should conduct himself in a manner in which the players, school, and community will be proud.

3. *Morale Builders*

(a) One of the better means of promoting a closeness among your squad is to have a "get-together" at the coach's house. It might be in the form of a cook-out in the spring or fall. Make it known that your home is open to all of them at all times.

(b) Pep meetings and rallies are a common denominator for all students and these appeal in the best of school tradition. As mentioned, a speech by the coach is always important, and a pep meeting is also a good time for the captain to say a few words.

(c) Special nights such as a Winter Homecoming, Parent's Night, and Civic Club Night are fine promotion stunts which lend cooperation and spirit to the program.

(d) If your school color is, for example, green, encourage a "Wearing of the Green" for all home games. The entire student body can sit in one section and wear clothing which is green in color. This brings about school spirit to a fever pitch. According to whatever is the dominant color of the school, such an activity might be called a "Wearing of the Blue" or a "Wearing of the Scarlet."

(e) Utilization of bulletin boards for stories and other features can serve a useful purpose for the basketball team and student body.

HINTS FOR SUMMER WORKOUTS

In every coach's mind the ideal thing would be to keep his basketball players playing the year round. Coaches realize that the extra hours of practice will make boys better basketball players. Many coaches spend countless hours mapping out individual programs that seek improvement over past-season performances. Many boys will go to a summer camp for extra tutelage from some of basketball's finest instructors. It is our feeling that regardless of the type of program designed, if the player is not willing to put his best efforts into it, the plan will not be effective. The same holds true for any basketball camp instruction. The desire to improve must come from the individual.

The following is a guide sheet which is handed to a basketball player who is interested in improvement. It is categorized according to position and will depend upon what your pattern of play dictates regarding shooting. It is not the answer to every player's weaknesses, but improvement will come to the individual who works diligently on this schedule. It is set up primarily to serve as a guide for coaches who are just beginning in the coaching profession.

FORWARDS

1. Practice 100 shots from each side of the floor. This will include those coming off the inside and outside screens for the jump shot.
2. Practice baseline jump shots with a minimum of 50 on each side.
3. Practice driving both the baseline and off the inside screen. Place a chair in your path and tell a teammate to stand on it with raised hand and shoot over this simulated defensive man.
4. Practice tipping the ball continuously against the backboard and see how many tips you can attempt before missing or tiring.
5. Tip the ball with both hands five times and then attempt to tap it in the basket.
6. We encourage the "dunking" of the ball. It can be done by many small men who acquire the knack of knowing how to jump.
7. Practice dribbling to the baseline, reversing off the dribble for the jump shot 50 times on each side of the floor.
8. Master the overhead pass to the pivot man. Forwards who can feed the pivot man when he is open are at a premium.
9. Practice 10 changes of direction from both sides. Learn to play without the ball. This is the test of the good basketball player.
10. Squeeze a tennis ball to build strength in your fingers and hands. If you have an old bowling ball, rotate the wrist in all directions and you will develop stronger wrist action for your jump shots.

CENTERS

1. Practice 100 jump shots from the high post. As you receive the ball, turn and face the defensive man and take the jump shot over him.
2. In shooting practice, begin in at the three-foot area and work out to the free-throw line. Include both baselines in your territory to score from. This is your practice area and nowhere else.
3. If you are making a hook shot, start in the three-foot area and progress outwardly once you have mastered this spot. Take 50 shots to begin with.
4. Learn to keep the ball chest-high on your jump shots. Do not lower it. This insures that when you shoot the ball with your hands extended

over your head, you do not have to bring it up very far before letting it go.

5. Rebound a shot and get rid of the ball quickly. Simulate a fast-break situation. The quicker you can get rid of the ball accurately the better opportunity you have of scoring.

6. Be conscious of good shooting form on all your shots. Don't "throw" a ball at the basket. Shoot it with "touch."

7. To improve your coordination, skip rope 300 times daily.

8. Do bench jumping at the end of your workout. This is a close correlation to rebounding in the games. You must clear a two-foot bench 35 times without stopping. This will develop leg strength, which most centers need.

9. A rope climb will aid you as a center in developing the upper extremities of your body.

GUARDS

1. Practice a minimum of 15 drive-ins from each side, going at top speed.
2. Practice 100 jump shots from the outside perimeter.
3. Learn to be an efficient screener so that you can free a teammate.
4. Learn to handle the ball flawlessly and without mistakes.
5. Practice your center feeds, as you will be handling the ball more than the other players.
6. Learn change-of-pace dribbling, as it will lend to frequent scoring opportunities and will be of need in a "delay" game.
7. You must learn to shoot from or dribble down both sides of the floor. Do not have a favorite side.
8. Run side-shuffle races cross-court to develop legs and endurance.

In summary, a total of approximately 500 shots should be taken in each session under such a program. This will take about an hour and a half for the individual player. Sessions should not be a daily occurrence, but run over a three- to four-day period. This will depend upon several factors, chiefly whether the player wants to spend this much time on his game. In past years at Northern Michigan this type of schedule, with variations for individual weaknesses, has produced great improvement in average basketball players and turned them into excellent performers.

5

Meeting Conditioning
Standards

Basketball play and practice call for endless endurance. It should be remembered that conditioning and specialized training are specific for any sport. A well-conditioned football player, for example, requires considerable additional conditioning to prepare himself for basketball. The conditioning of basketball teams has become an art in itself. The coach's preseason conditioning program and training have assumed greater prominence during the past five years than ever before. With the basketball season beginning in October for colleges and sometimes earlier for high schools, it is not unusual to have a preliminary conditioning program. Nearly all basketball players are participating on a year-round basis at the present time. They realize that basketball is now rapidly advancing to the point where players are working at it continuously and without any long layoffs.

There is considerable debate over whether an outdoor running program is of aid in helping condition basketball players for the long season. Many coaches would rather spend this time on the basketball floor than go over fundamentals out-of-doors. This philosophy will revert back again many times to the degree of basketball emphasis which was instilled in the prospective coach during his playing days or from his basketball theory class. Those who have spent time with an outdoor running program are sold on its merit. Likewise, the same holds true with coaches who do not like to go outdoors. It is their conviction that leg endurance and strength can be gained as rapidly and effectively on the basketball floor as through an outdoor running program. Some coaches also feel that it is impossible to run outdoors prior to the season, since in some cases they have such a short period of time to prepare the squad for their first game.

At Michigan State and at Northern Michigan University, the coaches believe an outdoor running program is not only important, but completely imperative as the first step in getting the basketball team in shape. In basketball, it is our theory that you are only as good as your legs and lungs and that you must therefore get into condition before the season ever starts.

Thus, we have a conditioning program that runs a minimum of one week to a maximum of three weeks, with emphasis placed on a slow approach to the boy's physical condition. The program includes a lot of running and various drills that demand stress on the legs and lungs as basketball does.

During the first week of this program, we run the team only every other day, i.e., Monday, Wednesday, and Friday. We allow Tuesday and Thursday as rest periods so the boys' muscles can literally "catch up" with themselves in rehabilitation for the punishment they receive. During the second week, we run the program every day. If a third week's work is necessary, we do the same.

We run outdoors when possible because if a boy pushes too hard (especially on grass) he will tend to slip harmlessly instead of having the punishment transferred to his legs or shins and thus causing injury to these vital areas. We feel this program will minimize shin splints, blisters, stone bruises and potential ankle injuries along with other minor ailments. Both Michigan State and Northern Michigan have had fine results from this running program, and we feel that it is in the best interest of all coaches to investigate this program.

The following is a sample three weeks' schedule:

Practice No. 1

Monday–Wednesday–Friday–First Week
1. Four laps of the track—or one mile—individually:
    (a) Emphasize proper breathing and running on the balls of the feet with an easy, relaxed arm carriage.
2. Deep breathing exercise:
    (a) Inhale while raising arms and standing on toes.
    (b) Exhale while lowering arms and coming down off the toes.
3. Sprints—four in a group—one lap:
    (a) Emphasize a quick start, a low charge, and ten full strides before relaxing.
4. Ankle exercise:
    (a) Turn ankle out as far as possible on the count of one.
    (b) Turn ankle in as far as possible on the count of two.
5. Change of pace—one lap:
    (a) Emphasize straight-line running.
    (b) Slow—Fast—Stops. All types of pace changes.
6. Change of direction—one lap:

(a) *Emphasize:* Slow approach to the left side of the track. The importance of making a good head, shoulder, and eye fake and of placing the weight on the left foot, lifting the right foot, and driving off the left foot. You literally "leap off" the left foot. It is necessary to gain as much distance as possible in the first two steps after the pivot off the left foot. You then repeat the same action on the right side of the track.

Practice No. 2

Monday—Second Week

1. Laps—Review.
2. Quarter Drill—Review Sprints—One Lap.
3. Deep Breathing Exercise.
4. Change of Pace—Review.
5. Ankle Exercise.
6. Change of Direction—Review.

Tuesday

1. Laps—Review.
2. Deep Breathing Exercise.
3. Sprints.
4. Ankle Exercise.
5. Change of Pace.
6. Change of Direction.
7. Leapfrog—One lap around inside of track.

Wednesday

1. Laps in a group with small men in front and no stopping.
2. Deep Breathing Exercise.
3. Sprints.
4. Ankle Exercise.
5. Change of Pace.
6. Change of Direction.
7. Leapfrog.

Thursday

1. Laps in a group.
2. Deep Breathing Exercise.
3. Change of Pace.
4. Ankle Exercise.
5. Change of Direction.
6. Short Sprints.
7. Volleyball or soccer.

Friday

1. Laps in a group.
2. Races—50 yards with centers separate.
3. Change of Pace.

4. Change of Direction.
5. Volleyball.

Practice No. 3

Monday—Third Week

1. Laps in a group.
2. Races—50 yards with centers separate.
3. Change of Pace.
4. Change of Direction.
5. Volleyball or soccer.

Tuesday

1. Laps in a group—can be extended to five laps.
2. Sprints.
3. Change of Pace.
4. Change of Direction.
5. Leapfrog.

Wednesday

1. Laps in a group.
2. Change of Pace.
3. Change of Direction.
4. Short Sprints.
5. Volleyball or soccer.

Thursday

1. Laps in a group.
2. Races—50 yards with centers separate.
3. Change of Pace.
4. Change of Direction.
5. Volleyball.

Friday

1. Laps in a group.
2. Races—75 yards with centers separate.
3. Change of Pace.
4. Change of Direction.
5. Volleyball.

This sample practice schedule for the fall outdoor running program can be varied to any lesser or greater degree. It is flexible enough to warrant this action and we know of coaches who have substituted other excellent drills into the program.

Some coaches will do fundamental work outdoors with a ball, but these drills are the type which can be practiced as effectively outdoors as in the gymnasium. This will include all types of ball-handling, peripheral vision drills, drills which include all types of passes, jump-ball techniques, and body balance techniques. It should be pointed out that no shooting fundamentals are covered outdoors under this type of program.

This program has helped with the total development of better muscular coordination and muscle tone among squad members. Special assignments for individual players needing extra work can come from this outdoor running program.

TRAINING RULES. One of the biggest headaches in the coaching field is the training of athletes—especially the enforcement of training rules. In this age of the two-car family, the pocket full of spending money, and more to see and do the plight of the athletic coach becomes increasingly more difficult. The authors will not attempt to tell you as a coach what is right and wrong relative to your situation, but we do hope that you will find these observations by high school coaches concerning their problems with high school athletes interesting.

A recent survey conducted by Allan Dighera, currently head basketball coach at St. Paul High School in Negaunee, Michigan, as an undergraduate at Northern Michigan University made a fine contribution to basketball in the field of training rules and procedures, as exemplified by high school coaches in Michigan. The survey included all four basketball classes in the state, and contained many remarks by various coaches on the subject of training. It is our hope that both prospective and practicing coaches will gain new insights from these remarks and utilize them in formulating training rules of their own, as well as learning something from the philosophy behind them.

The question of dismissal of any squad member for training-rule infractions brought one coach to remark, "It is hard to talk yourself into 'booting' a good boy off the squad, but surprisingly your team is usually stronger after this violator departs."

"The most difficult part of enforcing training rules is to decide what authority of proof one is to use as evidence against an offending athlete," Dighera stated. "A coach certainly does not want to be a 'watchdog' of his players. Anytime we find anyone who will testify against an athlete (who has broken a training rule) in the presence of the accused and the coach, we consider this as evidence of a training violation at our school."

A coach who had encountered his first major problem concerning training rules the very year of the survey commented: "This season I dropped a regular for drinking. After three weeks the boys voted to have him back and I went along. This incident in the long run helped make our ball club." But this same coach made further note of the situation. "In training rules, I believe a lot of things enter into consideration. I had rules, but never thought I would have to enforce them. This was my first experience in three years. I told the players after it happened that the rule would be changed for next year. Instead of just the rule, I would add the following statement: Anyone in violation of these rules will be dismissed for the remainder of the year."

Another coach said, "I dismissed five players including my captain and finished the season with sophomores and juniors. This was all due to lack of desire and breaking training rules. I finished the season with only eight players. It hurt in the win column, but everyone will profit from it in the end."

"I cut one boy from the squad for training rule infractions and we immediately won seven straight games," said a Class-A school coach. "I quickly noticed the difference in desire and hustle by the remainder of the squad."

Some advice for a young coach came from an "old pro" who explained it this way: "For a coach just entering the field, I think his best bet is to be very strict the first two years on training rules. If you are not, the easy moments and lack of discipline will come back and haunt you in future years. The best method is to suffer through a couple of bad years if you have to, but it will pay off for the younger coach as an end result."

"Make positive the administration and school board know the rules that are to be followed for athletes and that they are behind you in enforcing said rules," stated a coach who was caught in the middle of just such a situation.

From a basketball coach with a 77 per cent winning average over 11 years came this candid thought: "Training is getting tougher every year. I attempted a system of 'no training rules, just be in shape, philosophy' this season. It was a complete failure and never again will I try this pattern. Next year, I am going back to my original rules. Training pays. The advent of the automobile is the worst evil of all for the athlete of today."

As you can see, variances occurred with each coach. This is why a standard pattern cannot be established for all coaches concerning training rules. You must solve your own problems with the best possible weapons you have. This might mean that you are a strict authoritarian or perhaps a more lenient disciplinarian. All decisions on training rules must be made by the coach.

PROMOTION OF PERSONAL CARE

The basketball player should take utmost care of himself. If he is to be a member of the team it is important that he maintain his health during the season. The daily hygiene necessary to be physically fit is minimal for players, but not to be neglected.

After every workout or game, the player should take a brief, warm shower. This should be followed up immediately with a cold shower. In this way the player can emerge from the shower and not be perspiring.

A vigorous dry rub with a towel will stimulate the player. This brisk rub will achieve the same result as a rubdown. Should a player sweat after this rub, insist that he cool off further before dressing. The player should never leave the locker room while he is still perspiring. He must not go out-of-doors until he is thoroughly dry and completely cooled.

The major worry of all coaches during the season is the health of their players. The wet hair of a boy coming out of the shower room is a constant source of concern among coaches. It is at this time that players are most vulnerable to catching colds which in turn reduce their effectiveness. *Insist that players cover their heads with caps, especially during the winter season.* Prevention of colds must be taught.

PROPER WARM-UP. Athletic trainers are an integral part of our basketball programs. Nearly all colleges, and many high schools, currently have a trainer. It is through these men that many of our training and conditioning methods have blossomed into the advanced techniques we enjoy today.

It is probably through the trainers' insistence that more coaches than ever are turning to the use of calisthenics prior to the starting of their practice sessions. This might take only five or ten minutes, but serves a definite purpose. It insures the proper circulation and warm-up of muscles which will be taxed through the practice session. Exercises will cut down on minor and nuisance injuries which cause so many players to miss important practices and games. Warm-ups must be organized and complete.

These calisthenics can be of any nature, but some effort should be made to see that they correlate with definite parts of the body. Ankle, arm, and leg exercises are deemed most important. This mass drill is normally led by the captain and can lend you unusual esprit de corps. It develops a close unity of group action among the team, along with group discipline. Not enough can be said for this simple but effective technique in coaching.

WATER. While there has been much written on whether water is detrimental to the athlete there has been no concrete evidence to back this claim. However, certain rules should be observed for basketball players in the matter of drinking water. No water in the training room should ever be iced. Ice water hinders the digestion of players.

Years ago it was felt that an athlete needed six to eight glasses of water daily. Many similar theories have been advanced, although efforts to prove these claims have been unsuccessful. There are coaches, for example, who will not let their players drink water during a practice session or game. Conversely, other coaches will permit their players to drink moderately during both practices and games. The results of tests on both units seem to show a negligible difference in so far as performances are concerned. Therefore, we tend to favor the use of water sparingly in both our practices and games. Nevertheless, the players should have an opportunity to rinse out their mouth if they desire. It should be understood by everyone that a large intake of water before a game is not sound judgment. At the same time, a coach should not insist on his players drinking a set amount of water. He can let the thirst of the individual govern the intake of water.

One final suggestion concerning the use of water. Do not permit the player to load up his stomach with water after practice. If he is to drink, insist that he drink with moderation in order that he will have an appetite for his evening meal.

SKIMMED MILK. Skimmed milk is a fine food in itself. Milk is our leading source of calcium, which we all need for strong bones and teeth. It is essential that all of us, regardless of age, include a liberal supply of milk in our diet. Controversy rages continually among coaches as to whether milk should be part of the athlete's pre-game meal. Many coaches will not let team members drink milk with their meal. We would like to defend the use of milk, as we have found it to be a most easily digestible drink. With a pre-game meal eaten anywhere from two to four hours before game time it is perfectly permissible for players to drink milk without fear of harming their performance. It is best to explain to your squad that they should drink their milk slowly for proper digestion rather than gulping it down.

SLEEP. The phenomenon of sleep cannot be explained. However, research has been able to prove that sleep is the most satisfying form of recuperation from fatigue. There is no apparent reason why we must sleep —except that it is known to be vital to proper health. It is during sleep that body cells have an opportunity to restore lost energy. The length of time the player sleeps is more important than the intensity of sleep.

There is no barometer for how much sleep a player must have. Normally, the adolescent basketball player needs eight to ten hours. This is a standard among men of the profession, but disagreement on the number of hours needed for the player to remain at maximum performance is commonplace. The authors have found that in October, November, and December the players need more sleep. As the year progresses their adjustment is strictly an individual matter. It appears that players in peak condition do not need as much sleep as they do when practice sessions are just beginning. Nevertheless, regularity of sleep is important and coaches must be made aware of it.

Loss of sleep will occasionally happen to everyone, but coaches should take preventative measures with their basketball teams, especially when on an overnight trip. The selection of a quiet motel or hotel rather than one which is located in the heart of the city will aid the players' sleeping habits. It is important that players rest as comfortably as possible, especially the night before a contest. The coach should make arrangements for separate beds for his players. Seldom will a player sleep naturally with a bed-mate. The player should get a good night's rest the evening before the game, and should also rest during the day of the contest. A short nap on the day of the game is useful, especially right after brunch. It will also help the player adjust to the strange surroundings of hotel life and to the normal change of habits which is taking place.

FOOD. It is understood that the coach cannot control the diet of every player. In the type of diet to which he is accustomed, the player will be a product of his home environment and other influences. With few exceptions, players are fed quite well at home, and most parents work hand-in-hand with the high school coaches in planning their pre-game meals.

Many colleges are furnishing their basketball players with a training table. In this way, proper nutrition for the athletes is assured. One of the objectives of the training table is to provide a diet that enables playing weight to be maintained and at the same time to include adequate amounts of all necessary nutrients.

There can be no definite criterion as to how much a player should eat. This naturally depends upon the individual and the amount of energy he expends. It is estimated that basketball players will probably need anywhere from 4,000 to 6,000 calories a day during the season. It should be understood also that the smaller player will never eat as much as the bigger man and should never be forced to try to eat the same quantity.

Regularity of meals for all players is a must if they are to be healthy and strong for an entire basketball season. The regular, balanced diet of adequate protein, an abundance of carbohydrates, moderate fats, and fresh fruit is necessary for a healthy basketball squad.

PRE-GAME MEALS. Coaches have expressed varied opinions on the pre-game meal for their basketball teams. In high school, the pre-game meal is normally eaten at home if the game is to be played that evening. Coaches should visit the homes, talk earnestly with the mothers, and suggest a pre-game diet for the boys. You will find the majority of mothers very sympathetic and most willing to help prepare what suggestions the coach has given them.

When the high school team is on an overnight trip, the pre-game meal as well as other meals should be arranged in advance by the coach.

Some coaches are very strict in what they allow their players to eat, while others feel that they can still eat a regular meal without too much harm to their performance.

An excellent liquid food concentrate recently placed on the commercial market is Dine-A-Pac. This is a complete pre-game meal in one container, and it tastes like chocolate milk. Four cookies are furnished with this liquid, which the players drink much the same as any other liquid. It provides a high protein diet, which is most suitable for players.

Northern Michigan University made exclusive use of this product while participating in the 1963 NAIA Tournament in Kansas City, Missouri.

The Wildcats played the first game of the morning session at 10:30, which is considerably different than normal playing times. The adjustment of players to an early starting time was a problem. With this in mind, it was decided to give the players the Dine-A-Pac after letting them sleep longer in the morning, since the rest was more important than food. The players were fed the Dine-A-Pac approximately 1½ hours before the game, and they expressed satisfaction with it. In both of the instances in which this product was used, the team succeeded in winning, and we are consequently sold on its usefulness in the field of athletics.

For those young coaches just beginning in the field the question of diet and pre-game meals presents a problem. For this reason we are including a sample pre-game meal for a team, which should be served four hours before game time:

> Fresh Fruit Cup (minimum of citrus fruit)
> Beef Tenderloin Steak (6 to 8 ounces and broiled)
> Baked Potato (small, with one teaspoon of butter)
> Orange Gelatin
> Toast and honey
> Hot tea, black coffee, or skimmed milk

If there is only a very short time in which to eat a pre-game meal, the following abbreviated menu is prescribed by many coaches:

> Poached or Scrambled Eggs (no fat)
> Toast and Honey
> Orange Gelatin
> Hot tea or skimmed milk (one glass)

VITAMINS. Coaches in nearly all sections of the country have resorted to the use of vitamins during the basketball season. They are dispensed by the manager or trainer, who merely places the tablet in a small paper cup in the player's locker. After practice, the player will fill the cup with water and take the vitamin tablet. The vitamins are sometimes dispensed from a container on the wall, with the players "dialing" a vitamin or two as prescribed.

Vitamins are used by basketball teams as a supplement to their diet. Coaches feel that their players are susceptible to colds and other rundown conditions and vitamins are used to restore lost energy and also as a preventative. Their value is termed purely psychological by some nutrition experts, who believe that a balanced diet will eliminate the need for additional vitamins. They insist that if a player pursues a well-rounded diet he will not need this artificial assistance.

If vitamins are used by a coach, he should always check with the school doctor and school nutritionist for proper guidance in their use.

Providing a basket of apples and oranges for the players to eat after practice is an idea being advanced by coaches in some areas of the country.

They are of the opinion that an orange or apple will stimulate the appetite and satisfactorily curb thirst and hunger. A second advantage is that it relaxes the squad and brings them a change of pace from the regular locker room routine.

The money for the fruit basket is donated by the players and coaches, who are assessed a very nominal fee each week. The manager is then placed in charge of this fund and is responsible for the buying and distribution of the fruit.

Much use is also made of the ascorbic acid tablet during practice sessions, and particularly at game halftimes. This Vitamin C supplement reduces "cotton mouth" and aids in moistening the throat. Perhaps one of the reasons they like it best is that the tablet is easy to handle, since it is not messy and is quickly dissolved in the mouth much the same as candy.

SALT TABETS. Training supplies for the year should include a good supply of salt tablets. These are to be used by the players after practices. The tablets will replenish the salt the body lost during the session. Two tablets daily are normally sufficient for each player.

There are players who will perspire profusely, and this dehydration can be supplemented by salt tablets. If this condition is not corrected early, however, a more serious condition may result. The coach should be cognizant of these "sweaters" and see that they are taken care of by the manager or trainer.

STALENESS. A common worry of all coaches is staleness. It is nearly impossible not to encounter some period of staleness during a season of basketball. With the season extending five and a half months for colleges and almost that much time on the secondary level, it would take a magician and all his powers to prevent this condition. On the other hand there are coaches who do not believe this is a problem. The authors would like to point out that we have not observed staleness and its symptoms among the players who sit on the bench. It usually takes its toll on those men who are performing regularly and must meet the tension and pressure of each game head-on.

Staleness in a team is difficult to fight once it sets in. It can eat away at your team like a cancer. The players will appear listless, lack enthusiasm for the game, and show apparent physical tiredness as well as mental stress. It would also seem that a losing year or losing streak magnifies the staleness, and at this point the coach must not overwork his team.

A basketball team can be prepared for staleness. It is the theory of some coaches that they can talk with the team and condition them by a psychological approach. If this is true the coach will have to consider two items very carefully. The first is the schedule which the team plays. Since staleness never is a problem during early season games the coach must be extra watchful during the second half of his schedule. As the games come more quickly and the tournaments rapidly approach he must be at his best in guarding against this condition and handling his squad members. Make it a rule not to plan further ahead than the upcoming game. When games are played on consecutive nights, always prepare for them one at a time. The second item the coach must consider is knowing his personnel. The team will look to the coach for leadership. If the coach displays unrest, quick temperament, edgy feelings, or a rundown feeling that team members are able to detect, they will have the same appearance. The coach should not discuss team condition with anything except bubbling enthusiasm and confidence. He must impress the team with this attitude and endow them with it. Remember, a team which thinks it is going stale will play this way.

A successful high school coach in Central Illinois feels he can press for every game throughout a 26-game schedule. He believes staleness is a state of mind which does not exist as far as his team is concerned. He has sold them on what they can do with this demanding defense, and they play it with abandon.

Remedies prescribed for staleness normally call for a few days' rest. One psychological move the coach can make is to wait until the players report to practice and make a surprise announcement that practice will not be held. The coach should encourage extra sleep, rest, or any other change of habits the players might like. Such actions on the part of the coach will mean renewed interest when the players return for their next practice session. Interest in practice is difficult to maintain late in the season, and the coach will often have to come up with "gimmicks" such as these to do so.

A failure on the part of the players to maintain the proper diet is another possible reason for staleness. During this period it is important to check the player's food intake to see if any radical changes have taken place.

A surprise of some type to break the routine of practice is another possibility. A mixed party at the coach's home can be profitable, since it will ease the tension prevailing on the basketball court. The players will appreciate your inviting their girl friends. Boy-and-girl relationships are not to be overlooked by the coach and if you can contribute to harmony in this area, you will have accomplished something worthwhile. Such a party can raise player morale considerably.

Taking the team out for a fine meal at a quality restaurant is another tactic used by coaches in combatting staleness. The coach should invite the managers, statisticians, and other people who might be associated with the basketball program. This "breaking of bread" together has worked wonders for coaches during the pressure-packed tournament trail. This will have to be at the coach's expense if the budget will not cover it.

The biggest help a coach can give to the prevention of staleness is to check his own practice schedule and the organization of it. When it is late in the season, he should keep practices short and above all should not over-coach. The driving type of coach must be more alert under these circumstances because he can exhaust the team's spirit for an upcoming game on the practice floor if he is not careful. He must be able to recognize staleness and its symptoms.

BLISTERS. In no other sport is there more of a demand made on the feet from stopping, starting, and turning than in basketball. For this reason, special care of the feet must be taken. Blisters must draw the immediate attention of the coach. The number one annoyance a coach has is those players with extra sensitive feet. Every preventative necessary should be used to ward off blisters. We would like to mention that the prevention of blisters is easier than the treating of them. Our attitude is reflected in the fact that we recommend to all our players that they pad their feet with a piece of combine roll 3 inches square. Vaseline is added to the pad to act as a lubricant. This will also aid in decreasing any friction between the shoe and the feet. The entire ball of the foot should be covered with the pad and the tape then applied to hold it securely. This procedure is followed during every practice session and for all games. Under this method the practice time and game time lost because of blisters has been kept to a minimum.

The wearing of two pairs of socks is advocated. One method is to have the player wear a pair of liners under a pair of heavier sweat socks. A second method of prevention is for the player to use two heavy pairs of socks without the liners. We are not stressing one method over the other, as it is our feeling that this is an individual problem which only the player can decide.

A properly-fitting shoe will cut down on such foot problems as callouses, corns, ingrown toenails, and ankle sprains. This is the most important piece of equipment you will buy for the player (that is, if you furnish the shoes), so we suggest that you study the various types on the market and fit the player's foot accordingly. Nothing will cut down player efficiency more quickly than uncomfortable shoes which cause distress.

ALCOHOL. The use of alcohol should not be condoned by the coach. The effect it has on a young man participating in basketball is worth mentioning. It would appear that drinking among athletes is on the rise and for this reason we would like to present the following.

The percentage of alcohol in the bloodstream determines its effect on the individual. The larger the amount, the greater is the tendency for the individual to lose his mental and physical abilities. The continued presence of alcohol prolongs the incapacity of his essential functioning organs.

It should be noted that individuals differ in the amount of alcoholic beverages needed to produce a state of inebriation. Some may only need one-fourth the amount that it takes for another person. Physiologically, even in "safe" concentrations, however, mental processes are broken down and altered.

Why do athletes sometimes drink? Some of the reasons given by research include:

1. Proving they are "men"
2. Curiosity
3. Social pressure
4. Home environment and background
5. Attracting attention

In a West Coast study on alcohol and the extent of its use in high schools by athletes, the findings were startling. The researchers reported that the average adolescent experiments with drinking at age 14. The youngster sees it as a social beverage and the first exposure is usually in the home with parental consent. One only has to look at the average home to see how many fathers allow their children to sip beer out of their glasses. It goes without saying that today's youth are increasing their drinking, and any positive impact of alcoholic education on attitudes and behavior is certainly not in evidence.

This study pointed out that 99 per cent of the coaches surveyed included abstinence as one of their training rules and 98 per cent were making a real effort to enforce their no-drinking rule. The "authoritarian" coach was found ready to dismiss the drinker from the squad with no consideration in 81 per cent of the cases. There is no doubt we are dealing with an exceedingly complex and controversial subject, which is continually being debated. There are no easy answers and the coach is burdened with this problem. It merely means that no definite philosophy of handling alcoholic education by coaches can be interpreted as being correct.

Your squad should be made aware of the effect alcohol will have on them if used. First of all, alcohol is not a stimulant as many of them will believe. When alcohol enters the blood stream it acts as a depressant, since it depresses all mental activity. After reducing the drinker's power of self-control it begins working on the motor center of his brain. This leads to poor muscular coordination which readily affects a basketball player. This action should be carefully described to the team when you are discussing training rules at one of your early meetings.

COLD OR FLU SHOTS. Our health authorities are constantly reminding us to take advantage of cold or flu shots. We strongly recommend these shots for your basketball squad. They have been very successful at Michigan State and Northern Michigan Universities in the prevention of colds and flu during the long winter months.

We suggest that the team be given their first shot early in November. This would be one cc. of serum for those who do not suffer from any type of allergy. Those who do are limited to one-half cc. This is followed by a second shot during late January or early February. The cost of these shots is slight. One cc. will cost approximately $1.00, while one-half cc. will be fifty cents.

WEIGHT TRAINING.   Recent trends in athletics have brought to the surface the success of weight training in sports.   The improvement of athletes through such a program cannot be accurately calculated over a short period of time, as the program is geared to build strength and endurance.   This is never accomplished in a short duration.

Credit for the prominence of weight training in basketball is given to the State University of Iowa at Iowa City.   The research involved the university basketball team, and the success of its program is reflected by the Big-Ten championship the Hawkeyes won after one year of utilizing this program.

A sample weight training program for a high school basketball team would be to work with the weights three times a week.   You would start this program the first week of school in the fall and conclude it one week before your first regular scheduled game.   The program follows:

1. Rope skipping for 15 minutes, which serves as a warm-up.
2. Clean and press, ten repetitions, two sets with 50 pounds of weight.
3. Curl, ten repetitions, two sets with 40 pounds of weight.
4. Lateral rise, dumbbells, 8–12 repetitions with 25 pounds of weight.
5. Forward raise, dumbbells, 8–12 repetitions with 25 pounds of weight.
6. Squat, ten repetitions, two sets with 75–100 pounds of weight depending upon the player.
7. Pullover, ten repetitions with 25 pounds of weight after each set of squats.
8. Quick partial bends with barbell on shoulders with 100 pounds of weight. Ten repetitions and build up.
9. Employment of the Sargent jump test to establish jumping ability and the effect of weight training on physical improvement.

Other training aids which coaches have made effective use of are the so-called "spats."   These are weighted holders strapped to the ankles of the players to increase the demand on this part of the body.   Along this same line is the weighted training shoe which is sold by commercial companies. This features an ounce of weight for the shoe size.   For example, a player wearing a size nine shoe would have nine ounces of extra weight to carry in this training shoe.

A weighted vest of 10 pounds has been used especially in seeking the development of the big man.   This is similar to the navy life jacket in fit, with the weights placed in strategic places.   Players are required to wear the vest during various drills and during special extra sessions with the coach.

Regardless of the devices used in weight training, it is compulsory that you have proper supervision of these activities.   Never let a player work with any heavy weights individually as he is most susceptible to injury when he does so.

ISOMETRIC CONTRACTION.   Isometric contraction has revolutionized the body-building aspect of athletics.   You may ask, "What is isometric contraction?" A definition stating that it is contraction in which the muscle length always remains the same would suffice. This contraction to a muscular standstill can be attained in two ways.

1. By attempting to lift unliftable objects.
2. By pushing against an immovable object.

Physiologically, these methods are merely ways of overloading the muscle to the limit of its ability, and they therefore serve as stimuli to growth in size and strength. (See Fig. 5–1 for a fine example.)

Fig. 5–1 (Views 1 and 2). One isometric exercise. Note the contracting muscles.

Many of our top professional athletes, in every sport, have gone on record as stating that isometric contraction has yielded profitable returns in increasing the strength and endurance of their bodies.

As mentioned above, be certain that a well-trained member of your coaching staff is in attendance at all times during the program. This will insure proper supervision and will cause the players to work harder during their workout.

FATIGUE. Fatigue in basketball is usually either normal or psychological. In normal fatigue the player can go through a routine day—which includes school and practice—and be tired at the end of that day. He can eat dinner, get a good night's rest, and be ready to go again the following day. His overnight recuperative powers will enable him to follow this same daily pattern.

Psychological fatigue does not follow this same pattern. The player will rise in the morning with a tired feeling. As he proceeds through his daily routine, he feels better. Nevertheless, one important change takes place. The player may manifest a feeling of exhaustion sometime during the day. This feeling can occur during a practice session or a game. It is usually brought about by the fact the player is not happy with the prospect of practicing or playing a game which he either consciously or subconsciously dislikes at this time. This type of fatigue is not uncommon in basketball near the end of the season.

The game as presently played is complex and possesses constant mental strain. It places exacting pressures on players and coaches alike. While the body can absorb the physical punishment it gets and recover quickly, the mental outlook of the player must be a dominant factor in combatting the psychological warfare of basketball.

COACH'S LETTER TO PARENTS. Many of our coaches are using a direct approach to parents in discussing conditioning and training matters for a school year. It usually takes the form of a letter and gives not only the parents but the player an idea of what he might expect. For the beginning coach we have such a letter, which will serve as a guide for him if he is thinking about this particular idea.

November 1

Mr. and Mrs. Joel Smith
1303 North Eighth Street
Anytown, Michigan

Dear Mr. and Mrs. Smith:

Basketball season is upon us again and it is with enthusiasm and pleasure that we look forward to providing leadership for your son in these coming months.

It is a big job that we undertake each year at this time and we feel that if parents and coach team up, the job can be made easier. Your son is one of about 60 boys that our basketball program directly or indirectly encompasses. Besides the actual playing and competing in basketball, we hope to emphasize teamwork, cooperation, fair play, sportsmanship, honesty, integrity, obedience, authority, control of emotions, proper health habits, a competitive desire, and proper conduct.

Our athletes must live up to certain standards before they can represent our school in a worthy manner. We feel that 8 to 10 hours of sleep is necessary for our boys, preferably 10 hours. Our athletes generally possess superior mental abilities, which we expect them to use. The training rules for this year have been recommended by your son and the remainder of the squad and have been approved by us.

Naturally, smoking and drinking are out if a boy is going to be able to stand the fast pace of a basketball game without letting his teammates and school down. The hours which they have set for going to bed are 10:00 P.M. on week nights and Sunday, and 9:30 the night before a game. On Friday and Saturday nights it is 12:30 A.M., unless there is a special formal dance, in which case the squad and myself discuss the time and occasion. If we play a game away from home and your son is home after 12:30 A.M., it may be that we had a long trip and by the time the boys have eaten a post-game snack, it is after 12:30 A.M.

The following disciplinary actions have also been agreed to by the squad for an infraction of the above rules: Immediate dismissal from the team for drinking or smoking; If a squad member violates the bedtime-hour rule, he will be reprimanded and disciplined by the coach, depending upon the circumstances, and upon a second violation, he will be dropped.

We do not expect your son to be placed upon a special diet but we would like to recommend meats, milk, and fresh vegetables for him. Highly seasoned, fried, or fatty food should be avoided if possible, especially on nights of the games. We expect him to dress and talk like a gentleman and to realize that his responsibilities to the school and community are very important.

We feel that the above training rules are indicative of the high moral values and cooperation the squad is showing and will continue to show. You should feel justly proud of your son and urge him at all times to continue this fine moral attitude and cooperation.

We shall try to shoulder more than our share of this responsibility. We have had fine success in the past and with your cooperation we can continue to be that successful.

Please feel free to get in touch with me if you have any questions or problems. Looking forward to seeing you soon, I remain

                    Sincerely yours,

                    Basketball Coach

6

Individual Offensive
Maneuvers

In any discussion of basketball, individuals, or teams, the execution of fundamentals is usually talked about. It is our feeling that regardless of the type of offense used in the game it still must evolve around fundamentals. This is the "foundation upon which the house is built." Coaches spend countless hours with their players helping them master these fundamentals to improve their play. Without the proper instruction and mastery of these skills your team cannot expect to enjoy any unusual success. The beginning coach only has to look at the more successful coaches in our profession to learn that consistent winners are coaches whose teams are fundamentally sound. In short, they minimize their mistakes.

The coach should strive to get the proper response from the player in the practice session. He should set up every conceivable play possible so the player can see alternatives and be motivated by "seeing and doing" the right maneuver. These player responses should be cultivated always at game speed for simulation of actual game conditions. To create these proper responses the authors demand adherence at all times to the generally accepted fundamentals of play. Fundamentals are the basis upon which we predicate our offense.

The one-hand shooting we now have in basketball has played havoc with basketball defenses and caused coaches considerable loss of sleep. It has improved offensive play markedly since its inception, however, to the point where there is no real defense against the good one-hand shooters. With this in mind we want to elaborate on how an individual player can improve his offensive play through the observation of seven basic individual offensive moves we teach them. This is a pet project for both of us and all our squad members are drilled extensively in its use.

If you were one of our players, you would receive from us these general instructions. First, we would insist that you turn and face the basket as soon as you get the ball. Immediately face your opponent to take advantage of any defensive lapse on his part. We stress the elimination of the bounce with the ball until the player is ready to go some place. We don't want the players to develop the habit of bouncing the ball as soon as they get it. When the player receives the ball he should (1) look for a pass to a teammate who is open, (2) use his own individual shot or move, and (3) utilize the dribble as a means of going somewhere. We believe the player should not hold the ball for over three seconds—he should have made his move by this time or should pass to a teammate. Finally, we want our players who don't have the ball to work to get position on their defensive man so that when they do receive the ball they will be able to do something with it.

TYPES OF SHOTS

SET SHOT

1. We will take up the one-hand set shot, since it is used more in our offense than the two-hand set shot.
2. When you are just starting to practice the shot we like you to get as close to the basket as possible. As you get the touch and feel, start to move farther back.
3. If you are right-handed (we will use a right-hander as an example—the left-handed shot is just the opposite) plant your right foot in front of you. Your stance should be comfortable and in balance so a person can't push you over—the weight should be on the front foot.
4. Hand position should be emphasized. Your left hand is under the ball with your finger tips controlling the ball. A slight cup might be formed with this hand position. Your right hand should be directly behind and slightly above the center of the ball. Your index finger should be spread and using the thumb as a guide. The elbows should be in a comfortable position close to the rib cage. The eyes should be looking directly over the ball at the rim of the basket.
5. In the proper execution of the shot you should bend your knees. As you are doing this, cock your wrists—don't drop the ball down any more than necessary because of the bend in your knees.
6. Keep the ball up as high as practical. As you come up, your left hand leaves the ball. As you let the ball go, extend your ankle, knee, elbow, and wrist or body joints as much as you possibly can.
7. Don't turn sideways when you are shooting. Always face the basket.
8. Use a medium arch with the front of the rim as the target for the shot. The distance in the shot comes from the extension of your four joints (ankle, knee, elbow, and wrist), not from the windup you use.

FAKE SHOT AND DRIVE

1. If you are a right-handed shooter, use your left foot as the pivot foot regardless of which side of the floor you are on.

2. When you drive, drive off with your right foot.

3. On most fakes, use head and shoulder fakes and not ball fakes.

4. When the player has the ball, keep it in "home position"—that is, belt-high to chest-high—because everything that you do offensively starts from this position.

5. When you make the set shot, move toward the basket—not away—from it.

'6. When you are driving or faking a drive, operate off the front foot of the defensive player.

7. Fake a shot to bring the defensive man up to block the shot. This will get him off balance and make a drive easier.

8. When you see him approaching, squat with the hips and give a good shoulder and eye fake. When you get him off balance, step off with the right foot as far as you can with the initial step—then bounce the ball as far out in front of you as possible.

9. The player's first two steps determine whether he will get around the defensive man. Try to get as much distance possible in the quick two steps.

FAKE DRIVE AND SHOT

1. The purpose is to get your defensive man back three or four steps and make him think you are going to drive.

2. The offensive player should give the impression that he is going to drive his opponent. In this move he doesn't step off quite as far as on the drive because he will shoot without coming back to the original position. He will shoot at the end of the fake.

3. The shot should be taken over the left shoulder of the defensive man, and you will use the same techniques as on the set shot.

4. It is best used after a drive or a fake shot and drive.

DOUBLE FAKE

1. Fake a drive with a big step—then settle your weight on your heels and fake a shot but don't move the ball around—use a head and shoulder fake—look up at the basket.

2. As the defensive man brings up his left hand and foot, step off and place the ball well out in front of you when you take the first dribble.

3. Get as much distance in the first two steps as you can as this determines whether you will get around the defensive man.

4. You attempt to get the defensive man to put up his hand to block the shot and you go under his hand.

ROCKER STEP

1. You try to get your defensive man into a rhythm.

2. Fake a drive toward the basket, operating off the front foot of the defensive man—watch your opponent's feet to see which is the front foot. *Don't* place the ball on your hip because you can't do enough things with the ball in this position.

3. Start the move with your driving foot one step behind the pivot foot.

4. If the defensive man drops his feet back, come back to the starting posi-

tion and begin again—if the defensive man brings his foot back up, then the rocker step is good for the drive.

5. This time only settle back on your heels instead of coming all the way back. Don't bring your feet back—just bring your head and shoulders to this position.

6. Lift your front foot and take off toward the basket, dropping the ball way out in front of you.

CROSSOVER STEP

1. This can be used by all the players, including the centers or pivot men.

2. This maneuver is used to take advantage of any defense that is overplaying an offensive man.

3. You receive the ball and make a fake drive to the basket but more lateral and away from the basket than usual. Get your right foot back to start the play. Be sure to expose the ball because you want your opponent to go after the ball.

4. Place the weight on the balls of your feet. Then lift both heels, make a quick pivot on both feet, and step off with the foot you used to fake the drive so you won't be traveling with the ball—the ball has to go under the opponent's hands.

5. Step off with the ball way ahead of the step.

6. Keep most of the weight on the back of the left foot.

7. Quickness, not speed, is the most important factor in any of the moves.

JUMP SHOT OFF STEP

1. Your left foot should be your pivot again in this maneuver.

2. You execute the move at the particular moment when you feel the defense has struck a "happy medium" with you. We mean close enough to prevent the set shot and far enough away to prevent the drive.

3. Knowing this, you should step immediately toward your opponent and watch his feet for reaction. If he retreats, you quickly step off the front foot and take the jump shot.

4. If he does not give ground you can still get a fine shot off with the element of surprise when you fake the drive and then jump shoot over him.

5. You should keep the ball as high as possible in this move, and jump straight up and somewhat forward—*never* backwards on this maneuver.

6. Experience will tell the player when to use the move. It should be mastered as it is basketball's most productive point getter.

GENERAL POINTS

1. All of these maneuvers are a matter of timing and quickness and not so much a matter of speed.

2. If any individual has a move that is effective for him, it is all right for him to use it as long as he doesn't waste his time and his teammates' time. In this manner he can still make a return pass to his teammates. An example of such a move would be a change of pace while he is dribbling or a change of direction while he is driving.

3. Watch your opponent's feet and save your dribble until you can use it as a means to get to the basket—work off your opponent's front foot.

TECHNIQUES OF TEACHING

As a coach you are perhaps the busiest teacher of all. Your advanced techniques, skills, and knowledge must be simplified for the player you instruct. The coach should expect to modify his teaching after a study of the players' behavior and reactions, if such a study is necessary. If the material cannot be absorbed by your squad then you must re-evaluate your teaching methods and try other routes. The success of your team depends upon how well you teach the fundamental phases of the game and how well the squad retains these essentials.

In brief, you are a teacher who will wear many hats. As coach, counselor, adviser, and close friend, you will deal with a multitude of students. These students need direction and require information, and the coach must supply this instruction along with inspirational teaching.

It has been said many times by educators that good teaching is easier than poor teaching. Common sense, a dedication for teaching, and a thorough knowledge of basketball will make for efficiency on the part of the coach. Rules to govern basketball instruction should be specific and clear-cut for the coach.

In looking at each of these fundamentals of teaching, there are points in which we would be remiss if we did not examine each very closely. The following will be instructive for the neophyte coach and a review for veteran coaches of their teaching methods and progression.

SELF-PREPARATION BY THE COACH. The coach must be prepared much the same as a classroom teacher. In fact even more so, for you will never fool your players. They can quickly tell whether the coach is qualified to instruct them after a single practice session.

The cardinal rule of good teaching is a thorough knowledge of your material. Present your coaching methods in a communicable procedure. This assures the squad members of a basic understanding of the coach's particular philosophy. Another way of knowing your material is by keeping abreast of the latest techniques, methods, coaching ideas, and changes —which come along constantly. This can be accomplished by reading the vast number of fine athletic magazines on basketball, the books written by many of our successful coaches, and other literature in the field. Basketball movies of teams are available by writing the different service bureaus and schools, requesting whatever you might like to view. Coaching clinics offer another fine outlet for the coach to investigate as a way of keeping up with the times.

A mastery of knowledge in itself does not mean sufficient preparedness. The coach must be able to impart his knowledge to the player in a clear and concise presentation. In order for this presentation to be meaningful it must be organized. The detailed teaching points must be systemized, whether it is in the form of a coach's notebook or a syllabus. This will give him complete command of the teaching points, and the presentation will reveal thoroughness and continuity.

The final phase of a coach's self-preparation is his fervor for and interest in his teaching methods. Enthusiasm is contagious and the players will detect and pick up this characteristic if the coach can stimulate them. The majority of coaches demonstrate this kind of automatic interest, since it is a part of all of us. We can expect a breakdown of our teaching technique if we exhibit anything except this inspiration for our work.

The coach should not have to force himself into proper teaching techniques. Since basketball is a living dedication, it is a challenge for us to refresh our teaching methods. Be inspirational and enthusiastic. Explain, demonstrate, and inform the players painstakingly, since they rely upon the coach. Try to remember your own feelings when you were playing. Your experience is their best teacher!

PRODUCE INCENTIVE IN YOUR TEACHING. The spirit of a basketball squad must be maintained in order to obtain results. Coaches are aware of this distinct quality and are generating some stimulating and interesting methods of motivation for the players. The following are some of these methods, which you might use:

1. Various awards, such as best free-throw percentage for the year or the most improved player;
2. A player-of-the-week award for the best defensive performance;
3. The allowance of a five-minute break during practice;
4. The handling of an egg instead of a ball in a passing drill;
5. The enactment of game situations and the use of the time clock in practice.

Any time you attempt to motivate a player you should arouse in him a feeling that it is to his personal advantage to do well. Every individual player likes personal attention. Psychologists tell us that we are thinking about ourselves better than 90 per cent of the time. A hint which is helpful in our teaching of the individual offensive moves is stressing the point that if a player can master these moves he will score between 50 and 100 points more during the regular season. This is a real stimulus for the players because they want to improve their scoring output. By doing this we ignite an interest close to the individual. Be quick to compliment and praise your players when they deserve it. They are human and vulnerable to mistakes and seek the approval of the coach. It has been stated over and over that praise is better than criticism in teaching methods. This is especially true in the instruction of players.

CLARIFICATION OF YOUR TEACHING. Any success the coach may have will be contingent upon his ability to get the material across to the players. In order to do this effectively he must be patient. This virtue is a necessity in the coaching profession. A knowledge of the game through professional preparation and experience should be an excellent guide for the coach to follow. At the same time, let us caution you not to submerge your team with nomenclature they will not understand. One mistake the younger coaches make is trying to impress the players with their background of the game. They tend to confuse, make indistinguishable, and muddle their teaching progression with this flood of jargon.

The coach will start with the simple and work up to the more complex plays or fundamentals. In performing this function for the players, he gives them a basic understanding of how, why, and when. It is important for them to know this before undertaking any fundamental or play. It gives them the perspective to grasp the material. This should always be your first step, rather than presenting details immediately.

After a thorough explanation, the coach must analyze his interpretation and proceed to outline the material and break it down even further for his players' understanding. They must have the opportunity to absorb what you have presented. This will also prove helpful to the coach by showing him what points in his teaching progression need re-emphasizing. *Do not take anything for granted!* Cover the material in a meticulous sequence for their complete understanding.

PLAYER RETENTION OF THE MATERIAL. The next step calls for a demonstration by the coach or an assistant of what you are teaching. It is of consequence to be impressive during the demonstration. Make sure the demonstration is successful by employing the same techniques you are teaching. When a squad can see the coach display a flawless exhibition, they gain confidence in his skill. It is a necessary part of teaching and do not be fooled into believing it is not.

Finally, the squad members themselves should execute the moves. The coach will have a chance to get a first-hand glimpse of whether or not his teaching techniques were absorbed by the squad. Close surveillance of each player performing the move must be made by the head coach and his assistants. A tailored policy of constructive criticism will aid the players needing help. A second assistance will be in the form of repetitious drills so that the player can establish a standard of excellence. These two aids are vital in your teaching techniques.

FUNDAMENTALS NEEDED TO WIN

SHOOTING. In discussing offensive fundamentals, you must recall that the game of basketball has changed considerably during the past 15 years. The greatest change has been the use of "freedom offenses" in contrast to the earlier, more controlled style of play.

Never before in the history of the game has shooting and scoring been so prevalent. It is not uncommon to see scores of above 100 points in high

school, while some colleges have averaged near the century mark for an entire season. The reason for this increased scoring lies with the development
of excellent shooters. The ability of some players to average thirty or more
points a game will be evidence enough to cite. Besides their phenomenal
scoring average, the players are shooting over 55 per cent in many cases.
There is no question about it—the player today must be versatile enough to
play all styles of offensive basketball.

SHOOTING ABILITY.   The shooting ability of a player will depend upon
his confidence, relaxation, poise, and proper technique. As a coach, you
can understand why it is such a difficult task to develop a shooter. Those
players who want to improve their shooting ability devote a major portion
of their time to this art. However, for improvement to take place they must
observe certain rules and be willing to make individual sacrifices. The
coach should set up a uniform method of executing the various shots he
wants his team members to observe. For this reason, we will systematically
list the major teaching points for the shots we employ in our pattern of play.

Jump Shot.   The invention of this shot caused the "early retirement" of
many coaches, as it has taken its place as the most potent offensive weapon
in the history of basketball. If a player desires to be a top scorer, he must
first become a good jump shooter. Up to this date, there has been no defense developed which can consistently cope with the jump shooter. This
is best illustrated by the fact that after possession is gained, the ball is rapidly advanced upcourt and the 15-foot jump shot taken immediately. This
jump shot should be coached to the point where the players shoot a "percentage" shot and not one fired up at the basket without proper shooting
techniques being employed. The many successes of the Michigan State
teams can be attributed to this quick advancement upcourt for the medium
jump shot. Figure 6–1 illustrates this shot.

Fig. 6–1. Excellent jump-
shooting form but watch that
        defensive hand.

In teaching the jump shot, these points should be considered:

1. The feet, shoulders, and body should be facing the basket.
2. The jump can be made off both feet or off the front foot.
3. The jump approach should be straight up and slightly forward.
4. The position of the ball is high and above the head.
5. The elbow should be held *inside* and not allowed to stray.
6. The index finger should be on the middle of the ball.
7. The eyes should be focused on the front edge of the rim.
8. The ball should be released at the peak of the jump.
9. There should be a complete follow-through after the shot.
10. A jump shot should not be forced.

Lay-up Shot. The lay-up shot is the most fundamental of all shots. It is also one of the easiest shots to teach. With the rapid pace of the game increasing the number of fast-break baskets, the lay-up is more important that ever in your fundamental teaching. This, coupled with the big pivot man who scores frequently on three-point plays, has placed special attention on the lay-up shot. Figure 6–2 shows the driving lay-up.

Fig. 6–2. Two points on a perfect lay-up shot.

There are teaching points which insure proper technique of this shot:

1. The player should assume a stance 8 feet away, facing the basket.
2. Hand position finds the right hand under the ball with the left used as a guide.
3. The takeoff foot should be opposite the shooting hand.
4. The takeoff should be in the form of an explosive high jump rather than a broad jump.
5. As the ball is released, the left hand is dropped and the right hand is extended fully and places the ball in the rectangle above the basket.

6. The shooting target should be the right-hand corner of the rectangle.
7. The ball should be released with the player's palm facing the shooter and no english applied to the shot.
8. Eye contact must be maintained with the right corner of the rectangle throughout the drive (Fig. 6–3).
9. As you approach the basket, veer directly to the right or left and use the backboard.
10. A player is encouraged to shoot with both left and right hands on lay-ups.

Fig. 6–3. Example of concentrated eye contact after breaking through the defense for a lay-up.

Crossover Shot. There may be instances in a game when a player will be unable to approach the basket for a shot at the angle he desires. He may be forced to go in front of the basket and shoot from the opposite side. This is referred to as the "crossover" shot.

The same procedure should be applied as on the lay-up shot with a few exceptions:

1. The approach is most important. The player should take off just inside the 12-foot lane at the proper angle.
2. As his momentum carries him to the basket, he turns his body in the air. This should be a smooth and natural move.
3. Upon release of the ball, the right hand is rotated to give the ball english.
4. Ball placement on the backboard should be slightly inside and high on the rectangular area. The english will bring the ball down into the basket.
5. When the shot is completed, the player's chest should be turned in toward the basket.
6. Remind your players not to make a hook shot out of this crossover shot.

Hook Shot. This shot is the most difficult for a coach to teach—although once mastered, it is one of the most difficult to block. Because of the use of fan-shaped backboards in most high schools, only a few coaches spend a great deal of time teaching this shot. For this reason, you find very few natural "hookers" in the secondary schools. The following are our teaching points on the hook shot:

1. The player must first turn his head and look at a spot on the backboard or the basket itself, depending upon his floor position.
2. The feet should be spread approximately the width of the shoulders.
3. After receiving the ball, the player should hold it high and away from his body.
4. Depending upon the defensive man, the player will step toward the basket and not away from it. The exception is on the dribble directly in front of the basket.
5. The ball should be released *behind the head* and not out in front of the player. It should be shot off the fingers and not the palm.
6. The other arm should be brought up to insure protection of the ball.
7. In the case of a fan-shaped board, the eyes should be focused on the rim. In college, shoot for the right-hand corner of the rectangle if the proper angle exists.
8. The follow-through should bring the player around and nearly facing the basket. (See Fig. 6–4.)

Fig. 6–4. Correct fingertip control arm extension, and follow-through on the hook shot.

Offensive Tipping. A tip shot by the offense has joined basketball's circle of select shots. It was a successful tip shot of a missed attempt that won Loyola University the NCAA basketball crown in 1963 over the University of Cincinnati. Its importance cannot be minimized as it is the "cheap" basket that is so often instrumental in winning games.

As player jumping abilities are increasing, coaches stress the use of this shot. It is very effective for the big pivot man and the good jumper, plus being almost impossible to stop. The express time of its use occurs under the offensive basket when a shot has been attempted and it is impossible to gather in the ball with two hands (see Fig. 6–5).

1. The tip should be made with the arm fully extended in order to achieve maximum height.

Fig. 6–5. Tremendous body control for height on the tip shot.

2. For the jump to be as high as possible, the feet should be close together at the start. BEND THE KNEES!
3. Fingers on the tipping hand should be spread.
4. The wrist snap after making contact with the ball should be quick but soft.
5. The ability to "hang in the air" by the player aids considerably on this shot.
6. Do not attempt to use the backboard in tipping a shot.
7. Practice using both hands to see which one you can go the highest with, then use it.
8. Come down from the jump ready to tip again and again if necessary.

Free Throws. Free throwing has always been an important part of basketball. Frequently, games are won or lost at the free-throw line. Rule changes in basketball, providing for a bonus shot, have increased the importance of the free throw. Also, more and more fouls are being called by officials. It is not uncommon for a team to shoot 30 or 40 free throws in a single game in this new era of basketball. Therefore, coaches are stressing the significance of this toss.

Of major concern is the inconsistency of shooting, either by individual players or the entire team. This does not seem logical. The free throw is a shot that is taken at the same distance, from a basket of the same size and height. It would seem that a player should be able to perfect this phase of the game. It is one of the very few moments in any athletic contest where a player knows that he is unmolested and unguarded, and that this situation will exist everytime he shoots a free throw.

For many years a difference of opinion has existed regarding the relative effectiveness of the two-hand underhand free throw as compared with the one-hand push free throw.

In 1956, Coach Albeck completed his master's degree with a cinematographic analysis of the two types of free throws to ascertain which technique is the most accurate.

The survey included 47 major college basketball teams. Of the 23,471 free throws attempted, 15,942 were shot one-handed.

The following conclusions were drawn in comparing the two styles:

1. The survey results indicated that the one-hand free throw is the favorite of players today.
2. Statistics indicate that the one-hand free throw is the more accurate shot.
3. Release velocity for the one-hand free-throw shooter is slower, insuring a smaller margin of error in the technique.
4. A better angle at the basket is obtainable through use of the one-hand free throw.
5. Before the early 1940's, the two-hand underhand method was considered to be the only correct way to shoot free throws. Since that time the trend is toward almost universal acceptance of the one-hand push shot as a sound shooting form for the free throw.
6. The underhand method is rapidly losing its status in free throwing.
7. Coaches want the players to use the same type of shot from both the field and the free-throw line. This avoids having to master two techniques.

The history of the game has influenced the thinking on foul shooting. The original way of shooting in basketball was the two-hand underhand method. When the game advanced, and this shot became impractical for field goal shooting, new techniques were developed. However, the underhand free throw remained. Only one player shot the fouls and he became an expert. When the rules changed to allow the fouled player to shoot the free throw, different methods developed. These players did not perfect the shot as the single free thrower had done. As a result, these new methods were condemned as inferior to the original shot. Therefore, basketball tradition tends to preserve the two-hand underhand free throw. Its life, however, is being quickly shortened by a combination of better techniques, finer players and greater emphasis placed on foul shooting.

Turn-and-Push Shot. This shot (Fig. 6–6) is used and taught by many high school coaches instead of the hook shot. They feel it is easy to teach and a more natural shot for younger players to master than the hook shot.

The basic principles of the shot are much the same as those of the hook shot, with these exceptions:

1. The turn on the turn-and-push shot is slightly greater than on the hook shot.
2. Rather than having the arm extended, it is bent at the elbow and extended after the ball is released.
3. The ball is released with a tonic wrist snap.
4. Its effectiveness is reduced by the distance you are from the basket.
5. In this shot, the player seldom uses the backboard.

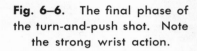

Fig. 6–6. The final phase of the turn-and-push shot. Note the strong wrist action.

Backhanded Shot. This shot (Fig. 6–7) is up to the individual player. It occurs when the player has his back to the basket and is directly in front of it. It is a shot to be used only by the advanced basketball player, although the utilization of it in the professional game has increased its popularity in the colleges. Each year we see more and more of its use. The need for a surprise move and quickness dictates this shot.

Its execution is as follows:

1. The player with the ball is positioned in front of the basket.
2. He may dribble or jump straight up in the air, slightly turning his body to the right.
3. He holds the ball with two hands until he reaches the peak of his jump.
4. He releases the ball to the right side of the opponent's head.
5. An application of english usually accompanies the ball on this shot.
6. It cannot be effective unless it occurs close to the basket.

Fade Shot Off Dribble. This shot rivals the backhanded shot as the newest point-getter for the individual offensive man. It is an advanced technique for the advanced basketball player and its addition to an already loaded offensive arsenal makes him nearly unstoppable. Its teaching points include:

1. The player is driving the baseline as the defensive man cuts him off.
2. As the dribbler stops, the defensive man's momentum carries him slightly past.
3. The dribbler then jumps sideways and in toward the basket for the shot.
4. The same maneuver has also been made effective by continuing the dribble and, after gaining a step advantage on the defense, moving in so that the defensive man will be on the dribbler's back.
5. Insist on good shooting form by the players using this move.
6. Be sure they do not travel with the ball when trying to execute this move.

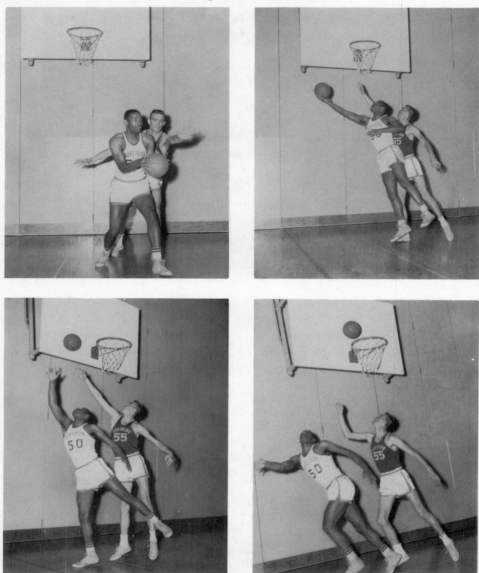

Fig. 6—7. The advanced backhand lay-up.

OFFENSIVE REBOUNDING

The outcome of the "battle of the boards" in basketball usually will determine the winner of the game, with other things being equal. Modern-day rebounding seems to have become a congregation of all ten players under the basket. Some colleges have 6' 2" to 6' 5" guards, with their three other men being even bigger. Therefore, you can see that height is a leading factor in rebounding. You cannot win without the ball.

The strong offensive rebounder will possess desire, aggressiveness, timing, and jumping ability. Only a portion of these abilities is innate, and it is the coach's responsibility to develop the others for total rebounding performance. The only way to promote tireless rebounding is through practice drills. Rebounding must be practiced, the same as shooting. There is no other alternative. Coaches are in agreement that offensive rebounders are harder to develop than defensive board men. One reason might be that they play away from the basket farther and tend to "float" when a shot is taken rather than crash the board. A second reason might be the offensive pattern the coach engages in, whereby the team is stationed in a position which makes it difficult to secure the rebound.

RULES FOR THE OFFENSIVE REBOUNDER. The good offensive rebounders are those players with a knack of knowing where the ball is at all times. This is interpreted as attempting to gain a favorable rebounding position.

1. Know where the ball is at all times offensively.
2. Once the ball is shot, crash the offensive board. Otherwise, you are susceptible to screening-out procedures by defense.
3. Attempt to gain an inside position by the use of fakes.
4. If you are blocked out, try and jump to deflect or tip the ball to a teammate or an open spot on the floor, then hustle to get there.
5. Never get caught standing flat-footed on a shot attempt.
6. Be aware that 75 per cent of the shots taken from the side will rebound across on the opposite side of the basket.
7. The offensive man should jump so that he will be at his maximum height when coming into contact with the ball.
8. Utilize the tip shot as the main offensive weapon.
9. In high school, it might be wise to bring the ball back out after securing a rebound, rather than gamble on the tip shot or other poor percentage shots underneath.
10. Be prepared to crash *between* two or three screening defensive men for the rebound.
11. Game-like drills and practice develop good offensive rebound location.

BALL-HANDLING

The team which can pass and handle the ball, and use it as an instrument to score, is one which is difficult to defeat. The "Whiz Kids" of Illinois in the early 1940's were regarded as a great passing team. Two consecutive Big Ten titles attest to this fact. Their cleverness in passing set up many scoring opportunities they were able to take advantage of.

The passing game must be uniform and mobile in order to be productive. Often we have observed an open player cutting toward the basket and waiting for the ball, only to have the scoring opportunity nullified by the pass being deflected by the defense. It also has been our experience to notice a man break free under the basket and to have the pass overthrown. These situations can be conquered by the coach through constant practice and drill.

Passing involves handling the ball and gaining a genuine "touch" of the ball. You can never acquire this ability any other way than by drills with a purpose.

PHYSICAL FACTORS

Hands. Large hands on a player are an asset. However, the fact that a player has them does not assure him of being an excellent passer. The term "strong with the ball" refers many times to the player's hands. It means that he seldom loses control of the ball once he gains possession. This is not to imply that small-handed players are under any handicap. Many of our great small men in basketball are not blessed with the "big mitt," but they have carved many a niche in our basketball history.

Quickness. Quickness of hands in passing is paramount. The size of the hands are instrumental in handling the ball, but the manner in which you release it is often the difference between whether the pass is made or intercepted. It also is the difference between the opportunity to shoot at the basket or having an interception made by the defense.

Fingers. The fingers should be spread on the ball and it should be passed this way. The palms of the hands should not contact the ball. Test your players by letting them toss the ball into the air and catch it. If the player catches it with the fingers, there is a dull sound. If he does not catch it in this manner, there is a resounding "thud" as the ball hits the palms of the hands. These two distinct sounds are noticeable, and a good coaching aid which we have found helpful in pointing out this passing fault.

Wrists. The wrists should be flexible. Some players are naturally stronger than others and yet poorer passers. The explanation is that some players use their wrists as whips. They "pop" the wrists with a snap when passing. This is a loose and elastic break of the wrist and yet it remains strong enough to make all the necessary passes. This inability of "breaking the wrist" is what causes poor passes among some ball players.

PASSING RESPONSIBILITIES. As they advance the ball from the back-court into the scoring area, the team must now use all the finesse they have acquired in practice drills to assist them in scoring. If they cannot penetrate the defense with passes for the short shot, then they can expect trouble, as few teams will win solely on their outcourt shooting.

Decisions must be made at the scoring end by all the players handling the ball. They do have an advantage over the defense in this respect, because they know what their offense calls for and where their teammates will position themselves. The player must be able to think "on his feet." His response to the defense and his sense of knowing when to pass the ball—plus how to make the successful pass—should be automatic reactions. The use of the right kind of pass to enable a teammate to score, and the fakes to take advantage of vulnerable passing spots for feeding the open man, indicate a good offensive ball handler.

Fig. 6–8. Four vulnerable areas to pass by the opponent.

The defensive player (Fig. 6–8) has four vulnerable spots in which the offensive player can pass the ball by him. These are:

1. Over his head
2. By his feet
3. At his hips
4. Over his shoulder

These openings present themselves as the offensive player gains possession of the ball and the defensive man approaches to guard him. The offensive man can now count on help through a number of fakes which will set up the defensive man for a pass to be thrown by him. These fakes are initiated to bring the defensive man up closer so that passing to the open man will be easier. It is done in the following manner:

1. The best fake in order to pass is to fake a shot. It brings the defensive man up more quickly than anything else.
2. Use a fake drive to pass over the shoulder. As the defensive man retreats, he will drop one of his arms—pass over it.
3. Fake a bounce pass, or fake a pass directly at the defensive man to let you pass over his head. As he protects against the bounce or direct pass, he leaves an opening over his head.
4. When the defensive man keeps both hands up, pass off either hip.
5. Bounce the ball by the *front foot* of the defensive man's stance.

UNDERLYING PRINCIPLES OF PASSING

1. A player should never "wind up" on a pass so that he telegraphs it.
2. Don't be afraid to be close to the defensive man when passing.
3. Force the defensive man in committing the initial move to present an opening for the pass.
4. Never lob the ball on any pass.
5. Never "over ball-fake" against the defense.

TYPES OF PASSES. The number of passes in basketball are many and varied. Some coaches have expressed belief in all of them while others believe in only a select few. Regardless of the number of passes and individual conviction, the better passers seem to have a quality for quickly getting rid of the ball. They also possess the ability to use split vision, which makes them an even bigger threat. Finally, they have the skill of gauging the velocity of the pass to be thrown to their teammate. Before a player can become adept at doing these things, he must learn the proper technique of executing fundamental passes.

Chest Pass. The chest pass in basketball is by far the most common and important in the passing game. It is used more times per game than many other passes combined. It is customarily a short pass. The range of distance over which it can be thrown accurately and quickly is approximately 30 feet, although this varies with the individual passer. For any distance beyond this, the pass has a tendency to float and is subject to inaccuracy and interception. Teaching points of the chest pass are:

1. The player's hand position is slightly behind the ball, with the fingers spread evenly over the ball. The thumbs should be parallel.
2. The ball release begins with a mild recoil of the arms, with the elbows close to the body.
3. The ball is released by a combined quick movement of the arm, elbow, wrist, and fingers.
4. The passer's palms will be pointing at the receiver and his thumbs will be close together.
5. The ball will leave the index fingers and thumbs last.
6. A moderate amount of back spin may result from the release.
7. A follow-through on this pass is *not necessary*. You can get the ball away more quickly and just as accurately by snapping the pass off with the use of your arms and wrists.

Two-Hand Overhead Pass. This is perhaps the best pass in basketball for feeding the pivot man. It is used by both guards and forwards, with the latter having the best position in which to deploy it. It should not be neglected by the pivot man as a pass, for he can use it by turning around immediately after receiving the ball and looking to hit open men or cutters near the basket. It is a fine pass for the center to use in returning the ball to the outside men if congestion occurs in the pivot. This is how we teach the two-hand overhead pass:

1. The ball is held above the head with fingers spread evenly, the thumbs close together and behind the ball.
2. Foot position is without benefit of a step forward, but with the feet parallel when the pass is made.
3. The actual release of the ball takes place with a snap of the wrist.
4. Ball direction will be down toward the receiver, with the arms and hands following through.
5. After completion of the pass the palms of the hands, because of the follow-through, should be pointing toward the floor.

Bounce Pass. The bounce pass has a definite place in any offensive pattern. If its use is properly controlled, it will provide the offense with an additional scoring weapon. The smaller men on a team generally are the better bounce passers. They can get down low and deliver the ball quickly and accurately. They are more proficient in using this pass than the larger men. Many coaches feel the long bounce pass is dangerous and that the shorter passes, such as at the end of a fast break, are the types they desire. The bounce pass can be used as a means of giving the pivot man the ball. There are always occasions in the game when it might be the only way to get the ball in to the pivot man. The bounce pass should be used frequently in the penetration of a zone defense! It is much more effective than many others and is easier to handle. For these reasons, the bounce pass

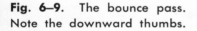

Fig. 6–9. The bounce pass. Note the downward thumbs.

should not be neglected in the coach's passing game. Figure 6–9 illustrates the correct form in making this pass. Points of emphasis on the bounce pass are as follows:

1. Body position calls for the player to have a low center of gravity.
2. The hand position on the ball is the same as that of the two-hand chest pass. The body should be bent at the waist.

3. The ball carriage is at knee- to waist-height.

4. The player should "squeeze out" the ball when releasing it. His hands and fingers literally compress the ball downward on its flight and out to the receiver.

5. The elbows should be in and not held out.

6. The thumbs should be pointing down to the floor after the follow-through. This again is not mandatory and a snap is recognized as being just as effective as the follow-through.

7. Refrain from using excessive overspin on the ball, thus making it difficult for the receiver to catch.

8. The ball placement on the floor should be closer to the passer than the receiver.

9. Great care should be taken concerning the use of the bounce pass on certain floors. The ball seldom bounces the same on a portable floor such as you find in fieldhouses. On harder surfaces, it reacts much more quickly.

Baseball Pass. Northern Michigan University's Wayne Monson, an All-American choice, made us well aware of what could be done with this pass. Repeatedly, he would throw a full-court-length pass to a breaking man for a basket. He was much like the professional football quarterbacks who throw the ball just beyond the defensive man's outstretched hands into the receiver's for a touchdown. Granted, these individuals do not come along very often; but we should learn from what they teach us. This player taught us the importance of the long pass and nullified the idea that it was much too long a throw and would be easily intercepted. Many times we are afraid to break with tradition, and for this reason our teaching methods remain pretty much standardized. Experiment. Let your players teach you some valuable points. Learn from them.

The baseball pass has much to offer the fast-break team. It can be used as the outlet pass and can give you an immediate advantage by enabling you to penetrate down the floor further on the first pass. With its continued use, a defending team has a tendency to retreat rather than fight you on the boards for fear of this pass, thus enabling you to get the ball more often. Also, knowing that you are a threat with the long pass and respecting this feature of your game, the opponents open up the middle more than ever, giving your team the perfect middle-man fast break.

Points to remember in teaching the baseball pass are:

1. The pass is started with the ball at shoulder height near the ear.

2. The throw can be likened to a catcher firing to a base in an attempt to catch the base runner.

3. The elbow and wrist are important factors to consider. Both should point in the direction in which you are throwing. The wrist will produce the accuracy, the elbow and arm the power.

4. A step toward your receiver must be taken to compensate for the long distance the ball must be thrown.

5. A definite "rotation of the hips" toward the receiver will increase both power and accuracy. Do not rely entirely upon the arm for both.

6. The player's hand should be behind the ball to avoid any side-spin or curving of the pass.

7. Pick your target quickly and give him a proper lead. Use the four corners of the floor as a guide in completing the pass.

8. Follow through with the hand, arm, hips, and feet. You should be completely facing your receiver after the toss.

Hook Pass. This pass has a close correlation with the basket attempt. Like the shot, it is difficult to master, especially with a weak hand. Seldom have we seen a left-handed hook pass made to the outlet man by a right hander who has recovered the ball. In fact, the authors cannot remember when they last saw this occurrence in a game. Players "from experience" will always use their strong hand when pressured.

The advantages the hook pass gives are numerous. For instance, it can be utilized to originate the fast break. In the same vein, it can be used to get the offensive man out of trouble if he is being double-teamed. It is employed by fast-break men when they are covered and have to make a return pass to a teammate at the end of a fast break. Press offenses have made use of the hook pass by inviting a double-team situation and then having the player jump and hook pass to an open man.

Teaching points for the hook pass are:

1. Both hands should be on the ball as you step away from your opponent.
2. The jump into the air will be off the left foot if the player is right-handed.
3. The man with the ball will turn and look for his receiver while in the air.
4. The ball should be held with the fingers and hand, not against the wrist; it is released with a sudden snap of the arm, elbow, and wrist.
5. When the ball is released, the player will have his right arm fully extended.
6. He should land in a balanced position ready to return to action.

Sidearm Pass. Rapid approval of this pass is taking place among coaches. The professional basketball ranks have popularized its use and some coaches are including it among their list of passes.

This pass is easier to handle for some players than the hook pass and yet they are fundamentally much the same in execution. The main difference is that the player lets the ball rest on his wrist when throwing it. Since it is used for distance passing, the stance is much the same as that of a discus thrower. The weight is shifted to the back foot for the throw and the release takes place as the player brings the ball from slightly below the waist to a full extension of the arm. The follow-through will bring your rear foot parallel with your lead one.

Sidearm Bounce Pass. This has been a fine pass for the authors as it has been especially effective in our "man through" series. This functional pass is only for the advanced player however, and we recommend it strictly for his use. Its main purpose is to help the offensive man to pass by the defensive player who is directly between him and a teammate. The forwards in the offense are the men who make this pass work, since they must have the ability to hit the cutter as he breaks to the basket. The center can also utilize it by reaching around the opposing defensive man and passing to an open man. Figure 6–10 illustrates the proper position for the sidearm pass.

Fig. 6–10. The sidearm bounce pass. The offensive man is low in order to make the pass.

Teaching points for the sidearm bounce pass are:

1. Assuming the player is in the right forward's position and has the ball, he should immediately face his opponent.
2. To bring the defensive man up, he should fake a shot with the left foot acting as the pivot foot.
3. Once the defensive man approaches, the player steps directly toward the baseline, stretching as far as possible without moving the pivot foot.
4. The player then extends his arm and releases his left hand from the ball.
5. The ball placement should be under the defensive man's hand and close to his foot.
6. The right hand should put "over-english" on the ball so that it will come up off the floor just as your teammate cuts to the basket.
7. This overspin is applied by a quick flip of the wrist across the molded seams of the ball, with the fingers applying the spin.

Flip Pass. There are times in the offense when two men pass close together and make an exchange of the ball. The pass frequently used is a flip pass. It is a favorite of teams using the "guard around" play, and we might add that it is just as effective today as in the past.

It is usually made more between guard-to-guard and guard-to-forward combinations than any other, although sometimes you will see a pivot man use it in handing off. The initiation of the flip pass can be either by use of the dribble toward the offensive man, or by a direct pass and moving behind the receiver for a return flip pass. Teaching points for the player are the following:

1. Wait for the offensive teammate to get proper position for a return pass.
2. Handle the ball with both hands and pivot to insure protection of the ball.
3. As the potential receiver approaches, let go of the ball as if it were "red hot." The elbows should be out, not close to the body.
4. Don't shovel or hand the ball to your teammate. Flip it and then clear out of the area, taking your defensive man with you.
5. Keep your eye on your teammate and never lose sight of the ball.

SITUATION PASSES

These types of passes are questionable and draw considerable debate from interested basketball coaches. The behind-the-back pass, the backboard pass, and transverse passing on the fast break are termed flashy, tricky, dangerous, and fundamentally unsound by many coaches. In defense of them, we would like to say that although they are normally all of these, when that one individual or team comes along who can perform them well and still retain the proper basketball perspective, you have that valuable something extra.

BEHIND-THE-BACK PASS. This pass is seen more on playgrounds than in gymnasiums. Most players come in contact with this pass and have experimented with it earlier, usually in the backyard. Since youngsters are great imitators, and have seen our top professional and college teams play

Fig. 6–11. Once mastered, the behind-the-back pass is a valuable asset as shown here in the playing situation.

on television, they tend to mimic these players' basketball habits—especially behind-the-back passing. Thus this pass becomes a popular one.

The pass is normally made on the tail-end of a fast break when the offensive man cannot complete a conventional type of pass to a teammate. At other times it is a necessity, such as when the defense puts extreme pressure on the ball handler and it is his only alternative. (See Fig. 6–11.)

Assuming the player is right-handed and dribbling beyond mid-court in the offensive court, he will pass the ball with his right hand to the left side to a teammate. The ball is brought around behind the back, and the pass is dependent upon a sturdy wrist. The wrist snap is aided in the throw by strong fingers and proper follow-through. The passer sets up the defensive man by veering to the right to decrease possible pass deflection.

In conclusion, we would like to point out that it is a situation pass and dependent upon only one man, the ball handler. If he is competent and schooled in its use, then it can be employed. If he is not, then we consider it to be a "non-percentage pass."

BACKBOARD PASS. Because of the explosive jumpers currently playing basketball, the backboard pass has become a good alternate move in some offenses for coaches having this kind of personnel.

The plan is for the pass to be made normally in a fast-break or trailer situation. Supposing we have a two-on-one fast-break situation on the defense. The ball is on the right side and the offensive man is unable to make a regular pass to his teammate on the opposite side. Under these conditions, college coaches have authorized the man with the ball to glance it high off the backboard so that it will rebound to his teammate who has sprung up to catch it and shoot it into the basket, all in one motion.

The timing of both players must be perfect, and many college coaches are currently spending time with gifted players who can make effective backboard passes. The passer can tip off his teammate by yelling "board," thus letting him know what to expect. When executed perfectly there is nothing more exciting for the spectators to watch than a well-conceived "pass-and-dunk" play.

The pass should be soft and high, with no spin on the ball, as it would be difficult for the receiver to handle in the air. The passer should use the rectangle above the basket as a guide for his pass.

It is the most difficult pass in basketball to master and is not advised for any level of player other than the most skilled and advanced.

TRANSVERSE PASSING. Passing is the quickest method of advancing the ball to the offensive end. This is what we want our players to do with a minimum of effort if at all possible. We often have trouble when the defense plays certain areas or men in attempting to stop the fast break.

As a result, we have put into use what we term "transverse passing" to alleviate any undue pressure by the defense. After an outlet pass is made to the side, we attempt to move down the floor quickly, hoping to gain an advantage over the defense. It is our feeling that passing is the best method.

We try to center the ball to a middle man immediately and he, in turn, looks to hit the left wing man with the ball. The middle man's release of the ball must be quick, as many teams play this man strong defensively and hope to stop the break here. As you can see, we have gone across court with the ball by short, snappy passes, which emphasize no follow-through or strong wrist action. In this way, we have not given the defense a chance to get set and have enhanced our fast break opportunity. The three men move the entire floor length until in scoring position, taking advantage of this transverse passing game.

DRIBBLING

We minimize the use of the dribble in our offensive programs. It is our belief that passing is a better method of advancing the ball. Nevertheless, we are well aware of the dribble's value. When properly used, it is an effective offensive fundamental. On the other hand, it can be your *opponent's* best weapon if caution is not exercised in its use. Coaches usually teach two kinds of dribble. One is for speed situations and the second for control situations. We will analyze both, as they are assets for every player to learn and retain.

The speed dribble is executed by the player when he has a fast-break opportunity, such as a two-on-one situation. Along this same line, many high school coaches feel that it is one of the better methods of clearing the ball from congested areas under the basket. We know one coach who insists that when a defensive rebounder captures the rebound, he must immediately dribble to center court and become the middle man on his fast break. In this way, he eliminates the outlet pass and the possible interception. We might add, his teams have met with considerable success. This type of maneuver is one which deserves your attention. Finally, the speed dribble is used to advance the ball into the offensive court as quickly as possible. Some of your finest fast-break teams will throw the ball in with much haste and hope to beat the defensive team back to the offensive end by means of the dribble. It is their contention that the defense must stop the dribbler or he may go all the way for the easy lay-up. The offense feels that even if it does finally stop the dribbler, he may have penetrated far enough to take a medium jump shot. Another possibility could be a pass-off to a teammate who might be free because of this unforeseen pressure by the dribbler. The great basketball teams at Tennessee State University have personified this principle, and who can deny their success?

The uses of the control dribble are diverse. In the beginning, it is put into action to bring the ball from the backcourt to the offensive court. As a method of moving to a different area in the offensive court, the dribble may be exercised. The control dribble's greatest claim lies in its potency as an individual move to the offensive basket. The player who drives for the basket is always a threat and the control dribble is his major resource. Finally, this dribble is valuable when a team is in their delay or stalling game. In this type of game, never relinquish the dribble except in time of necessity and then know where to go when you put it into action. Never dribble without a purpose!

Teaching points for the speed dribble are:

1. The body should be upright and natural, not bent over.
2. The dribble from a starting position is made by dropping the ball out away from the body as far as possible.
3. If the player is right-handed, he will then lift off with his left foot, affording the ball protection with his body.
4. In contacting the ball, it is necessary to develop a "feel" or "touch" of the ball through the fingers. This insures acceleration and control.
5. The fingers should be spread in anticipation of the ball's coming up off the floor from the designated ball drop.
6. The second return of the ball to the floor on the dribble should be made with the utmost management of the wrist and relaxed finger movement.
7. The ball should be pushed down and forward to the point where the player finds himself literally running after it.
8. The ball should bounce up to your waist or rib cage on the speed dribble. Otherwise, you will overrun the ball.
9. Always dribble with vision. Do not show laxity in enforcing this point with your players.

CONTROL DRIBBLE. In this dribble the following exceptions are made:

1. The body will be bent more and not upright. The dribbler will be lower than in the speed dribble.
2. For body protection, the ball should be dribbled with the outside hand away from the defensive man. Make use of the left hand and shoulder as added protective aids.
3. Hand position on the ball is the same as in the speed dribble, except the thrust on the ball is more delicate.
4. The ball should be dropped off the right foot with a slight snap and away from the body.
5. The height of the dribble will depend upon the situation and the defensive man. In danger situations the dribble should be knee-high.
6. Finger efficiency must be maintained on the ball to warrant proper action and maneuverability.
7. Players should never be allowed to "roll the ball" in any dribbling phase. This occurs when they are practicing control dribbling and it encourages the "palming" habit, which is bad for dribblers.

DRIBBLING DRAWBACKS. Now that we have established the dribble in our offensive fundamentals, let us take a critical view of its implications.

There is no question that too much dribbling by one player on a team can become a major morale problem for the coach. Dominance of the ball by dribbling is not what a coach seeks in a player. Another detrimental use of the dribble is the one-bounce habit which players acquire from the time they start playing unless otherwise instructed. However, in deference to the good coaching which is found throughout our schools, this problem is diminishing somewhat. Nevertheless, it disappears only through recognition and correction.

In his quest for the spotlight the possessive dribbler will miss open team-mates during his exhibition and cause consternation among the team members. The dribbler may do this by not keeping his eyes open or by the mere fact that he is all wrapped up in what he is doing and does not think of his teammates.

Those "Dandy Dick" dribblers who envision themselves as Harlem Globe-trotters also deserve criticism. They are the individuals who believe that they can dribble behind their back and between their legs against any and all opponents. Usually when making use of these tactics they are relieved of the ball by their opponents or are vulnerable to a two-time situation by the defense.

Preoccupied dribblers never make good team players. The reason is evident and if they are to fit into the pattern of play as set forth by the coach, they must be regimented in proper dribbling techniques and procedures.

The following are good dribbling recommendations:

1. Always possess complete vision when dribbling.
2. Achieve expert skill by learning to dribble with both hands.
3. Dribble with a purpose, not just for the sake of dribbling.
4. When pressure is exerted by the defense, do not become panicky and dribble needlessly.
5. Change of pace dribblers are at a premium. Few players are good enough to do this efficiently. Learn this fundamental.
6. Practice dribbling on top of the front-row bleachers in your gymnasium to develop the "feel" so necessary for dribblers. This is a drill used by Rudy Ellis, Shawano, Wisconsin high school coach.
7. Black-out blinder glasses for dribbling drills can help develop control and command of the ball.
8. When over-dribbling is committed during a half-court scrimmage, give the ball to the other team. Make them aware you want it passed!
9. Should you have a one-bounce player and he performs this act during the scrimmage, the ball should be taken away from him and given to the other team.
10. The dribble is useful and should be exploited with a one-on-one situation when the opposing team has a star who is a weak defensive man.

SCREENING

Screening in basketball is universal. In order to get an opening for a shot, every offense needs some form of screen. Screens usually are of two kinds: those set directly on the man, or those which are set away from the ball.

The aim of an offensive screen is to legally free a teammate. This is effected when the offensive screener sets the screen approximately 3 feet from the defensive man. He must be stationary or the screen will be illegal and a foul will be called on the offensive screener. In other words, the defensive man must be given a chance to escape the screen.

The screen, if made effective, serves several objectives:

1. It demands that the defensive man recognize the screen as a threat to him.
2. The screener hopes the defense will be confused by this maneuver.
3. When confused, the defense may make a poor switch, allowing offensive freedom.
4. The defense may drop off the defensive line, allowing a jump shot over the defense.
5. When no switch is made and the screen is good, the offensive man with the ball can go to the basket.

There is no denying that screening is another difficult phase to teach. You will find that your players will tend to rush to make a screen, while speed is not necessary for this maneuver. Proper footwork, change of direction, and excellent timing are the secrets of screening. Auburn University, with its shuffle offense, is the best example of these three qualities and its success is due to them.

Because a fundamental is difficult to teach, do not as a coach neglect learning about its techniques. Do not be afraid to tackle a tough problem because this one factor might be hurting your team. Just because you do not know how to teach it or do not want to spend the time on this relatively unimportant phase does not mean you have the right to strike it out of your teaching. Teach and coach without such fear. If properly prepared and organized, the screen is never a problem.

7

Formula for a Team Offense

FACTORS DETERMINING TEAM OFFENSE

In selecting an offense, a coach has many considerations and decisions to make. He will naturally be prejudiced by the type of pattern he will want to use. He may favor the fast-break game, but the slowness of his personnel might cause him to doubt their effectiveness in employing this offense. In this predicament, the coach would be foolish in attempting to use the faster moving game. Player competency should be studied and those with outstanding abilities should be fitted into your offensive pattern.

If you are moving into a new coaching position, considerable deliberation should precede any thought of installing a new offense. Should you have a group of seniors forming the nucleus of your club who are successful and express confidence in their present pattern of play, we advocate leaving the system alone. In this circumstance, the coach should begin exposing his entire offensive pattern to the freshman and junior varsity squads. By doing this, the coach can work with this group to bring them along and they will appreciate his demands. This preliminary work will also avoid a complete reorganization a year later, when your seniors have graduated.

A style of play will be determined by other factors which the coach must consider. These include the type of defense which a section of the country is using. In high schools, you can be assured that you will run into zone defenses in nearly 80 per cent of your games. Therefore, a high school coach must produce a fine zone offense.

Court restrictions are another handicap in the development of a specific pattern of play. The coach may like to play a single post offense and use cutters, but on a small, narrow court, for example, the opponents will make use of a zone, thus eliminating the possibility of using this offensive pattern. At the same time, the small gym can be a psychological advantage if the players are small and like the pressing game. Most opponents will fear the small gymnasium and the type of defensive game it forces them to play.

There are many successful styles of play in basketball today, with every coach believing that his is the best. Before any attempt can be made to construct an offensive pattern, the coach must have a detailed breakdown of work with individual, two-man, three-man, four-man, and five-man plays. Offenses are built on these plays and their precise execution.

Our offenses are predicated on "freedom of action" in the individual and two-man plays. This refers to the fact that we expect the man with the ball to test his defensive man. He must know if he can beat him. Whether the answer is positive or negative, he has carried out his assignment just by getting it. In case he is unable to beat him, then he will ask for help through a teammate. This cooperative effort is called a "two-man play." As the end result, we expect the percentage shot at the basket with the least amount of time and effort expended.

Finally, in the formation of our philosophy we believe in the single post, prefaced with two-man plays. In other words, we will make use of the pivot man primarily as a feeder, and only secondarily as a scorer. He will pass off to the open cutter as his first duty, but if all cutters are covered then he will operate against his defensive man and attempt to score by himself.

Coaches would be well advised not to attempt installing another colleague's offensive pattern. So many times we have attended coaching clinics and observed the young high school coach, hungry for quick results, endeavoring to put in a successful college coach's pattern. There are quite a number of young coaches who attempt this during the season and fail, unable to recognize that the college coach has hand-picked personnel which can execute the pattern perfectly and adjust to situations instantaneously. The high school coach does not have this personnel and consequently cannot achieve equal success with this pattern. Do not change offensive patterns every summer, but instead perfect the one best suited to your situation. Installing various phases may be justified and encouraged, but never a completely new pattern. There are too many chances for guesswork when doing this and basketball cannot be successful without attention to detail.

BASIC FOUNDATION. A sound basketball offense is built on a foundation of thorough instruction. The fundamentals you teach are the blocks of strength in this construction.

The coach will find his offensive teaching demanding a great deal of his time. He will also discover that it is not an easy task, since it requires the unhurried thought and understanding of all squad members.

Your method of instruction on a maneuver should show coherence before the squad. Whatever is to be taught the squad should be described by the coach in its entirety. His description of the play must be detailed and the urgency of these particulars upheld. In short, he must run through the entire procedure, or, as it is commonly referred to, the "whole method."

The next step is a demonstration of the maneuver by the coach or assistant. It will have a greater impact on the squad if the coach can do it. It will have this effect only if he carries out the maneuver exactly as he described it in the whole method. He should not omit or violate any of the steps in the instruction he has given to the squad.

The third aspect is the execution of the maneuver by the squad members. This is accomplished through close supervision by the head coach and his assistants. Errors and mistakes must be corrected, principally in the practice session. The immediacy with which this aspect is completed and corrected will determine the success of the player in learning the maneuver. Basketball is a game with great possibilities for mistakes, and the team making the least number normally will win. With this in mind, you can see for yourself that skill is developed through repetitious drilling to avoid errors.

ONE-VERSUS-ONE DRILL. With the tremendous flow of basketball talent from the various sections of the country, it is not infrequent that we are able to see some of the truly outstanding players perform.

More and more coaches are teaching a "free-lance offense," wherein the individual relies on his natural ability to free himself from the opponent. This is due to the modern offensive player's capacity to get open for the shot. There is no doubt that in forming an offense we must start with individuals. An offense's test is the coordination it receives from the five members and how they function using it.

The one-versus-one is the best individual drill in basketball (Diag. 7–1). The player, either offensively or defensively, can blame no one for his failures in this drill. It is much like the 440-yard dash man in track. He has no teammate to rely on for help; he must do it himself. This drill is the same way.

Our one-versus-one drill takes in the entire squad, which numbers 16. With this specific number we have an excellent breakdown for drills in that we can split the squad into four separate units of four players each. We use both ends of the playing floor for this drill. Careful attention is paid to each individual's placement.

We place one offensive man in a forward's position. The player will assume a spot at least up to the free-throw line and hugging the sideline. This is done so the offensive man will have more room in which to operate after receiving the ball. The second player is the defensive man, who is instructed to stop the offensive man. The offensive forward is instructed to use the seven individual offensive moves (Chapter 6) to free himself from the opponent. After completion of his turn, the offensive man becomes the defensive man. The player on defense returns to the side of the court to await his offensive rotation and the next offensive man comes onto the floor.

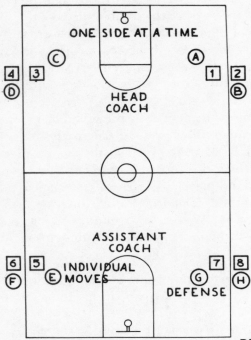

ONE SIDE AT A TIME

HEAD
COACH

ASSISTANT
COACH

INDIVIDUAL
MOVES

DEFENSE

Diagram 7—1. One-versus-one offensive
drill, using the entire squad.

Coaches should have only one group performing at a time and never both
units at the same time or there will be some collisions. As the season
progresses, and to avoid having individuals work against the same defensive
man through the year, we exchange partners. Another change we make
is for the defensive man to go across to the other side, play defense against
this group for two turns, and move to the opposite end where he plays defense for four turns. The number of baskets scored on the individual defensive player are tabulated and recorded on the bulletin board.

The coach should make all players participate. There should be no
separation of the players, such as of the centers from the remainder of the
squad. In this drill the guards will operate at a forward's position and this
will aid in the development of their driving game. You never know when
you might have to call on one of your guards to play this position in a game.
This practice will head off any possible lack of confidence should the situation become an actuality, and may thus avert further unnecessary changes.

The one-versus-one drill is also practiced from the guard position. The
offensive player's position must be clear, since the play will depend upon
whether he has enough room in which to maneuver. Assurance of this will
be realized if the offensive guard is set in fairly well toward the center of
the floor and in line with the 12-foot lane. As in the drill from the forward's
position, everyone takes his turn from this spot.

TWO-VERSUS-TWO DRILLS. As we mentioned earlier, two-man plays are an integral part of our offense. If the offenses are to function, the coordination of the two players involved must be exact.

Two-man plays involve a combination of players. The drills should include everyone. This prevents loss of team morale, since nothing is more discouraging to an individual than to have the coach say that he is incapable of performing a particular maneuver. The player must have a feeling of belonging to and must have confidence in the pattern if it is to be successful.

Our two-man plays are made with guard-to-guard, guard-and-forward, forward-and-center, and guard-and-center operations. The object of basketball is to attempt a shot and score. These plays give you the direction which coaches find necessary in the organization of their weakside games. (The weakside is that part of the floor where two offensive men align themselves in contrast to the strong side where the remaining three offensive men set up.)

What do two-man plays do for you? This question can best be answered by stating that they give the players exacting practice for improving their timing, learning other player habits, coordination, and execution. Once these plays are mastered they become a potent arsenal for a team to unleash upon the opposition. A great crowd-pleaser is a properly executed two-man play wherein the player suddenly bursts free off a screen for the lay-up. We might also add that it is one which brings endless joy to us personally and ranks as our favorite play in basketball.

GENERAL POINTS. Before we go into the actual teaching of two-man plays, it should be said that we have some pertinent ideas which are instilled ritually in our teams prior to their execution of these plays. These steps must be steadfastly followed to insure top performance.

1. Save your dribble.
2. Don't use numerical plays—let the position of the forwards determine the play:
    (a) If the forward is near the sideline, use an inside play.
    (b) If the forward is near the middle—use an outside play.
3. Anyone can try anything as long as it is not time-consuming and there is a chance for a rebound.
4. One of the best scoring plays is the pass and return pass.
5. Change of direction maneuver is one of the better methods of creating openings for the offensive player. This is designed for the player moving from right to left:
    (a) Player approach need not be made with blinding speed.
    (b) He should get to within 6 feet of the defensive man.
    (c) The player starts to the right, shifting his weight to the foot, and uses a good head-and-shoulder fake to fool his opponent.
    (d) He then pushes off quickly with the right foot.
    (e) The first two steps must be quick after the planting of the right foot.

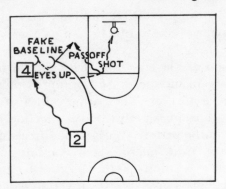

Diagram 7–2. Inside screen. Note
option and points to remember.

INSIDE SCREEN. Now we are ready to bring you the actual running of
the play and the teaching points in progression. Diagram 7–2 gives you a
visual interpretation of what we are doing.

1. Both the guard and forward are in their basic position and the guard has
   the ball.
2. The forward works for an opening and the guard should hit him on the
   "safe side" with the ball. This is the side away from the defensive man.
3. The forward makes himself an individual threat by immediately turning
   and facing the basket and his opponent. After passing the ball the guard
   makes a change of direction toward the middle and moves to set the screen.
   Don't be in a hurry.
4. The guard should give the forward time to get set and take advantage of a
   possible defensive change. The change of direction by the guard gives a
   better angle for the screen for such a situation.
5. The guard sets the screen for the forward 3 or 4 feet away from the defensive man. He should set the screen higher than the defensive man.
   When the guard is setting the screen the man with the ball cannot start
   until the guard has stopped. As soon as the guard is set, the forward fakes
   toward the baseline to get the defensive man in motion toward the baseline, thus giving the guard a chance to set the proper screen.
6. The forward should use a crossover step and come as close as possible to
   the screener. As he goes off his shoulder, he must get as much distance in
   the first two steps as possible.
7. While dribbling, the forward should keep his eyes up for:
   (a) A return pass if the defense is shifting.
   (b) A set or jump shot if the defense is sagging.
   (c) An opportunity to go all the way if no one picks him up after the
       screen.
8. As soon as the forward has gone by, the guard is to cut away for a possible
   return bounce pass or for the rebound.

Competition is added to this maneuver by placing two defensive men
on the court with instructions to try to stop the offensive players. The offensive men should use the inside screen with its options. Do not let them
use any other play. You should be careful not to rush into this competition

unless the coach feels the entire group is ready. An old adage, "Haste makes waste," would apply in this situation. The coach can kill offensive incentive should the play not work and cause loss of confidence on the players' part by placing defensive men in this drill too soon.

The inside screen builds fundamental basketball, and, when coupled with poise and confidence, it is difficult to defense. It has a definite place in your play pattern and many coaches have run entire games applying only this simple maneuver.

OUTSIDE SCREEN. The outside screen has been a powerful influence for the offense. Back screening has caused considerable discussion among coaches as to its merits. Some feel it has no place in basketball while others mention it as a most productive offensive point getter. We do not wish to enter into a debate concerning the value of the play but merely to point out its major teaching points.

    1. Its effectiveness is dependent upon the initiative of the forward, and he will determine the play.

    2. The basic positions will find the forward approaching the short 17 (Diag. 7–3) before any pass is made.

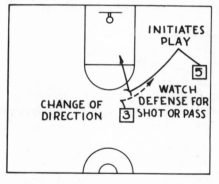

Diagram 7–3. Outside screen as the forward starts the play.

    3. The forward sneaks up on the guard's defensive man while the offensive guard is setting up his opponent with a fake.

    4. At the point of the screen which is outside, the guard changes direction to the inside and steps off the screen with his head up.

    5. After the offensive guard has gone by, the forward cuts away for the return pass or the rebound.

    6. The guard dribbles with his eyes up for one of these options:

      (a) Go all the way with the ball if there is no shift.

      (b) Stop for the jump shot on a sagging defense.

      (c) Make a return pass via the bounce to the screener if there is a shifting defense.

This play is used by teams who favor the screening game. It enables them to drive their best guard and jump shooter off the screen for the medium shot or produce a switch which places the small guard on a big forward who cuts away to the basket. Both are devastating moves which present problems for the defensive men.

GIVE-AND-GO (OUR VERSION). The Michigan State offense has been extremely successful in using this maneuver (Diag. 7–4) and its effectiveness is caused by making the inside screen good. It has a long history of suc-

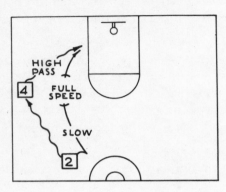

Diagram 7–4. Give-and-go two-man play. Note angle to basket.

cesses which dates back to Bradley University, where Coach Anderson originated this maneuver.

Teaching points for our version of the give-and-go include:

1. Positions for the offensive guard and forward are basic.
2. The guard should pass the ball to the "safe side" of the forward.
3. The guard uses only a short "stutter" step as a change of direction. As the screener approaches, the guard's speed is slow—at the time he is going to screen, while the forward changes direction toward the baseline. The guard immediately pushes off with the outside foot and really takes off to the basket. He looks over his shoulder for a return pass—if he doesn't get the pass he at least has an inside position for the rebound.
4. As the guard takes off to the basket, the forward should keep the ball high for a quick return pass. If the defense drops back, the forward can shoot a set or jump shot or use any other individual move he wishes.
5. Should the defense drop back in, the offensive men can take an occasional set shot to keep the defense up on them and "honest."

The team playing a strong switching defensive game is ideal for this two-man play. They are defenseless and caught completely off guard. Another type of pass which is effective in this play is the sidearm bounce pass with over-english applied to the ball. The pass is easy to handle and the offensive guard should look for the ball on the floor.

Bob Carney of Bradley University and Lance Olson of Michigan State have been two of the better players who have administered this maneuver with finesse. Both were sure-handed, deceptive, and excellent drivers who possessed poise around the offensive basket. These are essential characteristics for player personnel in this stratagem.

DROP-PASS SERIES. This two-man series is a trademark of Michigan State basketball teams. It encompasses three different drop-pass situations, namely the drop pass, the fake drop pass, and the set shot off the drop pass (Diag. 7–5). It is a complex pass maneuver which, when perfected, means greater point productivity from the personnel. This maneuver is dependent upon timing more than any other in basketball. If the timing of either guard or forward is not perfect, the execution of this play suffers. The way to faultlessness in this play is by reiteration of the basic teaching points and the carrying out of these details.

Drop Pass

1. The forward is recognized as the key man and both offensive players will start in their basic positions.
2. The offensive forward leans his shoulder in and takes off across to the free-throw line. The guard gives the forward a lead pass while the forward is running. There is no faking, as it is a straight forward play.

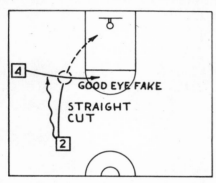

Diagram 7–5a. Drop-pass play in a man-to-man defense.

3. The guard runs right toward the spot where the forward caught the ball. Do not let him veer out on this cut.
4. The forward drops the ball immediately off his outside foot with a slight snap. *The bounce should be straight up and down.* After dropping the ball, he should look across court, fake a dribble, and continue on to the free-throw line.
5. The guard should pick up the ball on the dead run and be so close to the forward that he would be able to screen off the defensive man. The forward looks for a return pass or goes for the rebound.

Fake Drop Pass

1. This play is set in motion when the defense shifts onto the guard.
2. The basic positions are taken again by the offensive guard and forward.
3. The forward leans his shoulder in and takes off across to the free-throw line. The guard gives the forward a lead pass while the forward is running. There is no faking, as it is a straight forward play.
4. The guard runs right toward where the forward is when he catches the ball. Do not let him veer out as this enables the defensive man freedom to pick him up.

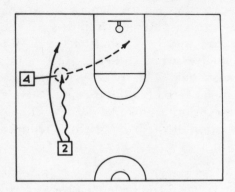

Diagram 7–5b. Drop-pass play when a switch is made by the defense. (4) fakes drop pass and drives hard for the basket.

5. The forward yells "shift" and then places the ball well out in front of him as he goes for the shot. Having passed the ball, the guard delays until after seeing the forward take off for the basket.
6. This is very effective as a surprise move, especially on the opponent who continuously "plays the play."

Set Shot off the Drop Pass

1. This play is applied to the offense when the defense sags.
2. The forward leans his shoulder in and takes off across the free-throw line. The guard gives the forward a lead pass while the forward is running. There is no faking as it is a straight forward play.

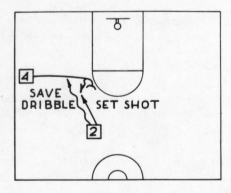

Diagram 7–5c. Drop-pass play when the defensive men sag back.

3. The guard goes right at where the forward is when he catches the ball. Remember not to let the guard veer out.
4. The guard gets a return pass from the forward. The forward then sets a screen for the guard, who should take advantage of it.
5. The guard, when he receives the ball, stops and saves his dribble because of the possibility of an individual move or the cut-away pass to the forward.

PIVOT MAN. The backbone of all teams is the pivot man. Single post teams depend upon this player more than any other. His most important prerequisite is knowing how to cope instantly with the changing situations in the pivot area.

In high schools, a 6' 2" pivot man is not uncommon. This is perhaps the average size of most high school pivot men. Meanwhile, college coaches accentuate height, and many centers are in the 6' 8" to 7' 0" category. The difference between these two examples is evident. It does not mean, however, that the 6' 2" center cannot be as effective as the 6' 8" player on his own level.

With the observance of some simple rules by the pivot man he can develop into a well-rounded center. For example:

POSITION

1. Keep moving, moving all the time. The easiest man to guard is the one who stands.
2. Don't waste time trying to get open.
3. Don't fight the defense. Step back.
   - (a) Confine your movements to a small square.
   - (b) Relax until you have a chance to get the ball—bob and duck to keep the defense "honest."
   - (c) If you still can't get open, go to the baseline and operate from there.

HOW TO MOVE

1. Go to meet the ball from the passer every time.
2. Come to a jump stop, since you can use either foot as your pivot foot.
3. The feet should be spread wide, elbows up, hands ready to receive the ball.
4. The center should signal with his hands as to where he wants the ball passed.
5. The pivot man should be much like a swivel chair—able to move his feet and body but not his hands and elbows.
6. Once the player establishes a position, he should keep it by using his hips.

CENTER SCREEN FOR FORWARD. Now that we have added the third man to our offensive plays, let's put him to work immediately. The center can be of great assistance to a team which has an outstanding jump shooter at a forward's position. Since our pivot man operates out of a single post, it is relatively easy for him to take two steps out from the free-throw line and establish a stationary screen (Diag. 7–6a). The cut-away possibility by the center is also shown.

The rules which govern the two-man plays are in effect on this move by these two players. A majority of the time the forward will come off the screen for the jump shot at the free-throw line. If a switch is necessitated by the defense, then the center will be open by rolling to the basket.

Timing is of major consequence in this play and it is up to the forward to wait with the ball until the center sets his screen. If he moves before the

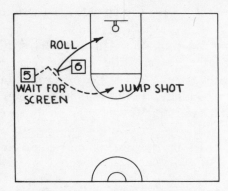

Diagram 7–6a. Center screen for forward. Two-man play with forward and center.

screen is made, it gives the defensive man time to adjust his path of defense to compensate for the screen.

A second type of center screen (see Diag. 7–6b) for the forward can be achieved when the pivot man sets a screen midway down the free-throw lane. The forward utilizes the pivot man to get a close-in shot. The screen can be

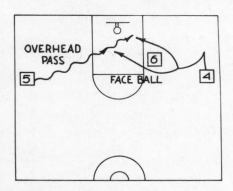

Diagram 7–6b. Back center screen, showing how the center (6) can also be used to screen away from the ball. (5) passes to (4) coming off the back screen.

made with the pivot man facing the cutting forward, or establishing a position with his back to the forward and letting the forward attempt to maneuver his defensive man into the center, thus getting him open for the short shot. As the forward comes off the screen, he should have the ball.

CENTER SCREEN FOR THE GUARD. The execution of this play (Diag. 7–7) is exactly the same for the pivot man as in the forward screen. The center comes out to the free-throw line and sets the screen much like the outside screen. The guard must hold on to the ball and not dribble until the center is situated. Then he must come off the screen looking for the drive all the way, the jump shot, or the possible return pass to the center. These options will be governed by what the defense does.

THREE-VERSUS-THREE

RULES TO PIVOT PLAY. As we progress in bringing the squad closer to the five-man operation, it is necessary to set up a criterion for pivot play. In

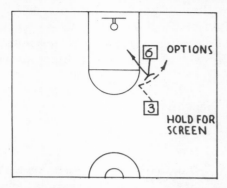

Diagram 7–7. Center screen for guard. The center (6) can screen for (3) effectively.

our offensive thinking we have established two rules for all squad members to observe in passing to the pivot man. The most important rule is: the man who passes the ball in to the pivot man is *always the first cutter*. The second rule is that in this three-man play, the accent is on timing and not speed.

ONE-TWO CUT. This three-man play is not new; and yet, when executed properly, it is nearly undefensible. It fits our offensive thinking and fills our demand for floor balance, sharp ball-handling, footwork finesse, hard

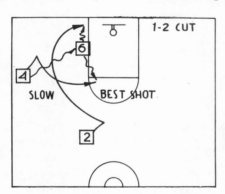

Diagram 7–8. The 1-2 cut. The timing and changes of direction by (2) and (4) make this play work.

cutting, and excellent rebounding position. Diagram 7–8 illustrates this play, which is explained as follows:

1. When the ball goes in to the pivot man, the guard changes direction to the middle and the forward changes direction to the baseline.
2. Whoever passes the ball in to the pivot man comes around *slowly* and away from the center—then the other man comes across. The cross is made from the center. The object is to cause the defensive men to run into each other.
3. The pivot man will pass to whichever cutter is open. The forward, when he receives the ball, will usually have to stop at the free-throw line for the jump shot.
4. The guard will continue in for the rebound and the forward, after shooting, is the long rebounder stopping at the free-throw line.

OTHER OPTIONS. Off the basic triangle of a guard, a forward, and the pivot man, four options can be exercised to neutralize the defense (Diags. 7–9a, 7–9b, 7–9c, and 7–9d). On this variation, the guard dribbling toward the forward passes to the center *before* he changes position with the forward.

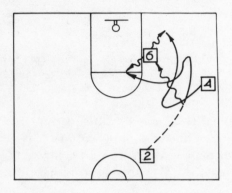

Diagram 7–9a. On this variation of the 1-2 cut, the guard dribbling toward the forward passes to the center, *before* he changes position with that forward. Then they make the 1-2 cut *after* the pass.

Then they make the 1-2 cut *after* the pass to the pivot man, who will feed the open cutter.

The second option also begins with the guard dribbling toward the forward and passing to the pivot man off the dribble. This time, as the pass goes to the center, the cutter keeps going straight toward the basket. The

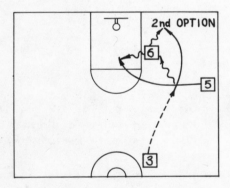

Diagram 7–9b. On this option of the 1-2 cut, as the pass goes to center, the cutter keeps going straight to the basket with the forward (5) coming off (3) cut.

forward makes a change of direction to the baseline and comes off the guard. The center will feed the open man.

Option three finds the guard and forward changing their positions. The guard originates the play by passing to the forward and moving to the forward's position. The forward returns the ball to the guard and moves beyond the top of the free-throw circle. The guard takes a dribble or two, then a pass is made to the pivot man and the change of direction is made by both players. The center, again, feeds the open man after the 1-2 cut.

The last option starts with the guard passing to the forward and making the change of positions. The forward will dribble out beyond the top of the free-throw circle, turn, and pass to the pivot man. Both players make

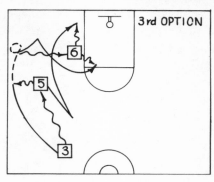

Diagram 7–9c. Another variation of the 1-2 cut. Guard and forward change places by a pass return pass. Then the pass to center and the 1-2 cut is made.

the change of direction and cut, with the pivot man, again, feeding to the free man.

A three-man, full-court game is used by Coach Albeck as a conditioner. The game is played to five baskets, and the first threesome scoring that num-

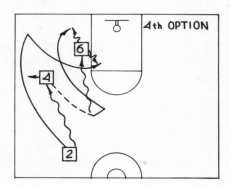

Diagram 7–9d. On this variation of the 1-2 cut, the forward keeps the ball and takes the guard position. Then he passes to the center and makes the 1-2 cut.

ber sits down. The losers stay on the floor against a new unit and the game is continued in this manner. It is a demanding drill game.

FOUR-VERSUS-FOUR

This drill (Diag. 7–10) is practiced 30 per cent of the time at Michigan State. The weak-side play is acknowledged by the authors to be every bit as important as the strong-side.

Recalling that we are interested in getting a shot off with a minimum amount of time lost and with ease, this drill fulfills that requirement. It incorporates the use of our two-man plays; perfects timing; and teaches rebounding position, ball-handling, and player-decoy movement.

Both ends of the court can be used in this drill, since four men are specified as offense and four as defense. The four offensive players work together as a unit. Their positions are the standardized ones that they comply with on the two-man plays. Two guards and two forwards are used on the offense.

They run the inside, outside, drop pass, and give-and-go patterns against the defense. On the weak side, the two players are always changing directions. The guard always moves inside of the forward for a quick pass or to continue in for the rebound. The forward comes out to the guard position and keeps his defensive man out of the play—he is the safety man on defense if the ball is intercepted.

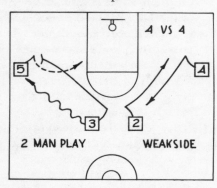

Diagram 7—10. Four-versus-four. Two-man plays stressed and all four men moving. Defense is added later.

Should one unit be unable to work anything, they pass across to the other two players, who then work to execute a successful play. When a shot is attempted, a rebound triangle should be formed with a man back to act as a safety man.

A competitive defense can be added and games played up to ten baskets, with the winners challenging the other winners at the opposite end of the court. Never let your players stop moving in this drill. They should be moving, since they all have a part to perform even when they don't have the ball.

FIVE-VERSUS-FIVE

We are now to the point where we can add the fifth man to complete our offensive planning. We have covered one-versus-one, two-versus-two, three-versus-three, four-versus-four, and now we move to the basic continuity involving both guards and forwards plus the pivot man. This bringing in of the fifth man demands an explanation of the purpose of a basic continuity. This continuity takes place when the players cannot get the ball in to the pivot man or when the center cannot hit any of the cutters with a pass. The forwards and guards exchange positions (Diag. 7–11), with the forwards becoming guards, the guards becoming forwards, and the play continuing from this point.

In our basic continuity we pay special attention to the speed with which the five-man play is operated. You will find the players in a hurry to run the pattern the coach has given them. The tempo at which they maneuver will determine their ability to take advantage of certain openings. Should

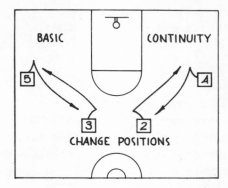

Diagram 7–11. The basic continuity, in which an exchange of positions takes place. (2) and (3) always move inside of the forwards. The center is not shown but his position is low and beside the free throw lane.

the players run the pattern more quickly than is necessary, the opening may not be present and confusion will result. The coach should take special care to see that everybody understands the complete five-man continuity and must remind the players of their duties orally when the action begins. He should attempt to synchronize the various parts into a working machine and mold the individuals into a poised and confident team.

This team must be tested in some manner with opposition, and an opportunity arises when you place five defensive players on the floor and scrimmage half-court. In this early stage you should advise the squad members not to play ironclad defense. This prevents any loss of confidence on the part of team members, and this is always a worry of the coach in presenting a new system of play.

In the half-court scrimmage, the coach should insist that the continuity be run to both sides with equal distribution. Players seem to have a tendency to run most of their plays to the right side and thereby disclose laxity in not being cognizant that there is another side in which they might maneuver.

Demand attention to every detail in all phases in the half-court scrimmage. Do not let the players amble wherever they want. Insist that they perform their assignments. The entire five-man operation should have been outlined for them, and questions should be few if the coach has done his job in preparing the players.

TOUGHEN DEFENSE. After running one week of the basic continuity, you can tighten the defensive rein and see how the team reacts to different types of defense. They will encounter an awkwardness similar to their first indoctrination when a switching defense challenges them. This is natural, and after several practices they will be able to solve this defense in a conventional way.

As the defense stiffens, the coach must firmly repeat his convictions on the offense and sell it to the players. Many of our coaches are fine demonstrators, and when a player continually faults the coach might have good reason to replace him in the line-up. The player is instructed to watch the coach and imitate his moves as he shows the players how the play can be worked. Young coaches should be careful in this respect, however, as they will not want to overdo the demonstrating. This kills player initiative and takes valuable practice time away from the player. Remember, *you* do not play in the games.

OFFENSE SHOULD HAVE OPTIONS.   When a defense encounters an offense and stops it, more than likely the offensive team was thwarted in its use of its basic continuity. Coaches everywhere attempt this strategy in the hope of upsetting the offensive timing and coordination of a team. For this reason the coach must have options off his basic continuity which will counterbalance any defensive maneuvering by the opposition.

The adjustments involve making minor changes in cutting lanes for the players, setting up new passing lanes for the pivot man, learning where to anticipate the ball offensive, and learning different rebound triangles. This may sound like a major overhauling but the variations are actually slight once the basic continuity is mastered.

MAN THROUGH.   This variation adds considerable motion to the pattern, as all five men will be picking, cutting, and moving in continuous movement. Its strength lies in the motion and continuity. It is most effective against a switching team and you can count on an excellent percentage shot nearly every time you run it.

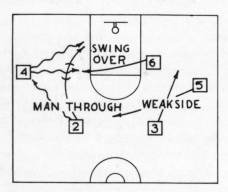

Diagram 7–12a. The man-through offense. (2) passes to (4) and goes through to basket looking for a return pass. (6) is weak-side and (3) and (5) execute a weak-side change. This is the first phase.

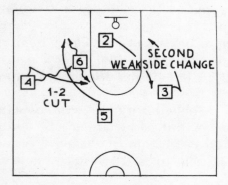

Diagram 7–12b. Second phase of the man-through. (6) swings to ball-side and receives ball from (4), who makes 1-2 cut with (5) who has come from weak-side forward slot. (3) makes double weak-side change and goes to board while (2) returns to guard position.

The play (Diags. 7–12a and 7–12b) starts with the guard (2) passing to the left forward (4) and going through to the basket. The forward (4) feeds the pivot man (6), makes a change of direction and cuts over the top to the free throw line. The right guard (3) moves down and sets a temporary screen for forward (5) who comes all the way around as the second cutter while the guard moves to the board. The pivot man (6) feeds either open cutter while the guard (2) returns as the safety man.

The shot will usually be taken by the forward (5) and in the form of a short jumper. This is an excellent play which favors the jump shooter and is a fine way to free him for the percentage shot.

VARIATIONS OF THE BASIC CONTINUITY

FORWARD SNEAK. The defensive forward is overplaying the forward (Diag. 7–13) and when this occurs, the guard will pass to the center. The forward, aware that the defensive man is anticipating his 1-2 cut, will make

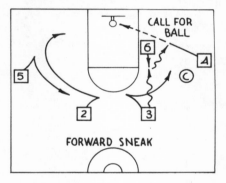

Diagram 7–13. The forward sneak variation of the 1-2 cut which finds (C) over-playing (4), and as (3) hits (6) with pass, (4) makes direct cut to basket. (2) and (5) exchange. (3) changes direction and comes off (6) looking for return pass.

a direct cut to the basket. If he is free, he shouts for the ball to alert the pivot man of his opening. The guard, seeing this, changes directions toward the middle, comes around like a 1-2 cut, and then becomes the long rebounder at the free-throw line. The weak-side men will change positions.

GUARD SNEAK. In this play (Diag. 7–14), as in the forward sneak, the defensive man is overplaying the offensive man. In this instance, it is the guard. The ball is passed to the center by the forward. The guard, seeing that his opponent expects him to cut the same way, changes his direction and goes down the middle instead of coming around on the 1-2 cut. The forward comes around on a 1-2 cut and is the long rebounder. The feed from the pivot man should be via a bounce pass. The weak-side men continue to change.

WEAK-SIDE GUARD SNEAK. This play begins on the strong side with the center having the ball (Diag. 7–15). The 1-2 cut is being executed by the guard and the forward. At the same time the weak-side men are changing. As the defensive men on the weak side relax on the change, the center

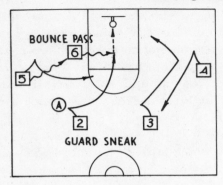

Diagram 7—14. The guard sneak, a variation of the 1-2 cut. (A) is overplaying (2) and as (6) receives ball from (5) he changes direction and goes down-lane looking for bounce pass from the center. (3) and (4) exchange positions.

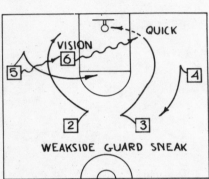

Diagram 7—15. Weak-side guard sneak makes defense play honest. (5) passes in to (6) and makes 1-2 cut with (2). The center (6) notices a defensive lapse by the weak-side defensive man and snaps quick pass to (3) breaking to basket. (4) moves out to act as safety man.

notes this by split vision and passes to the weak-side guard breaking to the basket.

The guard can sneak when either the center or the strong-side forward cutter have the ball. The guard, when making the change, should go slow until he sees that he has an opening. Then he can put on speed.

WEAK-SIDE FORWARD SHOT. Openings on the weak side are not always realized by the pivot man. One of the better shots in basketball is the jump shot, and this weak-side forward shot (Diag. 7–16) can be used to advantage in this pattern.

The ball is passed into the center and a 1-2 cut is made by the strong side. The center feeds the weak side forward after the weak-side change. The

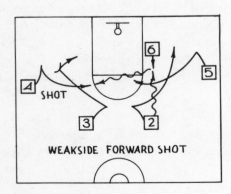

Diagram 7—16. Weak-side forward shot off 1-2 cut. (2) passes in to (6) and makes cut with (5). The center sees (4) coming off the free-throw area on weak-side change after a screen by (3) and hits him for medium jump shot. (5) should go on to basket to make play effective.

forward repeatedly will be able to receive the ball between the free-throw line and the top of the free-throw circle from the center. He will have a good shot, as his defensive man frequently will not follow him this far but will sag off him.

PASSING LANES OF THE CENTERS. *All* centers in our style of play must know what to do with the ball upon reception. Once a center receives it, he must be alert for cutters. If none are open he positions for a shot opportunity. Should this be unavailable, he will return the ball to the outside.

To help our pivot men pick up their teammates cutting to the basket, we tell the players to use their voices. This informs the pivot man, who is open, and he will then look for his teammate.

Another contribution we make to the pivot man's repertoire is getting him to use the four corners of the court as a guide post when he is making a pass to a cutter (Diag. 7–17). The center should pass the ball to a forward

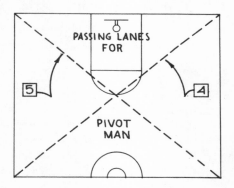

Diagram 7–17. Passing lanes of the center. Illustration of four corners of the floor which pivot man should use as a guide in passing to cutters. Note (4) and (5) cutting.

who is making a direct cut to the basket, using a bounce pass. He will aim the ball at the corner of the floor from which the cutter is breaking. This guarantees the forward an easy pass to handle and enough time to maneuver for a shot if something unexpected arises.

HALF-SHELL OFFENSE. This offense has been used by Michigan State teams for the past eight years as a surprise weapon. It combines everything that we as coaches are looking for, except for the pivot man. It is every coach's dream to have an excellent big man for the pivot position, but what does he do when he cannot find one? When this situation arose with the Spartans, Coach Anderson incorporated the half-shell offense.

It was his impression that they should keep their basic continuity as close to the original as possible and still maintain their strong two-man play game, their weak-side change, and their rebound position. With this in mind he devised a pattern without a big pivot man.

The alignment of personnel (Diag. 7–18) is such that it spreads the defense out and gives you an equalizer against a team which has a big man. This is an advantage for you, as is the fact that every man can play the pivot in this style of play. The alternating pivot normally will give the opposi-

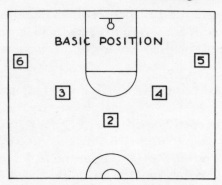

Diagram 7–18. Half-shell offense and basic alignment of players. Notice there is no pivot man.

tion problems and cause them foul trouble. Besides, it is perfectly suited for a hard-driving and hard-cutting team.

The next play, the inside screen off the two-man play as related to the half-shell offense, is illustrated and described in Diagram 7–19. Note the close relationship of the positions and duties of the remaining players to our original basic continuity.

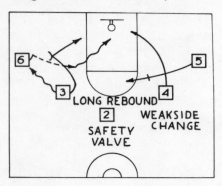

Diagram 7–19. Variation off half-shell offense. (3) passes to (6) and makes inside screen to free him. (2) is safety man while (4) and (5) exchange positions. (6) can pass to (4) as additional option if he does not have the jump shot.

The weak-side forward cut in the half-shell offense can be seen in Diagram 7–20. The guard initiates the play by passing to the forward and then clearing out down the middle. The forward hits the corner man, who will look for the center coming from the weak side off the guard's back. The corner man looks to feed the center for the short shot.

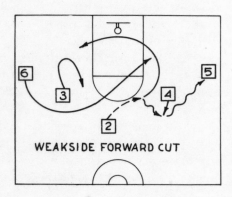

Diagram 7–20. Weak-side forward cut in half-shell offense. (2) dribbles toward (4), passes to him, and clears out down the middle. (4) promptly passes to (5) who looks for (6) making solo cut behind (3) to ball-side.

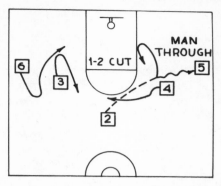

Diagram 7–21. (2) dribbles toward (4) and they exchange positions. (2) then passes to (5) and rolls into post looking for return pass from (5) and a 1-2 cut situation. (3) and (6) make double exchange with (6) going to the board.

Another variation which can be developed is shown in Diagram 7–21. Here the guard dribbles toward the forward and they exchange positions. He then passes to the corner man and cuts to the basket, looking for a return pass on the give-and-go. If he is not open, he buttonhooks to become the pivot man and it becomes a 1-2 cut setup. The weak-side men make a change, with the best rebounder going to the board.

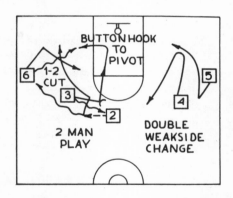

Diagram 7–22. Three-man half-shell offense play. (3) passes to (2) and moves down into pivot position. (2) then hits (6), who passes to (3), and (2) and (6) execute 1-2 cut. (4) and (5) make double weak-side exchange.

From this groundwork, our three-man plays can become even more effective. In Diagram 7–22 the guard passes to the other guard and sets the screen rolling off down the middle of the court. The man with the ball passes to the corner man, who immediately hits the guard who has rolled and becomes the pivot man. A 1-2 cut is then made by the corner man and the guard after a change of direction. The post man will pass to the open cutter, or look for a weak-side sneak off the double exchange, or take his own shot, in this order. The rebound triangle is definite and your safety man is clearly discernible.

The "man through" pattern is evident in Diagram 7–23. The guard passes to the forward and moves to the basket area on the give-and-go. He should be prepared to receive a return pass. As the guard goes through, the opposite corner man breaks across the free-throw lane and sets up as the pivot man receiving the ball. The 1-2 cut is made after the changes of direction. There is no weak-side change, as the other guard must remain back for defensive purposes.

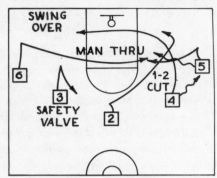

Diagram 7–23. Man-through pattern in half-shell offense. (4) passes to (5) and goes through looking for return pass. (6) moves to free himself and swings over to the ball, where a 1-2 cut is made by (5) and (2). (3) is safety valve.

Still another play (Diag. 7–24) is keyed by the guard, who dribbles right and passes to the right corner man. The corner man then passes without delay to (4) who had moved into the pivot and they make their changes of direction prior to the 1-2 cut. Meanwhile, the weak-side men make a double change but have vision on the ball.

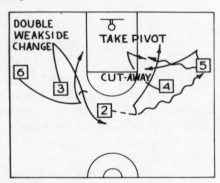

Diagram 7–24. Variation of half-shell offense. (2) dribbles right and passes to (5) who passes to (4) who has moved into pivot position, and (5) and (2) make 1-2 cut. (3) and (6) make double weak-side exchanges, with (3) providing a possible screen for (6).

The "back-door" play (Diag. 7–25) is our final pattern in the half-shell offense. It is used when the defense is playing the outcourt men extremely tight. From the open court, it is easier to employ than when you have a pivot man set in that position.

With the guard (3) bringing the ball into play, the right corner man (5) breaks into the free-throw area and receives the ball from the guard (3).

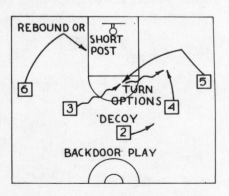

Diagram 7–25. Backdoor play. (3) starts play as (5) breaks toward basket and then to free-throw line to get pass from (3). (5) makes pass to (4) making direct cut or possible turn options. (6) rebounds and (2) acts as a decoy.

The other forward (4) makes a straight cut to the basket, receives a bounce pass from the right corner man (5), and goes for the lay-up. The guard (2) acts as a decoy, with the left corner man (6) moving for rebound position or the short post. The right corner man (5) can pass off, jump shoot, or drive his opponent if the back-door play does not materialize.

SIX SCORING PLAYS

All coaches have plays which they have devised and been successful in using over the years. Their identity is distinctive and different, as they are reserved for special circumstances. Normally, all have but one objective and that is to get the offensive man a better shot than he has been getting in the normal course of a game.

The situation might be in the closing seconds of a game when a basket is needed, or it might involve the use of a special play by the offense after a time-out. There are other circumstances which warrant the use of these plays, and we also have some favorites. It is our hope that they might give other coaches the same satisfaction they have given us during our coaching tenure.

STRONG SIDE SCREEN BY FORWARD. This play is operative as a special scoring play or as a continuity. If the coach has a good jump shooter from the free-throw area, this play brings about an ideal situation for him. Diagram 7–26 shows the coach how to get this player open through the use of a screen. Should the defense make any unexpected move to counter this play, the options listed can be applied.

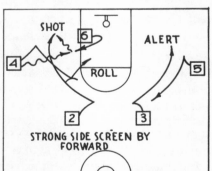

Diagram 7–26. Strong-side screen by forward. (4) passes to (6) and instead of making initial cut he screens for (2), and (6) shovels pass to (2) for jump shot. (3) and (5) are alert when making weak-side change.

The left guard (2) throws the pass to the left forward (4). The forward (4) tries to hit the center (6) who has made a change of direction to gain position for the pass. After the ball is passed by the left forward (4), he makes a change of direction and back screens the left guard's (2) defensive man. At the same instant that the forward (4) makes his change of direction, the guard (2) does likewise in order to set his defensive man up for the forthcoming screen. The left guard (2) comes off the screen looking for the quick pass from the center (6) and studying the reaction of the defense to decide on the jump shot or the drive.

In case the defense switches, the left forward (4) rolls to the foul line for a pass from the center (6) while the weak-side players (3) and (5) change position, always alert for a possible pass from the center (6).

STRONG SIDE SCREEN BY GUARD. Here again we have nearly the same play, except that the left guard (2) brings the ball upcourt and makes a straight feed to the center (6), who has freed himself with a change of direction (Diag. 7–27). The left guard (2) makes a change of direction to the middle to gain a better screening angle on the left forward's (4) defensive

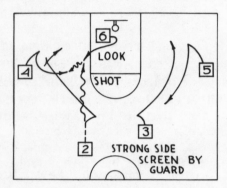

Diagram 7–27. Strong-side screen by guard to help free a good jump shooting forward.

man. The forward (4) makes his change of direction to the baseline at the same time as the guard (2) to insure setting up his defensive man for the screen. The guard (2) does not hurry down and rush into the screen but moves at operating speed.

The center (6) will pass to the forward (4), as the first and best option, for the jump shot or drive. If the switch occurs, the forward (4) looks for the cut-away man—the guard (2)—who does not release his screen until he has the defensive man on his back. The pivot man (6) will look weak-side for a sneak by the guard (3) as another alternative or, if both defensive men jump the forward (4), he can bounce pass to the guard (2) off the roll.

DOUBLE SCREEN. When in trouble, many coaches like to utilize a double screen for their best shooter. There are many versions of this type of screen. We are not debating which is the best but merely pointing out what has been incorporated into our pattern of play with slight variations in order to keep the offense simple and related for easier comprehension by the players.

Diagram 7–28 can be used to nail down the lay-up shot or present the coach with a clear-out for a one-versus-one situation. Either move will be dependent upon your alignment of personnel and the completeness with which they carry out their responsibilities.

The right guard (3) will pass to the right forward (5), make a change of

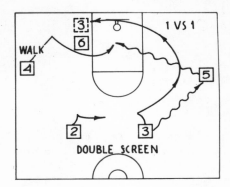

Diagram 7–28. Double screen.

direction, and go through on the give-and-go, looking for a possible pass as the best option. The guard (3), if unable to receive the ball, will continue on across the free-throw lane and join the center (6). The center's position is low where he and the guard (3) set a double screen just outside of the lane. The center will face the ball, the guard won't. The left forward (4) must decoy and walk his defensive man toward the baseline. As soon as the defensive man turns his head to look for the ball, the forward (4) comes off the screen. The right forward (5) has a one-versus-one situation during this time or will look to hit his teammate (4) with the pass for the lay-up.

The play has other options, such as the center·(6) and the right guard (3)—after the cut by the forward (4)—working together, but these are not diagrammed. The opposite guard (2) merely adjusts and acts as safety man.

BUTTONHOOK. If a team has the big guard to send through who can play the pivot, this is a fine opportunity to profit from his talents. The player need not be big if he can handle the pivot and has some familiarity in coping with it. This can be considered a type of clear-out series, and yet it has a basic relationship to our over-all pattern. Jack Quiggle, of the 1957–58 MSU Spartans, engineered this move with cleverness and gave them an added offensive weapon to throw at their opposition.

A smaller man, or guard, who has had experience in pivot play is a valuable cog to a team. By taking the post he has an advantage over his opponent immediately. Few guards or small men are adept at defending in the post. They usually will let the offensive man receive the ball (which is their first mistake), foul him (which is their second), and, finally, show signs of psychological pressures at their inability to stop the offensive man.

The buttonhook play (Diag. 7–29) is started in the same style, as, again, our left guard (2) passes to our left forward (4). The guard (2) observes the same rules and makes a change of direction, and watches for the return pass on the give-and-go as he moves to the basket.

The center (6) is low in his original position but moves to high post when the first pass is made to clear the area. The right guard (3) and the right forward (5) make the weak-side change.

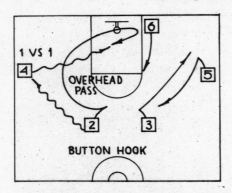

Diagram 7–29. Buttonhook play with the guard (2) moving into the pivot position.

As the play unfolds, the guard (2) sees that his defensive man is trailing him, suddenly reverses, and comes back with a buttonhook move, the same as a football player in that his hands and arms should be extended in anticipation of receiving the ball. The left forward (4) should be an individual threat while this is going on and if he does not have any move or shot, the ball should be immediately put over the head. This is done to expedite an overhead pass to the guard (4) on the buttonhook.

After completion of the pass, the forward (4) is instructed to stand until he sees the guard (2) shooting or driving for the basket. He then goes to the board for a possible rebound.

CENTER SCREEN. Whether you have a big pivot man or a small one, this play (Diag. 7–30) will score many points for your club. It is our choice when we have a fine jump shooter who can team up with a player and make the two-man play work. Should this fail, the man-through continuity is followed.

The play commences when the right guard (3) passes to the right forward (5) and goes through looking to rub his defensive man off on the center (6) who is set high at the free throw-line. After the guard (3) fakes receiving the ball, he continues back to his original position. The right forward (4)

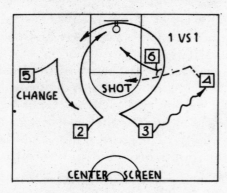

Diagram 7–30. Center screen play off man through series designed for the jump shooting forward.

immediately tries to defeat his man individually. If he is unable to do this, he uses the cross-over dribble and drives forward to the free-throw line. At the same time as (4) starts to dribble, the center (6) establishes a screen, attempting to pick off the forward's (4) defensive man. The secret to success will depend upon the forward (4) and his use of the dribble. He must maneuver his defensive man into the screen and the cross-over dribble will set this up.

As the forward (4) comes off the screen, he should have his head up looking for the shot if his defensive man is caught in the screen. If the defense elects to switch, it is easy to hit the center (6) rolling to the basket as you have the entire side of the floor in which to operate. In the event the defense sags, the jump shot is easily taken under these conditions.

The weak side is changing, with the left guard (2) going to the board while the left forward (5) comes away from the basket toward the top of the key to avoid interfering with the play.

GUARD-TO-GUARD. This play is shown in Diagram 7–31 and is keyed by the guard who is in possession of the ball. In this case the left guard (2) passes to his fellow guard (3). When the action begins, the center (6) remains in his position midway down the 12-foot lane.

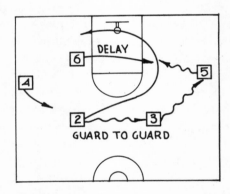

DELAY

GUARD TO GUARD

Diagram 7–31. Guard-to-guard play.

The left guard (2) moves toward the right guard (3) as if to set a screen. As this move is completed, the guard (3) will pass to the right forward (5) who in turn looks for the left guard (2) rolling down toward the baseline anticipating a pass from the right forward (5).

It is important that the center (6) remain away from the play until the guard has had a chance to handle the ball or does not receive it. In this event he (6) should move over quickly to gain position. A 1-2 cut can then be made by the guard (3) and forward. The left forward (4) merely adjusts to the safety position.

Timing is of prime essence and if the ball is late to the cutter, the play's effectiveness is greatly reduced. The guard should learn to "bear in" at the proper angle to gain an advantage on the defense. It is the type of play that will give a switching team considerable trouble. It can be worked to either side and fits a left-handed guard very adequately.

ATTACKING THE ZONE DEFENSE

As this is by far the most popular defense used in our high schools, coaches would be careless if they did not develop a solid attack against this defense. Few coaches in the game are without a basic philosophy against the zone. Those who do not adopt one usually do not last long.

It is a coach's duty to prepare his team for all zone defenses. The coach owes this to his squad. In order to do this, the coach must understand the basic principles of zone employment. After this realization is made, you can formulate your offensive thinking for this type of defense. Keep in mind the many types of zones and their varied uses, but most important, the fact that it is almost impossible to have a single offense against all of them. With this point we have set down a number of offenses, with our own.

GENERAL POINTS TO CONSIDER. It is our contention that the zone offense should be related to the basic offense in every attack made on a zone defense. This eliminates teaching two different styles of play, one for the offense and a separate one against the zone. Not all coaches will agree with our belief that we should express confidence in teaching one style of play, with slight modifications, for all defenses, but we feel that this endows our players with a style which is simple and yet remains basic to our original offense.

It should be pointed out that experience has taught us that use of the zone offense by all teams, whether high school or college, will be dictated by personnel. The coach must have players who are able to score against the zone. Without them you might as well forget about playing and forfeit the game to save everyone embarrassment.

The type of zone defense must be quickly recognized so that your plan of attack will carry early emphasis. The more quickly the team moves to the attack, the less chance it has to panic. Strike swiftly and display unhesitating speed in differentiating between the zone played and the offense to be used. This is an essential issue in conquering the zone defense.

Defensive weaknesses of the zone should be scouted prior to the game. This allows the coach time to plan possible strategy. However, this is not always possible, since the zone defense is used primarily as a surprise defense which sometimes helps beat the opposing team psychologically. In this event, game conditions present the only time for the coach to make a diagnosis and his analysis will determine the relative weaknesses of the zone. Players will then be instructed on the plan of attack.

Court restrictions admonish the use of the zone defense. Many of our schools play on narrow courts and for this reason apply the zone as their basic defense. Of course, this can be a hindrance when the team plays on a larger floor as the offense has more room to operate, but there are many excellent zone defense teams.

THINGS MICHIGAN STATE DOES AGAINST A ZONE

1. Fast break most of the time. Get the players and the ball down the floor quickly before the defense sets up.
2. Don't hesitate on your passes. Snap them off! Don't telegraph them.
3. Attack the weak areas of the zone by using an overload of players.
4. *Always* have one man going through with another one swinging around for balance. You need motion to be effective against the zone.
5. Emphasize the weak-side passes and learn to appreciate them.
6. Jockey for position (between the two defensive men) when you don't have the ball. This is called "splitting the defense," and is done to cause confusion on the part of each defense man as to who should be guarding the offensive player.
7. Be patient in your shooting. Make certain that you have someone in position for offensive rebounding.
8. Contrary to general belief, you can fake and dribble against the zone if you don't overdo it or try to force the ball into the basket.
9. A press is fine strategy against a zone defense team.
10. A court balance is maintained.

GENERAL TIPS AGAINST A ZONE.   In addition to the above philosophy, which might be termed "attacking the zone," there are other factors which determine the outcome of the game. These come in the form of tips which have passed our desk or through actual experience in games. The players of our teams have been responsible for the majority of them and they might be of aid to you.

1. At times, refrain from maneuvering for the overload until the ball passes the front line of defense.
2. Attack the zone where the opponent's best rebounder has to cover him. At the same time, employ your better rebounder on the opposite side of the basket. He will give you a board advantage in most cases.
3. Gamble. Crash the boards. Second and third shots against the zone are easier to pick up here than against any other defense.
4. Don't over-offense against the zone. When the shot is there, take it and don't pass off. This over-offensing is one of the most common faults of basketball players.
5. Bounce passes against the zone are to be encouraged, especially against the big men.
6. Control the ball in the late stages of the game and make the defense come out. Here you must have expert ball-handling and some restraint placed on your shooting.
7. Don't give the zone a chance to conserve their energy. Make it move fast.
8. Make the zone spread out as much as possible so you can penetrate it easier.
9. If your personnel can absorb other offenses against a zone, don't neglect using them. However, be sure they can run one efficiently before moving to another. There are many variations of the zone defense and the coach must have his team prepared to meet all of them.

MICHIGAN STATE ZONE OFFENSE.   The authors are going to tender their ideas as to what an offense against a zone should consist of and then discuss methods which are frequently used by other coaches. This assures the beginning coach of a variety of offenses with which to work and then choose the one which best fits his team.

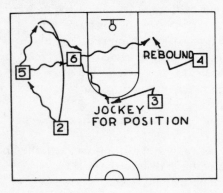

Diagram 7–32a.   Michigan State basic zone offense alignment and passing lanes against the zone.

Our basic alignment and options can be seen in Diagrams 7–32a and 7–32b. As you can see, our positions are the same as if we were playing against a man-to-man defense. This is our first step in planning our method of attack.

Guard Baseline.   This is our first phase, in which the guard (2) passes to the forward (5), goes through to the baseline, and remains on this side.

A point for the forward (5) to remember when he has the ball is that we want the defensive backline man to guard him, and we never want a front man in the zone. This may necessitate his dribbling once or twice down the side to make the defensive forward cover him.

The center (6) comes across to ball side and sets up a passing triangle between these three players. In their passing, they should not try to pass over the zone or through it as this is when an interception usually occurs.

The second phase takes place when the first play doesn't work. (See Diag. 7–32b.) The guard (2) on the baseline will go to the other side and

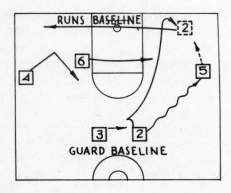

Diagram 7–32b.   Guard baseline zone offense to provide overload.

the play starts again on the same side as the original play. This is the basic motion with which we test the zone defense.

Forward Reversal of Ball. Diagram 7–33 will show you our continuity when we do not have anything on the strong side. The forward (5) reverses the ball to our right guard (3). As he does this the baseline guard (2) runs to the opposite side. The left guard (3) passes to the left forward (4) who is pinched in on the short 17. The man with the ball then has the option

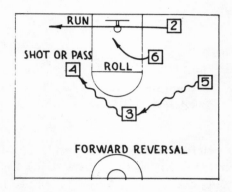

FORWARD REVERSAL

Diagram 7–33. Forward reversal of ball on zone offense continuity as (2) runs baseline.

of hitting the baseline guard (2) or the center (6) rolling down the middle, or of finally shooting if he has a good shot.

If you do not get a decent shot off with this reversal then it is an easy matter of offensive adjustment for the players as they swing around.

Center Baseline. In this play the center takes the baseline instead of the guard, with the guard assuming the center's spot in the offense. In the pattern (Diag 7–34) the left guard (2) passes to the forward (4) against a

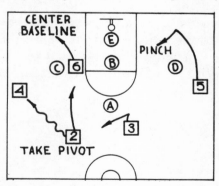

TAKE PIVOT

Diagram 7–34. Center baseline zone offense against 1-3-1 defense.

1-3-1 zone defense. As the pass is made, the center (6) moves immediately to the baseline and the guard (2) mans the pivot. The other players then adjust to the ball and gain position for rebounding or a quick reversal of the ball. Our passing triangle is completed again in this manner. It has never been much of a problem for us to get a good percentage off this phase but we do have a reversal which has been very effective in case we do not get the shot the first time around.

With the 1-3-1 zone adjusting to the ball (Diag. 7–35) the left forward (4) reverses the ball to the right guard (3) who attempts to hit the right forward (5) positioned adjacent to the free-throw line. Once he receives the

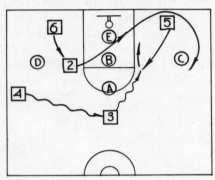

Diagram 7–35. Forward reversal against 1-3-1 zone, and player movement.

ball he quickly looks for the shot. Our left guard (2), seeing that he does not have the shot, moves behind the middle man on the zone looking for a pass from the right forward (5). If he does not receive it he moves out to his original guard position. The center (6) moves to the high post after the guard (2) cuts and usually will get a pass from the forward (5) for the jump shot.

Should none of these options work, then the ball is brought back out to the guards with everyone in their original positions to give the zone another test.

Forward Sneak. Diagram 7–36 will let you see a fine variation of what can be done with forward action against the 1-3-1.

The left guard dribbles the ball until the point man on the zone covers him completely. He then flips a pass to the other guard (3) who dribbles straight into the zone until the middle man stops him. He then passes off to either the center (6) or the right forward (5) who sneaks behind the wing

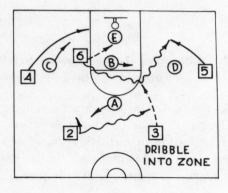

DRIBBLE INTO ZONE

Diagram 7–36. Forward sneak offensive option against 1-3-1 zone.

man. This is the better option and will result in an excellent shot for the offensive man.

Another variation (Diag. 7-37) against the 1-3-1 zone with the same kind of action finds the right guard (2) hitting the center (6) with a quick pass and, as the pass is made, both forwards cut behind their defensive wing men,

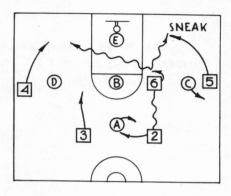

Diagram 7-37. Variation of forward sneak offensive option, using direct pass to (6), who splits (B) and (C).

for the basket. This allows the center two options and puts extreme pressure on the low defensive man of the zone.

Should the forward's (4) defensive man follow him, the guard (3) moves to the free throw area where the center (6) can hit him for a jump shot. Each of these two have been excellent options and have seen repeated use in our zone offense.

OTHER ATTACK SYSTEMS

In all probability the 1-3-1 offense against the zone is the standard offense in many of our high schools and colleges. It is used as a man-to-man-offense, and eliminates learning a second offense against a zone.

In Diagram 7-38a and 7-38b you see the basic positions of the 1-3-1 offense with an option. There is an often repeated adage, "You don't use screens on a zone." It is our feeling that, on occasions, screening the zone can be effective. In this offense, a back screen can be utilized for an exchange of positions and operating motion.

Another option of this offense takes place when the guard (2) passes to the forward (5) on the baseline and the other forward (4) cuts through the zone to the opposite side. The center (6) replaces the forward (4) on the wing and the other guard (3) cuts down the lane looking for a pass.

The reversal of the ball (Diag. 7-39) from deep in the corner (5) can be made around the horn and with quick passes will enable the weak-side men (4) and (2) to get a percentage shot.

Against a 2-3 zone, the 1-3-1 offense can cause considerable destruction, as Diagram 7-40 points out. In this move, the guard (2) throws a direct

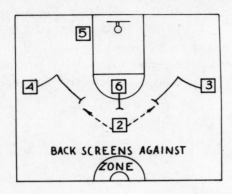

Diagram 7–38a. Possible back screens for (2) out of 1-3-1 zone offense.

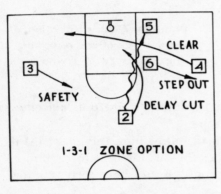

Diagram 7–38b. 1-3-1 zone offense with a continuity.

pass to the pivot man (6) who turns immediately to face the basket. He can shoot or, if the middle man on defense (C) should attempt to guard him, he can pass off to the forward (5) underneath the basket. In the event (E) tries to stop the forward (5), the wing man on offense (3) moves down a couple of steps and receives the pass from the center (6).

Here we have a perfect example of isolating a defensive man with the use of a triangle passing unit.

Off this same alignment the center (6) may set a rear screen for the guard (2) so he can drive off it for a jump shot.

A top play used against the 1-3-1 defense is seen in Diagram 7–41. Here the guard (2) passes to the wing man (4). The middle man (5) offensively breaks down the lane looking for a pass from the wing man (4). The wing man fakes a pass to the middle man (5) and hits the center (6) with a direct pass at the free-throw line for the jump shot.

By the forward (5) clearing to the ball side, he pulls his defensive man with him, leaving a hole in the center of the zone which can be capitalized upon. The baseline man (6) starts his cut at the same instant (5) clears his area.

OVERLOAD THE DEFENSE. One of the better ways of beating a zone is by flooding a defensive area with more offensive players than the defense has in this location.

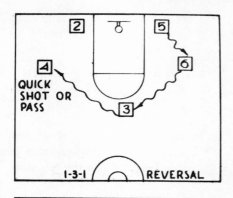

Diagram 7–39. 1-3-1 zone offense reversal.

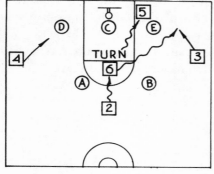

Diagram 7–40. 1-3-1 zone offense against 2-3 zone. Notice isolation of the defensive man (E).

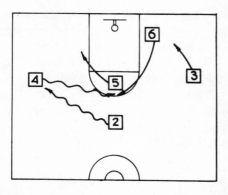

Diagram 7–41. 1-3-1 rotation zone offense with an exchange of positions by (6) and (5). (6) should be a good jump shooter from this area.

This overload also sets up the competent play of coming back to the weak side. One of the better methods we have observed is used by Glenn Brown at Danville, Illinois, High School. In Diagram 7–42 you will see his overload and its functioning.

The play is started with the guard (2) on the baseline, the center (6) low, the forwards (4) and (5) in a free throw high position, and the guard (3) at the top of the circle.

With the forward (5) passing to the guard (2) or the center (6) they immediately should look for the shot if there are only two men defensing the three men. One man should be open.

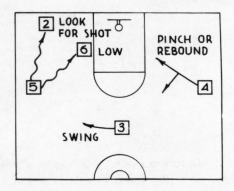

Diagram 7—42. 1-3-1 zone offense overload. (3) swings over to provide four men on the left side.

In the reverse (Diag. 7–43), the forward (5) brings the ball back to the guard (3), who will hit the forward (4). This player has the option of shooting or passing to the center (6), who delays the roll to the ball, or to the guard (2), who runs the baseline to the ball side. Once again you establish an overload and should outnumber the defensive men in the area.

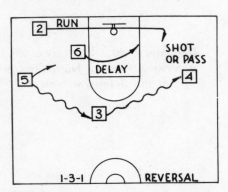

Diagram 7—43. Reversals of ball on 1-3-1 zone offense overload. (3) again will swing over as (2) and (6) go ball-side.

The "key to the kingdom" in zone offense, as we previously mentioned, lies in the hands of the players. They must show no cause for concern when a zone is played against them. Moreover, they must disclose poise, confidence, and shooting ability in everything they do. This is the answer to zone defenses.

DELAYED OFFENSE. The delayed offense is devoted to the team who is ahead in the game with a short period of time left. Of equal importance to the offense itself is the time in which the coach deploys it. It usually is at the five-minutes-remaining point, and anything over this is cause for alarm. There have been many theories advanced as to the correct time to use the delayed offense. We have observed teams with a big lead and a long period of time left in the game attempt to use this offense. Their margin was quickly dissipated because they did not play their normal game and quit shooting. There are some who are fortunate enough to hang on and win these games, while the others could only learn from their mistake of controlling the ball too soon.

The delayed offenses in the profession have been basically the same over the years. There are certain changes in the system which have taken place but all achieve the same result.

Each system requires floor balance, cuts to the basket, short passes with cuts away from the ball, and a continuity. It is easy listing these characteristics but the execution by the personnel can be much tougher.

Time must be carefully allotted to the delay offense in your planning periods. There is a science to this phase and it makes extra demands on the players. For these reasons it should be practiced diligently throughout the year.

M.S.U. and N.M.U. Delayed Offense. Our main point of emphasis in this type of game is: *When holding the ball to protect a lead, don't forget about putting it in the basket.* Teams will often pass up excellent shots only to have this backfire with an immediate interception and the opposition scoring. This gives the opposition momentum which is difficult to contend with, in addition to depressing your own team. From this viewpoint we have set forth rules which apply to our delayed offenses and their use.

Diagram 7–44 gives you our basic positions for the execution of the delay offense. You will notice that the middle of the court is kept open. The players' positions find the best ball handlers (2), (3), and (4) about 10 feet from the 10-second line, or as far in as the defense will allow them. The other players, (5) and (6), are to be in a normal forward's position but wide to spread the defense.

Coaching strategy enters into the picture at this time as you will want to put your best ball handlers into the game. It might mean sacrificing height for sure-handedness but you must have the latter in this situation. Many games are lost when a club attempts a controlled stall and a ball is fumbled or a pass thrown away by a player unable to withstand the defensive pres-

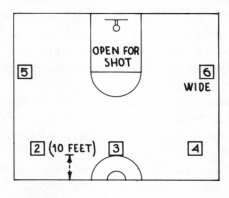

Diagram 7–44. Delay offense basic positions.

sure. Under these circumstances he panics and it costs the team a game which they might have won had they used a better ball handler. Players are drilled in panic situations in our practice sessions.

Points to Remember. As is our custom, we have oriented our squad as to our likes and dislikes concerning the delayed offense. It can be a strong tool for a team when used properly but only the execution by the players will net the results you desire. It is our feeling that they can best recall what you want done if you give them some kind of visual education during the time you spend practicing this phase. We itemize our delay offense rules in this manner on every locker:

1. Never quit trying to score. Go to the basket.
2. Everyone should be working to get open. When the ball is passed to you, *come to meet the ball.*
3. When you have the ball, look for the pass first, the shot second, and the dribble last.
4. There should always be two men for the man with the ball to pass to.
5. When a player is cutting away, fake a pass to him unless he is open—in which case give him the ball.
6. Always keep the floor balanced.
7. The guard-to-guard play is one of your best moves against a pressing defense.
8. When you are an outlet man and are covered by the defense, change direction and get out of the area.
9. Don't take a foolish shot; try to score with a percentage one.
10. You want to keep the defense spread; therefore you will not have a strong rebounding game.
11. Never cross close to a teammate; this will eliminate the possibility of a double-team.
12. If you lose the ball, get back into a 2-3 zone to:
    (a) Take away the opponent's driving game.
    (b) Reduce the fouling and thereby avoid stopping the clock.
    (c) As a surprise to confuse the opponent.

These rules are the premise on which we base our delay offense. It might be fitting to add that we do not believe in the complete "freeze" whereby a team does not attempt a shot. This is a suicidal philosophy which will back-fire on a coach, and it is not endorsed by the authors.

Our delay offense can be seen in Diagrams 7–45a, 7–45b, and 7–45c, the variations and continuity as they exist.

A beginning or veteran coach cannot trust to luck in a delayed offense attack. It must be organized and run under actual game conditions to gain its biggest test. After continuous "trial and error," a pattern will blend itself into an established unison.

One of the better methods we have used in teaching this offense is to use two squads on a half-court situation. One is designated the offense, and we run our delayed attack against the other unit. The clock is turned to the five-minute mark and the offense runs the delay for this period of time. Should a foul be committed the player is awarded a free throw, to simulate game conditions.

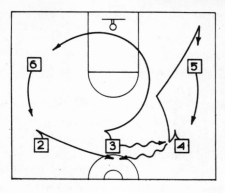

Diagram 7–45a. Delay offense. (3) starts play by passing to (4) and cuts down middle looking for a return pass. (4) passes back to (2) coming to meet the ball as (4) clears area. (6) and (5) move up as cuts are made. This motion is constant.

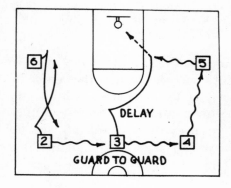

Diagram 7–45b. Guard-to-guard delay offense. Play begins with (2) passing to (3) and then on to (4). (3) then delays cut, makes change of direction and cuts down middle looking for pass from (5). (2) and (6) exchange positions.

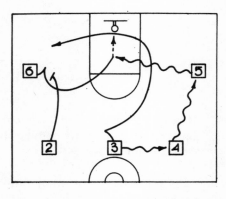

Diagram 7–45c. Delay offense with a set play. (3) passes to (4), who hits (5) as (3) cuts down middle and out of the area if not open. (2) moves down and screens for (6), who breaks across middle looking for pass from (5).

After five minutes have been clocked, the defensive unit becomes the offense and a third group takes the defense. Scores are kept by the manager on the scoreboard and the defense is awarded two points every time they can gain possession.

In this manner the drill gives us everything we want and is the best simulation of a game. With the use of the clock the players learn that five minutes is a long time to control the ball. The free throw taken under these conditions can be a "bonus" if the first is made, and again we stress the pressure on the shooter. It is perhaps as good a conditioning drill as we have because of the movement of the players and, subsequently, the constant expansion of energy.

SPECIAL OFFENSIVE ATTACKS

There are a number of exclusive situations in basketball where, with organization and preparation, the coach can avert a defeat with a well-executed play. Both side and end-line out-of-bounds plays, jump-ball plays, and zone press offense must be painstakingly covered by the coach.

As these plays unfold during the year we have found that the teams which win consistently are those which are prepared in these departments.

OUT-OF-BOUNDS PLAYS. Our thinking is that these plays (Diags. 7–46a, 7–46b, 7–46c, and 7–46d) should be as simple as possible, with few if any signals and with a relationship to your basic offense.

End-Line Out-of-Bounds. This is our favorite out-of-bounds play from this position. The forward (5) hurries to take the ball, as the center (6) is the screener, with the other forward (4) acting as a decoy. Both guards (2 and 3) line up at the top of the free-throw circle, one behind another.

The signal for the play to begin is given by the forward (5), who holds the ball over his head, slaps it, and shouts, "let's go." The guard (3) goes

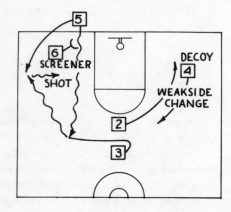

Diagram 7–46a. End-line out-of-bounds play with (5) getting shot behind screen set by (6).

left to receive the first pass. If the ball is held down by the man out-of-bounds, the front guard (2) will go to meet the first pass.

As the pass is being thrown out to the deep man, the center (6) moves in to deceptively screen the forward's (5) defensive man. The forward (5), after passing, goes behind the screen for a return pass from the guard (3), and takes the jump shot.

The second option occurs if the forward (5) does not have a shot. He passes to the center (6) who moves into his normal position and makes the 1-2 cut with the guard (3). The other two men (2 and 4) complete a weakside change to make their men play them honest.

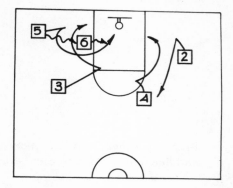

Diagram 7–46b. Option off end-line out-of-bounds play with 1-2 cut if jump shot is not available.

A slight variation takes place if the defense begins to "play the play." In this maneuver, the center (6) becomes the decoy and the forward (4) the screener.

The forward (5) fakes a long pass to the guard (3) and flips the ball to the other forward (4), who comes to meet it. As this happens, the guards (2 and 3) plus the center (6), form a "close the door" screen. The forward

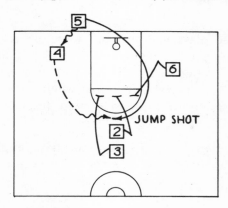

Diagram 7–46c. Second option off end-line out-of-bounds play with three man screen set at free throw line.

(5) who took the ball out-of-bounds comes around behind the screen for a return pass from the man with the ball who has dribbled back toward the screeners.

Northern Michigan employs a fourth end-line out-of-bounds maneuver. (See Diag. 7–46d.) This play scored four baskets for the Wildcats in their first two games of the 1963 NAIA finals at Kansas City.

The best ball handler should take the ball out-of-bounds with the center (6) set about 12 feet away and at an angle to the free-throw line. The remaining players (4, 5, and 2) position themselves on the free-throw line facing the basket.

On the slap-of-the-ball signal, the center (6) moves to set the screen on the forward's (5) defensive man. Your best jump shooter should be in position ready to break off the screen for a quick pass from the out-of-bounds man and the shot.

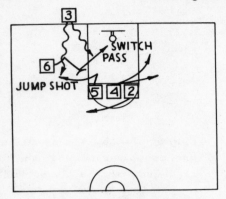

Diagram 7–46d. Third option off end-line out-of-bounds play using a side screen by (6).

The option occurs when the defense switches, setting up a roll for the center (6). This roll is most productive when timed perfectly, as the ball goes immediately to the center (6) from the out-of-bounds man.

The other players have been assigned specific duties and areas. The guard (2) leaves early to carry his defensive man out of the middle while the other forward (4) moves to his regular rebounding position in case a shot attempt is missed.

Side Out-of-Bounds. Although these plays seldom score with the regularity of the end-line plays, they cannot go unattended. If the play is unsuccessful in a scoring attempt, it still presents a uniform and organized method of putting the ball into play. It cannot be denied that when coupled with a possible scoring play, it produces another offensive phase for which the opponents must prepare a defense.

Michigan State Out-of-Bounds. Diagram 4–47 will show the basic alignment of personnel for the Spartans' maneuver from side court. As you can

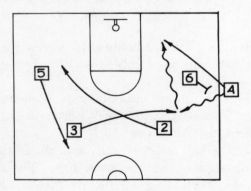

Diagram 7–47. Michigan State side out-of-bounds play. Notice movement by all five players and continuity.

see, the forward (4) takes the ball out. The other four men assume their basic positions with the exception of the center (6) who is pulled up into a regular forward's slot.

The ball is inbounded to the guard (3) who has made a change with the other guard (2). The opposite forward (5) moves out as the guard (2) continues on and exchanges with him to keep the weak-side defensive men busy.

As the guard (3) receives the first pass, the center (6) steps up and sets a screen for the out-of-bounds man (4), who cuts to the basket to receive a pass from the guard (3).

Northern Michigan Out-of-Bounds. This play has been especially effective for Northern Michigan in that it gives the team a percentage shot. It has also been successful when a defensive team is pressuring the team.

In Diagram 7–48 the center (6) takes the ball out with the guards (2 and 3) set wide as are the forwards (4 and 5).

On the slap of the ball, the guard (3) and the forward closest to the ball (5) set screens on the defensive men of the out-court men (2 and 4). The

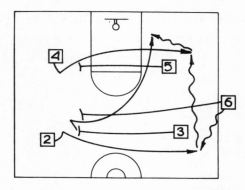

Diagram 7–48. Northern Michigan side out-of-bounds play.

center (6) will pass to the guard (2) coming to meet the ball and continue rapidly over to the top of the key to establish a screen for the other guard (3). He cannot tarry on the way; he must *move!* With the guard (2) in control he passes down the side to the forward (4) who looks for the other guard (3) coming off the screen. The best option seems to be the jump shot at the free-throw line although the drive cannot be ruled out.

A second method would be by making a direct pass to the forward (4), who then relays the ball to the guard (3). The defense will dictate this move but it should not be overlooked as a variation.

We would like to point out that most failures in out-of-bounds plays result from a lack of hustle by the players to their respective positions. If all players hurry to their proper places then the play has a chance of scoring. If they do not, then the timing and execution of the plan will be thrown off.

Coaches spend substantial time on these types of plays. The squad members must be reminded that there is more to the play than the explanation. The correct way to turn on a screen will mean points for the team. If this fundamental is not taught, the squad might lose close games where an easy basket would have meant the difference. Every coach is looking for the "cheap basket" and this is an area which is capable of producing it.

MID-COURT PLAYS.   These plays are usually reserved for last-second situations which always seem to arise. A team's ability to meet these situations with organized strategy can produce a highly desirable outcome.

In Diagram 7–49 you will notice the players lined up facing the ball with three yards between each of them. The key points in running the play are:

1. When the ball is held up by the out-of-bounds man, the 1st and 3rd players go to the right; the 2nd and 4th will move to the left.
2. Should the ball be held down, the 1st and 3rd players will go to the left, the 2nd and 4th players cut to the right.
3. When the man out-of-bounds is ready to pass the ball in, he slaps it and shouts, "Let's go!"
4. The man out-of-bounds should take his time throwing the ball in. He must always follow his pass.

The center (6) should look for either the guard (2) or the forward (4) who should make the basket cut their first move. If the defense is caught

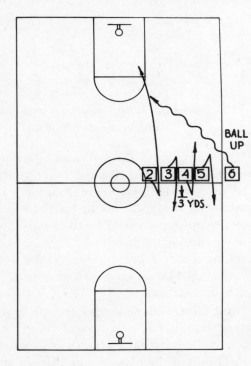

Diagram 7–49. Mid-court play for last-second play. Basic speed position is (2) as he must be able to outrun his defensive man to receive pass.

sleeping, you can make a baseball pass to them. If they are covered, the man out-of-bounds (6) will then pass the ball in to either remaining man in the back court.

As simple as this play appears, it is still one which is feared by coaches when they have to defense it. They cannot be sure that every boy will be on his toes defensively, and the instant you relax against this play, it proves to be a point-getter for your opponents.

JUMP-BALL PLAYS. Control of the jump-ball situations which come about in the course of a game can play a major role in whether you will take your share of the close contests.

The organization you support for these special situations must be complete. This includes an offensive and defensive alignment as well as a set of signals. With these carefully stored for prompt use, it could mean keeping possession of the ball in a critical part of a game or perhaps a key basket that decided the winner.

There are numerous alignments for control of the ball, but screening seems to be a favorite of the coaches. Diagram 7–50 illustrates this, as we

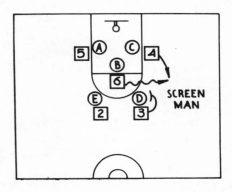

Diagram 7–50. Screening the defensive man to insure gaining possession on jump-ball play.

see the center (6) tipping directly to the forward (4). Note the guard (3) screening his defensive man to prevent him from going for the ball.

This screening may work with any pair of men and has helped in our acquisition of held balls. It is the best method for this situation and involves less risk than some of the others.

A formation which sees much use in Illinois high schools is an "I" formation. This unusual jump-ball play (Diag. 7–51) from the center jump circle is primarily used as a possession tip.

The positions of the players are in a direct line with the man jumping and the basket. The center (6) can tip to three spots. His first option is to the forward (4) breaking to the left side on the rotation. The second is to the guard (3) also rotating to the left. Finally, depending upon the defense, he can tip deep to the guard (2). As the ball is thrown, the rotation begins and the forward (5) moves into the guard (3) spot as he begins to rotate.

Offensive alignments (Diag. 7–52) usually mean the offensive team believes they are going to gain the tip. Many teams will shout "offensive" to alert their teammates to anticipate an offensive held ball. From this advance message a special play is automatically run.

With a definite height advantage assuring control of the ball, the defense will concentrate its strength close to the basket. This is an ideal situation for the offense. The forward (5) tips high and direct to the center (6) sta-

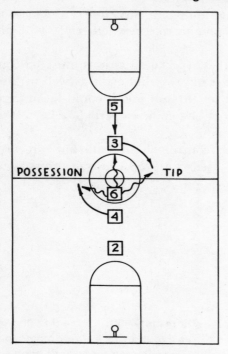

Diagram 7–51. The "I" jump-ball play. An unusual jump-ball play situation to gain control of the ball.

tioned in the middle of the 12-foot lane. As the two defensive men converge on the offensive man, he flicks the ball with his hand to the guard (3), cutting to the basket for the lay-up. The other forward (4) cuts at the same time in case the guard (3) is not open. The defense is handled by the other guard (2).

The key to this play is timing. The cutters should leave for the basket as soon as the referee tosses the ball into the air. If they are late, they will

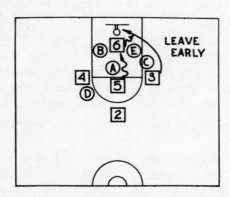

Diagram 7–52. An offensive jump-ball alignment for the easy basket.

not be open. The same play can also be run in the same manner at the center jump circle. The point man should not catch the ball and pass it, but rather tap it in the air to the cutter.

Fast-break teams gamble on this play getting them quick baskets, disheartening the opposition. Although it will not be successful on every attempt, it does net you ball control and possession from which you can get a good percentage shot.

The defensive jump-ball alignment (Diag. 7–53) is the conventional formation where the defensive men are in the inside positions, forcing the offen-

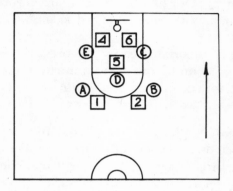

Diagram 7–53. Defensive jump-ball alignment. (1) and (2) may gamble to get the ball.

sive men away from the basket. This prevents their getting the ball underneath the basket for the lay-up. Note (4) and (6) protecting inside area.

Diagram 7–54 gives you a good preventative formation against a lay-up on the jump-ball situation near the opponent's basket. Should an offensive man get control of the ball, a defensive player (B) planted under the basket

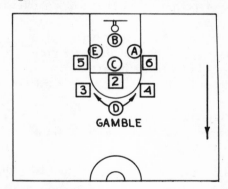

Diagram 7–54. Defensive jump-ball alignment with (B) close to basket while (D) gambles to gain the tip.

picks up any offensive cutters or helps the other two defensive men. Anticipating a tip to the rear, the point man (D) is able to gamble and go either way.

PRESS OFFENSE. With more teams using a pressing defense it is only natural that the formulating of a press offense be authorized. The number of presses being used will rival the number of passes we have in the game. There are variations of the man-to-man, half-court, three-quarter-court, and full-court presses.

In combatting the press, the coach must first be aware of the other team's philosophy on the press. If their theory revolves around pushing the offensive men to the side line, then you can counter with a plan of your own. Survey the vulnerable spots of the press and proceed to attack them methodically. Employment of your personnel must be planned prior to the game in order for you to profit by the weaknesses which exist in the press.

This type of defense is predicated upon rattling the players and is effective only when the offense panics. We tell our players not to be surprised to see a press and definitely not to fear it. Our practice sessions are devoted to every press defense known and our players have practiced against them and should know how to break them.

Controlling the tempo of the game is important against the press. Resist speeding up from your normal game. By doing this you eliminate the defense's biggest psychological weapon, for, coupling speed with an orderly barrage of baskets, the press can be destroyed within minutes.

Northern Michigan Zone Press Offense. We have established numerous rules after experience with the press offense, some of which are listed below. Depending upon the type of defense thrown against us, we feel that these rules are flexible and give us strong support for sudden changes.

1. Diagonal cuts are effective against a zone press.
2. It is vitally important that the first man immediately turn and face the defensive men without dribbling.
3. Keep the ball away from the strength of the defense and their better pressers.
4. Your philosophy of play should not permit an isolation of an offensive man to permit a double-team.
5. Constantly look ahead for an open man. Keep your head up!
6. Short snappy passes are the best type to use against the zone press.
7. Dribbling is acceptable on occasions but passing is better.
8. Zone presses are weak off their defensive board. Hit them hard for the second and third shots.
9. *Run* to meet every pass from a teammate.
10. Shoot the shot when you have it and express confidence in making it. Do not pass it up.

Full-Court Zone Press Offense. In this defense you first confirm the type of press and, after deciding its weak areas, attack it. A 2-2-1 zone press is standard and one which most of the coaches utilize in some form or variation.

Forward's Cross Offense. Against this defense we place four men in our backcourt (Diag. 7–55). As a zone press usually will let you have the first pass in, we place our guard (2) in a straight line with the man taking the ball out-of-bounds. The forwards (4 and 5) are set just inside the ten-second line with the center (6) at the top of the free-throw circle.

As the first pass is made to the guard (2), the forwards (4 and 5) move toward the ball and then reverse and cut behind their defensive men. As they cross, the center (6) comes right up the middle and the guard (2), who is not allowed to dribble, throws him the pass. The man who has taken the

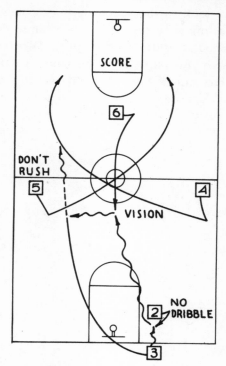

SCORE

6

DON'T
RUSH

5   4

VISION

NO
2 DRIBBLE

3

Diagram 7–55. Northern Michigan forwards-cross zone press offense.

ball out-of-bounds goes quickly down the left side after he passes the ball to the guard (2).

The center (6), upon receiving the ball from the guard (2), turns and passes to either forward (4 and 5) or the other guard (3) coming up the side. As the last alternative he may dribble directly up the middle, forcing the defense to commit themselves so he can pass off for the easy shot. The best option is the pass to the guard (3) who is free a great deal of the time since his defensive man usually has to help with the center (6).

We are never satisfied with just bringing the ball down the floor—we want the shot. If we can get a numbers situation off this offense we want our players to drive hard for the basket and stay with the play until they score. This type of attitude has helped us improve our play against this pressure defense and the players look forward to playing against it.

Side-by-Side Offense. Perhaps the zone press has made some adjustments to the forwards' cross offense to cover it; if so, they can use those compensations to force you out of what you like to do.

If this should happen the coach must make some offensive adaptments so his team can meet the defense. At the same time it should be related to what he has been doing so that a radical change will not take place.

The side-by-side press offense has proven just the ticket for us in such a situation. Its biggest factor comes in the opponents' surprise when they see all four players lined up abreast in the 12-foot lane. There is no one in their area to cover and the defensive players look to the coach in wonderment. Their confusion is matched only by guessing what the offense is going to do.

In Diagram 7–56 you can see the basic alignment of the players. We have a forward (5) take the ball out and with the slap signal, he passes to the guard (3) who goes to meet the ball. He immediately turns to face the defense but he *does not dribble.*

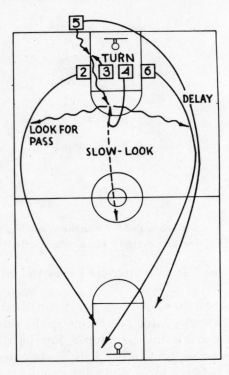

Diagram 7–56. Side-by-side zone press offense.

Meanwhile the guard (2) and the center (6) take off quickly down the sideline looking for a pass from the guard (3). The other forward (4) goes promptly to the top of the free-throw circle. The guard (3) can pass to him or he has the option of passing to the other guard (2), the center (6) or the forward (5). After a delay following the pass, the forward (5) follows the center (6) down the sideline. In the event none of these men are open, the guard (3) can dribble up the middle till an open man appears. They proceed down court at maneuvering speed with one idea—to score.

Offensive Zone Press, "I" Formation. This offense against the press is another variation that can be used with the same related parts as our side-by-side offense.

A look at the weak points of the zone press will tell you where to launch your attack. In this particular press, either side appears assailable, but the second line of defense must be made to react the way you desire in order to make certain of passing lanes.

You will note that in Diagram 7–57 the players' positions are along the 12-foot lane, one behind another, as the play originates.

The forward (5) takes the ball out-of-bounds again and at the given signal, the guard (2) goes to meet the pass from the forward (5). As this occurs, the guard (3) and the forward (4) take off down court while the center (6) backs up to take the middle. The wing men (3) and (4) should anticipate a

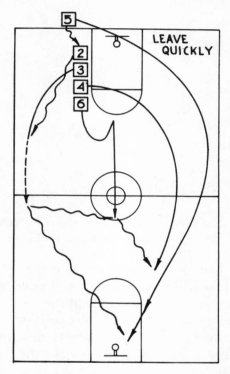

Diagram 7–57. Offensive zone press "I" formation.

pass from the guard (2) who in this case throws to the guard (3). This player can advance the ball by dribbling up the floor, but he should look deep for the forward (5) who put the ball in play, as he could be open. The middle man (6) can also handle the ball if the guard (3) experiences any pressure.

Half-Court Zone Press Offense. This pressure defense has increased in popularity and can cause considerable damage when an offensive team is not prepared for it. As the pressure is usually exerted at the 10-second line by two and three defensive men, the offensive team must penetrate through or over these men to get into the scoring area.

Diagram 7–58 shows you the Northern Michigan offense against the 3-2 half-court zone press. It is our theory that while the defense wants to dictate where they push you, *we* want to dictate what the defense does. Our positions in this attack are unorthodox but continuity is easily established as you will see.

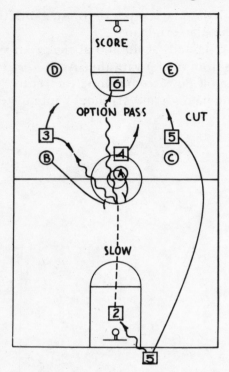

Diagram 7–58. Northern Michigan half-court zone press offense.

The forward (5) takes the ball out-of-bounds, passes to the guard (2) who dribbles slowly to the middle. The forward (5) runs upcourt and positions himself behind the defensive wing man with the guard (3) and the forward (4), who are also spotted here. The center (6) is at a high post position.

The guard (2) should dribble directly at the middle defensive man and *not to either side*. He should wait until the defensive men make the first move. If (A) and (B) two-time the dribbler he should bounce pass to the open offensive man (3). A second option can be used where the guard (2) makes a direct pass over the front line to the center (6) on the high post. The other offensive men at half court then turn and fill the lanes going to the basket.

Excellent jump shots can be obtained by the center (6) off the direct pass or by the lay-up as the back defensive men cover the center (6), who feeds the offensive wingmen (3) and (5).

Screening of the defensive front line by the offensive men is permissible for a variation. The major factor in combatting this defense is impressing your players not to panic! The press has definite weaknesses that can be conquered.

LAST-MINUTE OFFENSIVE PREPARATION. All coaches have a special play they hold in reserve for an emergency. It is a play which they hope will bring them a basket in the closing minutes of the game. It is not one that has been used during the game but a play organized for such a situation.

If the coach has appropriately prepared his team for such circumstances, the team members will not fear this situation. The only way that this can be done is through the practice sessions simulating late-game conditions.

Use of the Clock. Do not leave this time-piece idle during the practice sessions. In special situations practice with the clock is more useful than at any other time for the players and coach. It can be set with a certain number of minutes and seconds left to resemble actual game conditions. In this way, the players become acquainted with the time element and become educated in knowing what to do when these situations arise.

Scrimmage. Your squad should be divided into two or three teams. If you do not have this number of near-equal-ability players we propose you take your first five and two substitutes, placing the remainder of the group with a reserve team. These two groups then scrimmage under these circumstances:

1. 5 minutes left on the clock, first team is behind by 5 points. After they score, they employ a 2-2-1 zone press. The second team tries to protect their lead with the delay offense.
2. 2 minutes left on the clock; first team is ahead by one point; second team uses zone press defense after they score and the first team runs the zone press offense.
3. 1 minute is left on the clock; the score is tied with the first team in possession and the second team in a 2-3 zone defense.
4. 30 seconds left to play; the score is tied and the first team has the ball out-of-bounds under their own basket with the second team in a man-to-man defense.
5. 7 seconds left to play; the first team is ahead by one point with the ball at mid-court and the second team in a tight man-to-man defense.

There are innumerable specific situations which you can originate and function for your team. By giving your personnel a preview of what they might expect in a game you assure both sides of a guarantee against guesswork. Victories come through simulation of game conditions and guesswork should not appear in any last-minute strategy.

Last-Second Plays. The number of contests decided in the dying seconds is almost unbelievable. Every year there are some coaches who lose a large number of games by 5 or fewer points. Yet there are other coaches who seemingly squeeze out this same number of one pointers with regularity. What is the difference when the two teams have equal personnel? Usually it boils down to last-second strategy and how well equipped the players are to handle these situations. Diagrams 7–59a, 7–59b, and 7–59c show you three such last-second plays from the mid-court which might be used in a tight situation.

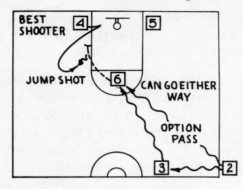

Diagram 7–59a. Last-second mid-court play for your best jump shooter.

The first play has the forward (4) and (5) camped low on the baseline while the center (6) is at the high post. The guards (2 and 3) have the responsibility of getting the ball into the center (6) either by a pass from the guard (3) or directly from out-of-bounds by the other guard (2). The center (6), upon receiving the ball, should dribble down the lane where he provides a screen for the forward (4) while handing the ball off to him for the jump shot. The forward (4) must make a change of direction to set his guard up for the screen or, as a variation, he can change positions with the other forward (5) who would then become the shooter.

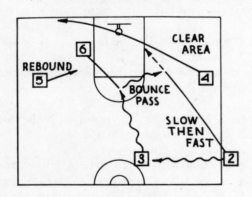

Diagram 7–59b. Last-second "back-door" play from mid-court.

A last-second play to use with less than 10 seconds is the back-door play from mid-court. It is disguised by the fact that the players are in their normal positions with the play capable of being run from either side.

The play begins with the man out-of-bounds (2) passing to the guard (3). As the first pass comes in, the forward (4) on the side of the ball clears out across to the opposite side. The guard (3) promptly fires a pass to the center (6) coming hard to the high post.

The man out-of-bounds (2) walks in and then sprints for the basket, expecting a bounce pass from the center (6) for the lay-up or jump shot. This man should watch the head of his defensive man, for when he turns to watch the ball the offensive man then cuts behind the "head turner" for the basket.

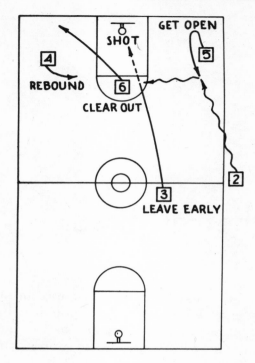

Diagram 7–59c. Third last-second play from mid-court for a quick guard.

The third play we have used is also a mid-court play. In this situation we spread the offensive men as pictured. The center (6) is on the high post and as the pass is made from the out-of-bounds man (2) down the sideline to the strong-side forward (5), he (6) quickly clears from the area.

As many teams pressure the guards, this play can be run well against this defense. As soon as the ball leaves the hands of the guard (2) the opposite guard (3) sprints right down the middle of the court looking for a pass from the forward (5) so he can jump shoot or drive all the way. In many cases, the guard (3) can outrun his defensive man for this pass should he be laying some distance off him.

These plays are simple to enact and it is our belief that in tight situations it is best to have such stratagems. Cool heads must prevail in times like this and a too-complicated play will only confuse the players—the last thing you want in these circumstances. Let us remind you again that these plays must be run during your practices and that they will not give you the results you want without prior preparation and experimentation.

8

Coaching the Fast Break

This is by far the most popular and widely heralded offense used in the game today. More coaches have adopted a fast-break philosophy than any other type. The primary purpose of the fast break is to get the ball into scoring position near the basket before the defense has time to get back and "hold the fort."

Why fast break? This question is asked many times of us when we attend basketball clinics and one that we answer easily. We both have adopted this type of game because of four reasons.

First, we feel it features the "finished" brand of basketball. This can best be defined as a style that possesses many thrills through top-speed ball-handling and shooting.

Second, the players prefer this method of play over any other. They flourish and prosper on activity both individually and teamwise. The fast break delegates initiative, responsibility, and cooperation for a successful attack.

Third, the spectators who attend basketball contests relish this colorful, fast-moving action. They seem to appreciate the more outward display of talent.

Last, and most important, it is very difficult to defend against.

POSSIBLE FAST-BREAK SITUATIONS

MAN-TO-MAN DEFENSE. In examining the number of opportunities which result in fast break situations, we find there are seven such occurrences in a man-to-man defense. It is impossible to attempt the fast break in any other situations and since these are the most common, they deserve your attention.

174

Defensive Rebound.   We have two thoughts about the defensive board we would like to point out.   First, we believe that players make two common mistakes on defense.   The most general error is watching the ball while defensing an individual opponent.   The second is the defensive man's retreating back toward the basket as soon as a shot is taken.   Both of these wrongs must be corrected before a team can think of fast breaking.

Our attitude toward defensive rebounding is reflected in the time we spend on it in practice drills.   Two drills which we gain considerable mileage out of are shown in Diagram 8–1a.   In the first drill, four defensive men are placed on the free-throw line with four defensive men one step away.

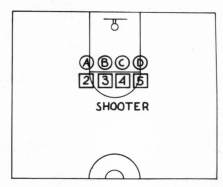

SHOOTER

Diagram 8–1a. Four-man defensive rebounding drill. (A), (B), (C), and (D) must screen out on shot attempt.

The coach or student manager is at the top of the free-throw circle and is the shooter.   As a shot is attempted, the defensive men must check out their men and recover the rebound.   A game is played to 10 points and the defensive team runs laps for the number of recoveries they do not come up with.   This drill is used throughout our practice plan for the entire year and teaches responsibility, teamwork, and position.

We are often asked to describe our screening or blocking-out methods at clinics and other basketball functions.   We have listed in progression the points to remember in this very important phase.

1. Always stay between your man and the basket.
2. Keep your feet on the floor at all times.
3. After the shot is taken, establish a line.   With a half pivot and check, keep one eye on the basket for the rebound and one on the shooter by using split vision.   This reminder, "Give your man one second of attention," helps the defensive man do his job.
4. *Do not move into the shooter,* but do not retreat either.
5. You don't need great height, weight, and jumping ability if you get position and can time your jump to meet the rebound.
6. Only experience and practice will tell you how long to keep your position before going after the ball.
7. Always assume that the basket will be missed.
8. Guard with your feet and not your arms.

9. When you are going after the ball, take short steps when it comes off the rim. Step with the foot in that direction which the ball comes off. Always have vision on the ball and *go to it.*

10. Shots from the right side usually end up on the other side of the basket. The longer the shot, the longer the rebound.

11. Keep both hands on the ball (Fig. 8–1). Come down with your arms and legs spread. This "spread eagle" position will aid in protecting the ball from the opponents.

Fig. 8–1. Perfect example of defensive rebounding.

12. After you get the ball it is important to get it out quickly to the outlet men. If you can turn and throw the ball in the air to the outlet men, this is the best method. If the dribble is to be used, "crash" between two defenders rather than risk an outlet pass should the opponents be playing this lead pass.

The other defensive drill to obtain better individual rebounding strength shown is the one-versus-one drill. (See Diag. 8–1b.)

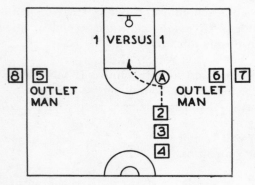

Diagram 8–1b. One-versus-one defensive rebounding and outlet pass drill.

1. Use both ends of the court.
2. Match up the players according to height and weight.
3. The offensive man should shoot a good shot as if in the game, then follow his shot for the rebound.
4. The defensive man will screen out the shooter, then go to retrieve the ball. Rebound the ball whether the basket is made or missed.
5. The next offensive man is the outlet man, and the drill ends when the defensive man gets the ball to the outlet man.
6. The coach should put pressure on the defensive man by insisting on a strong effort.
7. The outlet men become the next offensive and defensive men.

Fast Break After Made Free Throw. The number of free-throw attempts in a game could conceivably outnumber the total field-goal attempts our players take. It is not uncommon to see as many as 50 free throws in some of our games, furnishing excellent occasions to fast break. College teams are making 65 to 75 per cent of these attempts, with many high schools also averaging this. Because of these opportunities we approach the break with careful consideration. The following fast-break patterns (Diag. 8–2a) off the successful free-throw attempt are used by the authors.

The center quickly grabs the free throw as it comes through the net, runs out-of-bounds and fires a pass to the waiting guard (2). The longer the delay by the center the less chance you have for a successful attempt. Make him be quick in his recovery of the ball.

The other guard (3) sprints across to the ball side, bringing the defensive man with him. The forward (5) leaves early, trying to beat his defensive man down the floor, and looking for the long pass, fills the outside lane. The other forward (4) screens off the shooter, then cuts in front of him, becoming the middle man on the fast break. The guard (3) fills a lane whether he has the ball or not.

Occasionally the pass can be made from the guard (2) to the forward (5) or to the middle man (4) without benefit of the extra pass to the guard (3). The guard (2) is a trailer along with the center who took the ball out-of-bounds.

This plan is workable to either side of the floor and should never be run on the same side continuously. We have found that we are able to get the jump shot off around the free-throw area with regularity if the fast break lay-up is not available. This offensive play does not tolerate, and tends to eliminate, the loafing of offensive men coming upcourt. By the same token, it is geared to make the defense hustle back or become outnumbered, forcing them to yield a percentage shot.

The second method is the conventional play whereby your best rebounders are in the inside positions. Your better shooters are the outlet men and the player checking out the shooter will be the middle man on the fast break.

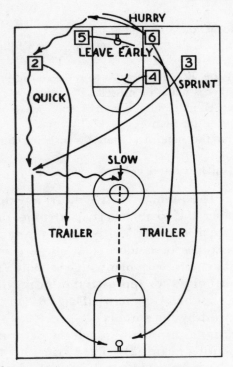

Diagram 8–2a. Northern Michigan fast break after made free throw.

As illustrated in the Michigan State attack (Diag. 8–2b), the center (6) tips the ball to the forward (5) who hustles out-of-bounds, then throws an immediate pass to the outlet man (3). The forward (4) screening the shooter quickly moves out to look for a pass from the outlet man (3) and becomes the middle man on the fast break.

The other guard (2) releases right away, filling the outside lane once he sees the ball is put into play on the other side. The rebounders (5 and 6) are trailers, since the fast break is underway toward the opponent's end of the floor.

This play depends upon the quickness of the first two passes and the readiness of the defensive men to convert to a fast break unit.

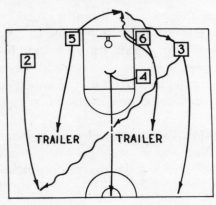

Diagram 8–2b. Michigan State fast break after made free throw. Note (6) tipping the ball to (5) to get ball in play quicker.

Missed Free-Throw Attempts. High school teams will miss on an average of four free throws out of every 10 attempts, while the college groups will fail on approximately three and one-half free throws out of the same number of attempts. This provides the coach with another fast-break situation.

A set-up which supplies us with related continuance to our fast break rules can be seen in Diagram 8–3.

As the free throw is missed, it is tipped out to the guard (2). The forward (4), after screening out the shooter, moves to the ball side and near the 10-second line looking for a pass from the guard (2). The middle man

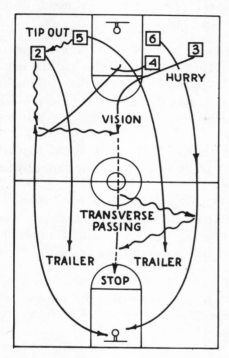

Diagram 8–3. Fast break off missed free-throw attempt.

on the fast break is the opposite guard (3) who should exercise caution and vision for opponents playing a pass to him. Once the ball is in the middle, the wing men (4 and 6) should sprint downcourt expecting a pass at any time. The trailers are the forward (5) and the guard (2) who follow the play to the opposite end awaiting its developments.

There are many variations which are practicable off the missed free-throw attempt. The authors are not trying to ascertain the best method but merely to make coaches aware of the possibilities which exist in this offensive situation.

Interceptions. The ability to convert from defense to offense is the key to interceptions. Although it is difficult to organize a specific situation, we have, nevertheless, a set of rules which apply to this potential fast break basket.

On any interception we want all three lanes filled. We are not particular who gets there first but that lane must be filled with an offensive man! Should the man who has intercepted the ball be on the right side and see there isn't a middle man, he is instructed to take this position on the dribble. As soon as the other players notice this, they know the outside lanes must be occupied. Our regular fast-break rules are mandatory once the lanes are filled.

The interception and its conversion can be accentuated in your practices by letting the defense fast break to the other end on every interception. This teaches learning habits to the players, proper lane fulfillment, quick conversion, and their enactment under game conditions.

Loose Balls. A few years ago a player at Bradley University taught us the importance of the voice on defense. He was a center who had the habit of yelling "ball" whenever he saw a ball rolling free on the floor. This instantly drew his teammates' attention to the fact that a recovery was possible for a fast break. In effect, all five men became "hunters" for the ball and were thinking about a fast-break situation.

Since that time we have used this term much the same as the football team does when they yell "fumble." It can be a passage to the rapid basket the same as a fumble is to a touchdown.

It may seem trivial but this yelling "ball" has brought us more than our share of loose balls and quick baskets over the years. If you insist that your players use it in your practice and scrimmage sessions, you will notice the quickness in which they re-organize and transform to the offense.

Jump Balls. The defensive position your opponents present will determine the extent of your use of the fast break. Normally you employ this opportunity when you know you are going to gain control of the tip. Our offensive tip patterns were described in Chapter 7 and these are put into effect on all jump ball plays where we feel we can gain an advantage.

We would like to point out that the passing in this situation is most important. Many of us have seen the team control the tip to the point man only to have him blindly tip the ball directly into a defensive man's hands. This obviously nullifies a probable scoring chance. To combat this, we tell our front man to tip to a pre-determined spot which is made up between him and the "scooter" before the jump ball. Another method is to have the point man hang on to the ball and advance it himself as the defense drops off to cover the "scooters" who have released. This still gives the team a numbers situation and a percentage shot.

Out-of-Bounds. This occurs after your opponents have scored a basket or when your team comes into possession after a fault by the opposition. This might be on the endline or the sideline. With training, these can be turned into either fast break baskets or fine percentage shots.

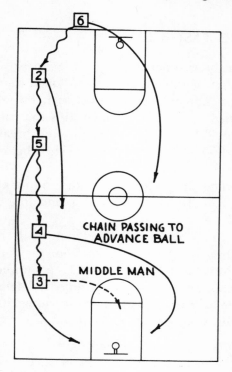

Diagram 8—4. Fast break from out-of-bounds down the left side

We have a saying relative to any man moving down court who does not have vision on the ball. We tell our offensive men, "Throw the ball and hit him in the back of the head." A player should never be unaware of the location of the ball. This style of getting underway offensively helps us get the ball out of the danger area quickly.

On numerous teams, coaches have noticed that there are players who are slower in getting back on defense. To take advantage of this weakness, they insist that the ball be thrown in-bounds by the closest man to insure against any hesitation. Diagram 8–4 shows you an overload method of advancing the ball up the floor from out-of-bounds.

All the offensive men line up down the right side forming a chain. They pass the ball upcourt rapidly, penetrating as deep as possible until they meet defensive pressure.

As the pass is made from the center (6) to the guard (2) the other offensive numbers hustle to the right side to complete the chain. The pass comes up the side and finally the guard (3) dribbles into the middle of the court. The forward (4) realizes he must fill the outside lane, so after his pass he cuts to the opposite side of the floor. The other forward (5) breaks down the right side to fill this lane with the center (6) and guard (2) trailing the play.

There can be variations of this play as the defense prepares against it. The middle man and the wing man can vary to change the pace of the play.

OTHER WAYS TO FAST BREAK

ZONE DEFENSES. The most frequently used defense to get the fast break going is a zone defense. It doesn't matter which one is used, although some are better than others. We would recommend the 3-2 zone, as it has all three fast-break lanes automatically filled. Once the team obtains the ball, it doesn't necessitate changing personnel, since it is a straight-line break. However, it has definite weaknesses which you will want to review before making a decision.

The 1-3-1 zone is perhaps our second choice. The point man can quickly release, and the other lanes can easily be adjusted to by the second line of defense.

As we mentioned, all are basically good but they must be adapted to the personnel on hand. Repetitious drilling on the fast break from the zone eliminates any continuous change of positions by the personnel. A number of coaches consider this element all-important in their selection of a defense with fast-break possibilities. They conclude that it cuts down learning situations for the players and, by doing this, suppresses the likelihood of errors.

PRESSING DEFENSES. These defenses are becoming stronger each year and as they do so, the scoring averages seem to soar with them. Through the years such high schools as John Marshall of Chicago, Illinois, East Tech in Cleveland, Ohio, and Kokomo in Indiana have been advocates of this harassing type of defense and great fast-break opportunists.

On the college courts, West Virginia, Bradley, and Arizona State have achieved fame through their use of this defense with the idea that it will increase their fast-break offense and scoring output. We believe everyone will agree that each of these clubs has met with unusual success, and a major share of this can be attributed to the pressing defense.

ESTABLISHING A FAST BREAK

The installation of the fast break as the coach's number one offense can become a problem because in this style you are going to make more mistakes than in any other method of attack.

There are many elements to consider in establishing the fast break. These include the mental and physical factors which the players must recognize. For a team to play fast-break basketball they must be in top condition. Every player must have the stamina for this type of game. A team which uses the fast break continuously hopes that it will eventually wear down their opponents during the course of the game.

The coach must also decide whether he wants to engage in the "race horse," or "controlled," fast break. A number of teams advocate the "race horse" style and surprisingly enough are regularly strong contenders. High schools in Indiana, Illinois, and Ohio have excellent teams of this type. There seems to be at least one of them in their state tournament finals every year.

DRILLS TO CONSTRUCT THE FAST BREAK. Drills are the only method with which you can teach the fast break. Those best suited are the ones with a combination of what you desire. The drills you use should fit into your pattern of play and be related to what you are doing with this style.

We attempt to bring this phase along in the same manner as all of our offensive maneuvers. Our breakdown for fast-break drills calls for one-versus-one, two-versus-one, three-versus-two, five-versus-two, five-versus-three, and the trailer situations.

One-Versus-One Drill. In the one-versus-one drill (Diag. 8–5) we want the offensive man to learn how to beat the lone defender. He dribbles directly at the defensive man and as soon as he retreats, the dribbler can

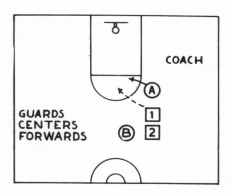

Diagram 8–5. One-versus-one fast-break drill emphasizing jump shot against a defense.

come to a quick stop and jump shoot or move past the defender with the use of a change-of-pace or direction dribble. He must attempt a percentage shot and *never* use any other type.

This drill has a defensive learning situation in that we encourage aggressive play. If the shot is missed, the defensive man checks out the shooter, rebounds the ball, and quickly throws it to the closest outlet man. We use a normal rotation of men and utilize both ends of the floor for this exercise.

Two-Versus-One Drill. As Diagram 8–6 denotes, you have two offensive men against one defensive man. You want to profit from this advantage before other defensive assistance arrives, so it is compulsory that you go for the lay-up and three-point play. Rules we have adopted include:

1. Attempt to get the defensive man out of position and get the ball behind him.
2. Minimize the dribbling of the ball.
3. Stay as wide as possible and yet hold excellent passing range.

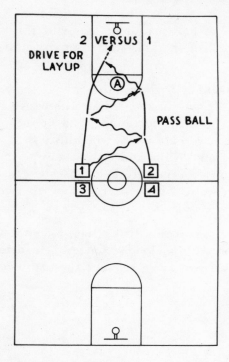

Diagram 8–6. Two-versus-one fast-break drill with minimal amount of dribbling.

4. Do not overpass. This is a common stunt in this situation and can prove costly.
5. The pass-off is a good weapon. This means going up for the shot and then, when covered, feeding off to a teammate.
6. After completing the drill, the offensive men change sides of the floor.
7. The jump shot is *never* encouraged in this drill!

Three-Versus-Two Drill. As we progress in our fast-break patterns, this play is one which coaches like to see—the quick-outlet pass whereby the offensive team has the defense numerically outnumbered (Diag. 8–7). To give you an idea of its extensive use, this three-versus-two drill is perhaps approved on all coaches' drill sheets. The variations are so numerous it would be impossible to list them. We will describe the drill we use and its rules.

1. Two balls will be used with the coach starting the drill by throwing the ball to one of the offensive men.
2. If possible, the pass should be used the full length of the court. If you are unable to do this, use the dribble to avoid trouble.
3. The wing men must stay wide. Note the use of chairs to help them gain the proper angle.
4. Make the front man declare himself defensively. When he comes up, pass off so that you will have a two-versus-one.
5. The middle man must stop and pass off by the time he gets to the free-throw line.
6. Use good fakes and changes of direction.

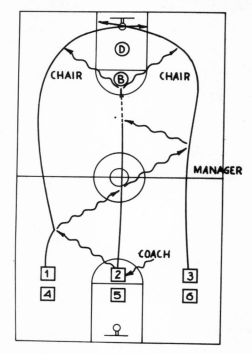

Diagram 8—7. Three-versus-two fast-break drill using two balls.

7. The bounce pass is the best one to use in this situation.
8. Should the shot be missed, every attempt must be made to rebound for the score.
9. Wing men cross underneath to the opposite side for a possible pass and the rebound.
10. After one group has had their turn, they hustle off the floor and return the ball to the manager, who passes it on to the coach.

The drill not only gives you ball-handling and simulated game circumstances, but also is a conditioner for the players. We have our players repeat the drill if they do not score as often as we would like them. This seems to quickly bring home the point that we want the ball in the basket.

Scramble Drill. This is the best drill we have come in contact with because it has everything a fast break contains. It contains continuous action, sudden situations demanding quick thought and reactions, and teaches the fast break as in every game situation. Diagrams 8–8a and 8–8b demonstrate this drill.

At the start of this drill we divide the squad so that we have six players on one end of the floor, with the remainder at the opposite basket. The three offensive men come down on a three-versus-two fast break against (C) and (B). If the shot is not made on the first attempt, they battle until the basket is scored or the defensive men come up with the ball. As (B) gains control of the ball, (4) steps onto the court and is the outlet man for a fast break going to the opposite end. His teammates are (B) and his defensive

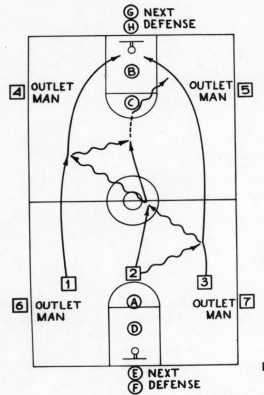

Diagram 8–8a.   Scramble fast-
break drill, first phase.

partner (C). They go three-versus-two, attempting to score against (A) and
(D) who have stepped onto the court. As this unit scores or as the defense
gets the ball, (A) and (D) will be joined by either outlet men (6 or 7), depending on to whom the defensive men pass the ball. Both should anticipate and expect the outlet pass. Do not let them wander down the sideline
but keep them in their respective positions. It should be clearly understood
that the defense can gamble on any method to gain the ball. They need not
sit back but can vary the defense, trying to rattle the offensive men or make
them commit a ball-handling error.

At Northern Michigan we run this drill daily for fifteen minutes using
the clock in a race against time. We keep the number of baskets scored in
this span of time and strive to improve it at every practice session. The
players like this drill very much.

Four-Versus-Three. A good defensive team will get back on defense and
often foil a fast-break situation from a numerical standpoint. The answer
to this problem can be solved with a simple drill (Diag. 8–9a) which calls
for a trailer to follow the ball for the medium jump shot.

Four men are lined up just beyond the free-throw area, with the first
three advancing the ball down the floor into the offensive end. As the ball
crosses the ten-second line, it should be in the hands of the middle man.

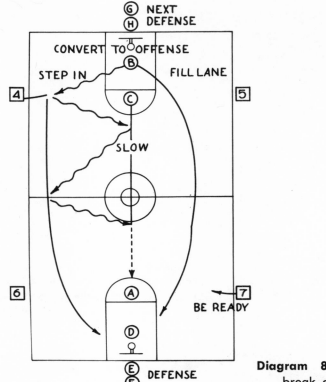

Diagram 8–8b. Scramble fast-break drill, second phase.

Any time the offense does not have a numerical advantage they automatically look for the trailer so he can get the percentage shot. Knowing this, the middle man passes to the left wing man and then clears to the side opposite the ball. This action will make the front defensive point man drop back to protect the middle and also move with the ball. The other wing man (3) also goes to the ball side via the baseline behind the defensive man in this area.

Finding everyone covered, the left wing man (1) stops and, knowing (4) is trailing, he passes back to him at the side of the free-throw line. He then fires a jump shot which should normally be unmolested.

A second trailer move (Diag. 8–9b) with the aid of a screen is also used. In this play the middle man (2) passes to the right wing (3) who stops when he receives the ball. Both the middle man and left wing man remain spread as the trailer comes down court and sets a screen on the defensive man who has rushed out to defense him. He comes off the screen driving hard for the basket and looking for an open man to pass off to in the event he is picked up by another defensive man.

Five-Man Shells. Another drill which serves a vital role in establishing the total offensive fast break is the five-man shell. With our breakdown now complete, we start using five men offensively for the first time. Let's talk

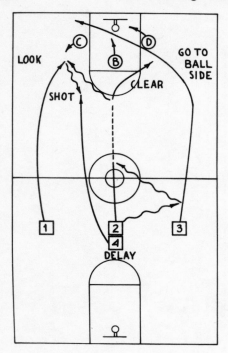

Diagram 8–9a. Four-versus-three fast-break drill with an offensive trailer (4) getting the jump shot off the top of the free throw circle.

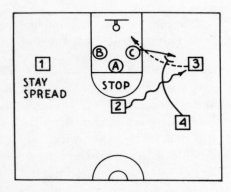

Diagram 8–9b. Four-versus-three fast-break drill with trailer (4) screening for (3).

first of all about the various methods we use in starting the fast break, and then add the three defensive men.

In keeping with our practice of naming drills to make everyone aware of what we desire, we have given our three methods the following names: Guard In, Forward In, and Anybody In. Let us closely examine each in order to familiarize you with their details.

Guard In. Diagram 8–10a shows all five men in defensive position and ready to convert to the offense. The left forward (4) has rebounded the ball and *fires* out to the left guard (2) who has gone directly to the sideline to receive the outlet pass. Notice he has not drifted down court, nor is he running away from the ball.

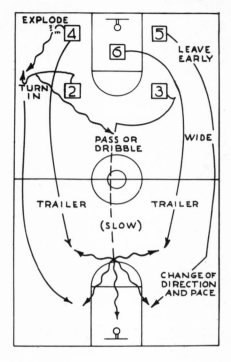

Diagram 8–10a. Fast-break shell with the guard in the middle.

The opposite guard (3) flares out and then back into the middle, where he should receive a pass from the outlet man before he approaches the ten-second line. The sooner the middle man has the ball, the better chance you have for a successful break.

The weak-side forward (5) leaves early to fill the lane opposite the ball side once he sees that his teammate has made the outlet pass. The center (6) comes down the same side as the weak-side forward in a trailer situation. The rebounder (4) is a trailer on the ball side to complete the first phase.

The second phase, penetration of the ball into the scoring zone, is now upon us. We insist that the ball pass among the front three men. Because he has the toughest job, the middle man should be one of your better ball handlers. His first duty is to go slow so his wing men will be slightly ahead of him. If he is ahead of them, it throws off your timing and hurts the execution of the play. As the middle man approaches the top of the free-throw circle, he should release the pass to either wing man. His momentum should carry him to the free-throw line, where he *stops*. The pass we like best in this situation is the "no look" bounce pass, although we are occasionally forced to use others. There is a difference of opinion on this subject but this is what we have been successful in using and it fits into our pattern.

The wing men (2 and 5) should stay wide and use a change of direction and pace, depending upon the position of the ball. If they receive the ball, they drive the basket first and shoot the jump shot as an alternate move.

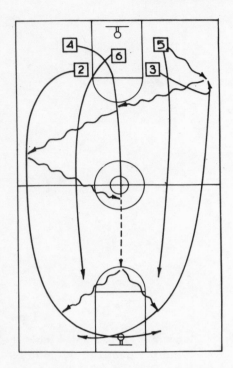

Diagram 8–10b. Fast-break shell with the forward in the middle.

Forward In. As coaches learn individual and team habits through scouting, it is nearly impossible to rely upon one set pattern of fast breaking. The best way is to stop a team from doing what it likes to do. Play situations are never the same and to orient the players we call upon a second method of advancing the ball into the scoring area.

First, the players are again concentrating on their defensive task so they can acquire the ball (Diag. 8–10b). Without it they are not going to run anywhere! The right forward (5) comes up with the ball and passes out to the right guard (3), who buttonhooks in from the side to receive the pass. The other guard (2), seeing the middle is clogged, fills the left lane. This move also takes the defensive man back and frees the middle so the weakside forward (4) can become the middle man.

The guard should attempt to give the ball to the middle man at the top of the free-throw circle and before the center jump circle. This will make it easy for him to avert any defensive pressure by passing off to one of the wing men breaking down-court. In this play the trailers are the center (6) down the left side, and the forward (5) down the ball side.

The same rules are put into use as in the Guard In fast break shell and are strictly enforced as the groups take turns running this pattern.

Anybody In. This occurs more times in a game than many coaches believe. It happens most of the time off a long rebound, recovered ball, and an interception (Diag. 8–10c).

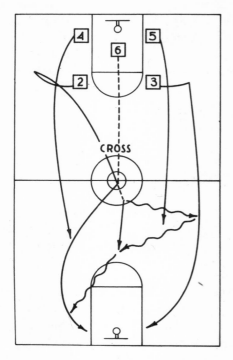

Diagram 8–10c. Fast-break shell with anybody taking the middle. (6) being the middle man until he reaches mid-court where (2) takes over.

In this situation we want our three lanes promptly filled without any wavering on the players' part. The center (6) picks up the long rebound and, seeing the middle open, breaks through any defensive men to take off down-court as the middle man. The guards (3 and 2) flare out and, seeing the middle is taken care of, fill the outside lanes.

Since most pivot men are not your best middle men, the guard (2) cuts behind the center (6) who leaves him a drop pass. The center (6) cuts sharply to fill the left lane where the guard (2) came from, with the guard now the middle man.

We have found that our big men enjoy this method of clearing the board and getting the ball out of the danger zone. Not all coaches will have personnel capable of doing this but fortunately you do have those outstanding few who come along once in a while.

These methods are run through in a dummy stage to begin with; that is, without benefit of the ball. Player assignments are reviewed on the floor for each position.

As we add the ball, the players walk during the first two attempts down the floor and then we let them run through the entire fast-break shell, using only the Guard In to start. After mastering it, we then move to the other two methods—but only after *complete mastery.*

Five-Versus-Three. Competition can now be reckoned with and should be urged in order to test the validity of the coach's instructions. Deliberation by the coach should take place before competitive drills are used to ward off any bewilderment on the players' part. Every coach can tell if his team is ready for advanced drilling. If they are not prepared, they should never be allowed to try it. If they are not adept in using proper fundamentals, then they will have difficulty learning the other progressive techniques.

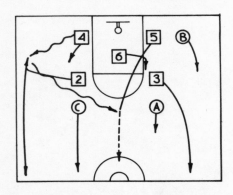

Diagram 8–11. Five-versus-three fast-break drill using fast-break shell to advance ball against the defense for the shot.

In Diagram 8–11 our fast-break pattern receives its first examination from the defense. Whether it passes or fails depends upon the execution by the personnel. This drill embraces practice in handling fast exchanges with the ball, outlet leads, learning lane requirements, and rebounding position.

The drill starts with five defensive men and three offensive men. The offensive men (A), (B), and (C) can move to any position they like on the floor. One offensive man has the ball and will take a normal shot. The five defensive men convert to offense and strike for their scoring end using the fast-break methods as described in Diagram 8–10. The beginning offensive men now assume defensive positions and have complete freedom to do what they can to stop the break.

At this time, all three may attempt to rebound the shot or elect to drop back to play the outlet pass once the defensive team captures the rebound. Then again they may drop back completely, never contesting a pass until the offensive men pass mid-court.

The drill is completed when the offense scores. If they do not succeed in their first attempt, they stay on the floor until they do score either from a driving lay-up, jump shot, or trailer shot. In this way they meet every defensive phase devised and, in going off the floor scoring, they gain full confidence in the method.

The fast break is a difficult game to teach and you must have patience, as the players will make ball-handling and footwork errors. You will have to live with these if this is the type of game you choose to play. The goal in fast-break basketball is to create prosperous and functional responses through concerted effort by the coach and players in the practice sessions. It does not come easily and without hard work. This style can be summed up as systematized organization through logical instruction.

OTHER ASSOCIATED FAST-BREAK DRILLS

Every coach likes a drill which he can utilize in everyday practice sessions. We are all constantly scanning horizons for these and inventing others to fit into our own pattern of play. The drills should be elementary and still incorporate essential factors geared to the fast-break fundamentals of the game.

Outlet Passing Drill. If a fast-break team expects to run the defense, it must clear the ball and have it in the outlet man's hands swiftly. Diagram 8–12 illustrates this as well as the shooting phase of this combination drill. To have uniformity, the rotation of the lines is to the right.

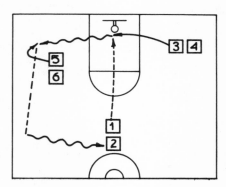

Diagram 8–12. Fast-break outlet passing drill. (1) dribbles in for lay-up. (3) rebounds made or missed shot and passes to (5) who dribbles to mid-court and passes to (2).

If the shot is made, the player must jump out-of-bounds and pass to the outlet man. The coach can vary the shooting distance to insure more rebounds.

Three-Man Fun Weave. Coaching anxiety is often expressed over team ball-handling. Fast-break teams need flawless passing to make this style click. We have all seen the player with "board" hands who cannot hang onto the ball when it is thrown to him. To help eradicate this kind of ball-handling a fun drill is added to the practice, with the players soon learning to handle all types of objects.

The drill (Diag. 8–13) is the accepted three-man weave but with variations, as you can see. For the basketball, we substitute a golf ball, ping-pong ball, volley ball, and, finally, an egg.

Many players do not "watch the ball" into their hands and this drill is ideal for these men. The different sizes of the objects demand and maintain eye contact. Soon the players capture the fundamental idea. It has cut down the number of fumbles in our games.

The use of an egg can be optional with the coach. The players enjoy it but we have never gone through a practice session without breaking one!

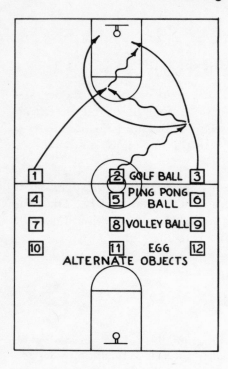

Diagram 8–13. Fast-break three-man fun weave with players alternating objects.

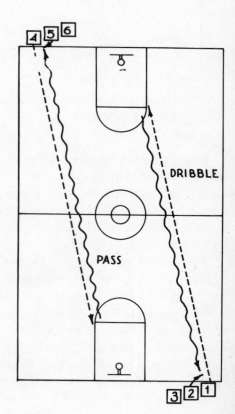

Diagram 8–14. Fast-break speed dribble and baseball-pass drill.

If this happens, the player making the bad pass or the man fumbling it cleans it up. This adds delicate touch to the drill and it is the same type of touch which fashions fast-break passes.

Speed Dribble and Baseball Pass. The development of the speed dribble to elude defensive men and as an effective means of going to the basket must be considered in the fast-break drills. When combined with the baseball pass, we have two ways to whip the defense. Both are brought together in this drill.

Diagram 8–14 acquaints the reader with this drill. Divide your squad and place one group at each end of the court. The players are instructed to dribble, under control, as fast as possible to the opposite free-throw line. After they have reached this point, a baseball pass is uncorked back to the next man in their respective lines.

After familiarization, a relay may be run for competitive purposes which will be useful in determining who are your fastest dribblers and "choice chuckers." This information is always of value to a coach.

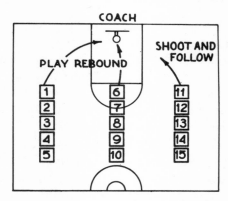

Diagram 8–15. Fast-break shoot-and-score drill.

Shoot-and-Score. Before you can win games you must be able to put the ball in the hoop. A major share of our time in the drill is spent on shooting to imitate game situations on the end of the fast break (Diag. 8–15). This includes the shot, the possible rebound, and the foul shot.

Divide the squad into three lines of five men each. The third-line man will shoot the ball and the first man in each of the lines goes for the rebound if the shot is missed. If it goes through, it counts as two points for that group. When a rebound comes off, the man who gets it attempts to score. If he is fouled, the free throws are shot. The game is played to ten points.

9

Player and Team Defense

FACTORS TO CONSIDER IN DEFENSE

STATISTICS. One only has to look at the record book to find many fine defensive stories. In the NCAA tournament finals from 1955 through 1963, five defensive-minded teams were victorious. All of the nine *losers* during this period were represented as high-scoring teams, with the exception of California in 1960 and Cincinnati in 1963.

Three balanced teams in these years merged strong offensive play with strategic defensive play to become champions. The masterful job North Carolina did on Wilt Chamberlain in 1957 to defeat Kansas was a defensive gem. Another highlight has to be the way the University of Kentucky handicapped Elgin Baylor as the Kentuckians emerged victorious over Seattle University in 1958. Probably the most complete and accomplished team defense was in another championship game in 1960, with the Buckeyes of Ohio State dumping California.

Taking a further look into the figures, we found quite a difference in the points scored from 1948 through 1963. There is little doubt that defense has suffered in this era of the great shooter. In 1948, major college teams were averaging 29 per cent of their field-goal attempts, while in 1962, the national average was slightly over 41 per cent.

The course of direction has definitely been on emphasizing the offense and neglecting the defense. Yet it is still difficult to sell many coaches the idea that sound defense will win for them. Their common reply, "a good offense is the best defense," is a reflection upon custom and how the offense has shaped their thinking toward the game.

PLAYER ATTITUDE. All players like to score. The first thing they do when they come from the locker room for practice is to pick up a ball and attempt to shoot it through. Seldom do you see the individual player off on

196

the side working to improve his defensive stance, balance, or footwork. If the coach is to field a sound team he must interest his players in the "other half" of the game.

RULE CHANGES.   No factor in the game has played such a major part as the rule changes the defense has been subjected to in recent years. Granted, we have some fine rules and are making progress, yet the rulemakers seemingly have favored the offense in most changes.

WHY PLAY DEFENSE?   The intelligent coach will prepare his team to effectively meet every offensive situation of the opponents. By doing this, he is regarded as a serious threat by the offensive team. All offensive-minded teams evidence strain when confronted by a sound club who will not let them do what they like.

Defensive-minded teams enjoy a psychological advantage over their opposition. Westminster College in Pennsylvania, under coach "Buzz" Ridl, perennially unsettles teams it encounters, especially in the NAIA national tournament. In 1961, in one of the great basketball games of all time, they held a potent Winston-Salem team, which had been averaging 90 points per game, to 33 points in the quarter-finals of this tourney and won the game. This tendency to "freeze up" is not uncommon on the part of high-scoring teams, and many upsets have been recorded through the use of this style. Coaches who have teams of this nature rarely give up the "cheap" basket, and fast-break teams thus seldom get the lay-up they fancy.

It is easier to organize a group of players defensively than offensively. By taking this group and drilling them, the coach can make them into a unit that is much more consistent than an offensive team. The teaching of offensive techniques is more difficult than organizing a similar group defensively. When the offense sputters it is the wise coach who, despite this failing, can count on a strong defense to carry his team to victory.

Coaches who basically teach aggressive defense are infrequently on the short end of a "bombing" by an opposing team. At the same time, their scores would indicate that they play many close games. Therefore, the players are oriented to pressure games and have a most flexible adaptability.

Defense is as important as the coach wants to make it. The degree of stress he places on it will be shown by his enthusiasm for defense and by additional coaching effort.

INDIVIDUAL REQUIREMENTS FOR DEFENSE

Any type of defense starts and ends with the individual. It is our feeling that the player cannot play a zone, man-to-man, or pressing defense without first being thoroughly indoctrinated with certain defensive characteristics. Individuals must be determined and possess speed, quick reactions, and aggressiveness. These are the ingredients of good players. We must add that defense is the non-glamour part of basketball. When an individual is not doing his job then the stability of your defense has been weakened. The defense of a team depends on how these characteristics are employed by the individual.

DETERMINATION. Coaches have described defense as 25 per cent ability and 75 per cent determination. Speculation concerning this figure is discussion for debate, but certainly no one will argue that determination is not a prerequisite for defensive play. The player who has this quality normally enjoys the challenge of playing against the offensive star. Call it pride, readiness to excel over an opponent, or self-confidence; regardless, players who have this trait are a capital gain for a coach. All good teams seem to have this one "stopper" on their club and everyone agrees he is essential.

The determination to dominate your opponents with utmost effort on every play situation and throughout the entire game *is* defense. This attitude is what we want our basketball players to adopt when they take the floor.

SPEED. Whether a player plays offense or defense he must possess basic speed. Without it he can expect difficulty in getting open on offense, and defensively, he will find it troublesome keeping up with his man.

A team which has defensive speed is a formidable opponent. They can be a bothersome pressing team, in that they can make a defensive mistake and still get back to thwart the offensive player. The harassment by the defensive guards enables them to pressure the offense into committing mistakes.

The natural speed of an individual is hard to improve upon. Not all players are endowed with great speed and the coach must spend time improving his players through sprints, races, and running form. The latter is important as you will be surprised at how awkwardly some players run. A slight correction can make quite a difference in the matter of starts. The ability to start in anticipation of a play is of major consequence in defensive play and can be taught and learned through drills.

REACTION TIME. The top defensive players have quick hands and feet reactions. These are requirements every coach looks to discover on his teams. The two go hand-in-hand because without proper footwork you will not get the opportunity to utilize the quick hands. We have observed players with great second and third defensive efforts and this magnificent reaction is instrumental to winning basketball.

A player gifted with these reactions can be a thorn in the side of any offensive team. When a team is blessed with more than one of these soundly-coached individuals, they will be a tough team to match.

Drills to strengthen those players who are weak in specific areas should be given careful consideration. Northern Michigan uses the bench-jumping drill to develop jumping ability, reaction time, and leg endurance. The player jumps over a two-foot bench 35 times without stopping. This makes him conscious of the bench height and equips him for the same type of jumping he will be doing in rebounding. The number of times is increased as the agility of the players improves.

The use of the hands has many facets in basketball. They are used to "snap" at the ball, to scoop up loose balls, and to defend against passes and shots. The more quickly they react defensively, the more alert your defense becomes.

Finally, you will never find two players who have the same basic reactions. For this reason the coach should attempt to help the weaker players through intensive drills, amplifying their development of better reaction time.

AGGRESSIVENESS. The day of passive defense is gone. All defenses today are predicated upon being the aggressor and coaches strive to make the offense play the way they want them to.

The pressure defense is aggressiveness to the point where the defensive men play so tight they force the offense into numerous mistakes. College coaches are placing more and more pressure downcourt so teams cannot come down the floor to set up as they like. The manner in which they do this comes from a press or just straight man-on-man pressure. This is not to imply that it is a gambling defense as the team is not intent upon stealing the ball. It is an aggressive, individual defense which makes the pass or shot as difficult as possible, but without the gamble or foul.

Players must be instructed in this defense, and when it is properly employed it can make a shambles of most offenses. Coordination between all aggressors is a must, since one lackadaisical player can ruin the effectiveness of the defense. Aggressive play is a necessary essential in any defense.

INDIVIDUAL POSITION

This is the most important factor in defense. The coach should insist that the players guard their men "with their feet," so to speak, by gaining position and then using their hands. So many players simply reach in playing defense, rather than hustling to a vantage spot where both hands and feet can produce more gratifying results.

When talking of defense, stance is always the basic subject. Fig. 6–8 in Chapter 6 is an illustration of a good fundamental defensive position. The player has excellent balance, with his weight distribution and center of gravity low. His knees should be flexed, and his feet comfortably spread in a boxer's stance. This enables him to move quickly in any direction. He must never cross his feet.

The hand position is such that in the event of a shot he can extend his arm to attempt to block it. The lower hand is off the waist where it is used to block possible passes.

The concentration of the defensive man is on the belt buckle of the offensive man when he is in control of the ball. We have learned from experience that this is the best method of watching the offensive player. His head, shoulders, and eyes can be deceptive because of possible fakes, but his belt buckle will never deceive you!

SITUATION GUARDING

Rather than elaborate in great detail on how to defend against certain individual moves, we thought it would be somewhat different if we listed the key points which we deem necessary for each situation. No doubt opinions will vary on some of these points but these are our choice.

DEFENDING AGAINST THE SET SHOT

1. Keep one hand above the head when a shooter has the ball in shooting position.
2. Make the offensive man hurry the shot and force a higher arch than normal. This reduces the accuracy of the shot.
3. Be aggressive and keep a hand in his face.
4. If caught any distance away from the set shooter, yell at him in hope of distracting him on his shot.
5. Screen the shooter after the shot.

DEFENDING AGAINST THE JUMP SHOT.
The defensive man is at a disadvantage, since he does not know when the jump shooter will stop and go up for a shot. Nevertheless, a defensive pattern against jump shooters should be placed into effect. There are two possibilities, one being to stop the shot before the player can get it off. In this maneuver, the defense hopes to play the offensive man close enough to knock it out of his hands before the shot. The second, which we prefer, is as follows:

1. Knowing that we cannot anticipate the shot until the shooter has committed himself, we wait until he leaves his feet.
2. At this instant, the defensive man thrusts the hand which is closest to the ball up in an attempt to block the shot as the shooter brings the ball into shooting position.
3. If the defender does not deflect the ball, he *should leave his feet* and at least pressure the shot. But he must be careful not to jump into the shooter.
4. When the jump shooter attempts the shot, the defensive man tries to "hang" with him to force his shot, thus ruining the timing.
5. A big commotion is being stirred in rule meetings, where coaches complain that their jump shooters are hit on the elbow when shooting and as

a result their delicate timing is thrown off. It is a controversial point, and the problem does exist, but we will let the rulemakers iron out the wrinkles.

HOW TO DEFEND AGAINST THE LAY-UP. Figure 9–1 is an excellent illustration of guarding against the lay-up shot. The hand position is particularly noteworthy, and it prevented the shot.

Fig. 9–1. Fine defensive hand position against the lay-up shot by (15) and (24).

1. In protecting against the lay-up we stress that the players first "snap up" at the ball, never down across an opponent's arms.
2. If the offensive player is faking before a shot, two-time him before he can get it off.
3. Should this be impossible, stifle the attempt with outstretched hands and smother the shot.
4. If a lay-up has left the shooter's hand, attempt to block it on the board. This is easier than it looks, as it is a matter of timing.
5. Most lay-ups utilize the board, so we attempt to deflect them by jumping with both hands extended, using the corner of the board as our target.

HOW TO DEFEND AGAINST THE HOOK SHOT. This shot is more popular on the advanced level than on the secondary, but when your team runs up against a good hooker, the coach must be prepared to stop him.

1. Try to prevent the hooker from gaining his position. Prohibit this and you cut down his effectiveness.
2. Once he does get the ball, step up with the inside foot. As he makes his turn, reach with the nearest hand to "snap up" at the ball.
3. If this is unsuccessful, continue right with him and cover his eyes with your hands, hoping to obstruct his vision.
4. As the last resort, yell at the shooter, trying to break the concentration of the shot.

5. Your momentum should carry you into the air but not into the shooter.

6. If it is possible, seek help from a teammate who can sag off to pressure the shooter and force him to worry about two defensive men.

7. As hook shooters usually are not in a good position to follow their own shot, they can be screened out quite easily.

HOW TO DEFEND AGAINST THE DRIBBLER. A player who is an excellent dribbler and uses this method as a driving tactic can cause considerable dismay if action is not taken to stop him.

There are two ways of playing the dribbler. First, if the dribble is lateral on the court we endeavor to overplay the dribbler and stay slightly ahead of him. This puts us within reach of the ball, whereas, if we play the dribbler in a normal position we must contend with the player's body. It also gives us an opportunity to "snap up" at the ball with the hand closest to the ball.

In snapping at the ball, we do not attempt to steal it. What we desire is that the ball be deflected cleanly or against the dribbler's legs.

In case the dribbler does get by the defensive man, we instruct the player to go immediately to the basket. He should never follow the dribbler as he will be too late to be of any defensive help. In such a situation, he should turn and retreat in a direction opposite the dribbler's drive. By doing this the defensive man has a chance to beat him to the basket.

The second situation is the fast-approaching dribbler and how to confront him. This plight occurs predominantly on fast breaks with the middle man, although sometimes under other circumstances.

1. It has been our experience that in order to lessen the threat you must make the middle man forfeit the ball.

2. Our defense is instructed that any middle man on the fast break rapidly nearing the ten-second line on a dribble is to be stopped.

3. If we have two men back, the front defensive man will make the middle man consume his dribble or pass off to a teammate.

4. This delaying action has helped our other defensive team members get back. Otherwise, the opponents will storm the offensive court unless we contest the dribble or pass.

5. We tell our players that 95 per cent of the passes made by the fast dribbler will be overhead. Rarely do you see a bounce pass to a wing man at midcourt, so keep your hands up.

6. If the dribbler is coming straight down the floor we tell our front man to run right at him on a collision course. When he veers to avoid contact, he usually moves to his right side so we shade him accordingly.

7. Many times this action unnerves the dribbler and he is forced into mistakes by this defensive strategy.

Two drills in which Northern Michigan employs the above tactics to combat the dribbler can be seen in Diagrams 9–1a and 9–1b.

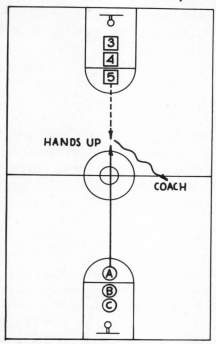

HANDS UP

COACH

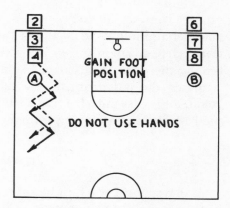

GAIN FOOT POSITION

DO NOT USE HANDS

Diagram 9—1a. Stopping-the-drib-bler drill. (A) runs right at (5) to stop dribble, and attempts to make him pass off to the coach.

Diagram 9—1b. Defensive foot-position drill. Two lines are formed. (4) zig-zags his dribble as (A) stays with him without using his hands for the entire length of the floor. (A) then goes on offense and (4) becomes defensive man.

HOW TO DEFEND AGAINST THE CUTTER. The offensive team that uses a series of screens and cuts to the basket can be defensed. One such method is by the zone and another by a man-to-man defense.

In playing a cutter to the basket the defensive man must drop off one full step from his man. When the defensive man has taken the first step backward, the offensive man will attempt to maneuver to get open. This gives the defensive man time to see the direction in which he is going and move with him.

By stepping away from the cutter, he decreases the offense's opportunity to place a good screen. The one-step retreat while overplaying your opponent can force him to go in the direction you desire. This eliminates any guesswork on the defensive man's part, as he knows there is only one way to go. These are just a few advantages the defensive man has when playing a cutter. He is in a much better position than the man with the ball.

HOW TO DEFEND AGAINST THE PIVOT MAN. With increased use of single and double post attacks, and the "giant" pivot men who frequent our courts, it is small wonder that coaches have ulcers. Learning how to defense these fellows, and even the smaller pivot men, is not a source of enjoyment.

In stopping the strong pivot man, the coach must determine a definite strategy relative to his characteristics. He must decide if one man is capable of stopping this scoring threat. As this is most unlikely if the player is accomplished, the coach must then attempt to cut down the number of times he handles the ball. This is a possibility if the defensive center can get support from teammates such as a zone defense offers. The sagging man-to-man defense might be of aid in this situation but recognition of this type would depend upon the scouting report. The final determinant rests with forcing the pivot man out of his favorite scoring spot. Defeat all attempts at giving the post man his esteemed position, even if you have to almost "scratch his eyes out" before sacrificing anything to him. Once his man has the ball, the defensive center might as well join the spectators in the stands.

TEAM DEFENSE

A player must *work* to become skilled in individual techniques because team defense is dependent upon the skills which have been learned. The five men defensively must be a cooperative unit and synchronize their movements. They must understand that together they can stop an opponent through helping each other, by "talking" on defense, and understanding the principles of team defense. If they are oblivious to these points, the coach should not hesitate to stop practice and orient them at that time. By delaying this action, you encourage sloppy defense.

In team defense it is completely understood that the player is to respond with the greatest possible effort whether it be in the man-to-man, zone, or pressing game. He must have an understanding of what is expected from him before he starts the game or practice.

The spirit which prevails defensively will determine the outcome of many of the coach's games. A team which has pride in its defensive efforts will perform well in every game. Those who are not consistent will find a fluctuation in their winning or losing margins.

We do not believe that any coach has cornered the "market" on any defense or has all the answers. No one has the best defense in the game. What will work for one coach might not for another. When two teams of equal offensive ability meet, normally the team displaying the better defense is the winner. While it might not have the appeal of the offensive game, we must all realize that defense is a major element in winning basketball games.

MAN-TO-MAN DEFENSE

ADVANTAGES. A man-to-man defense has certain characteristics which are favorable. A coach, in his selection of a team defense, will want to be fully informed of these advantages as well as the disadvantages. He will also take a long look at his personnel to see what best fits his needs.

The basic defense at Michigan State is a man-to-man with variations. The reasons we prefer the man-to-man to any other are:

1. We feel it is the toughest defense for the offense to beat.
2. We can delegate definite responsibility to individual players.
3. It develops the competitive urge of the individual to dominate his opponent.
4. This system allows the coach to delegate defensive assignments according to the scoring prowess of the opponents.
5. It can be used against all offenses and at any time of the game.
6. The system is flexible and can be adopted to situations as they happen on the floor.
7. It allows us a two-timing situation via a sag on a particular offensive player.

There are undoubtedly more advantages to the man-to-man defense than we have mentioned but we feel these are the most important.

DISADVANTAGES. Equally significant for the coach to understand are the drawbacks in the man-to-man defense. It can be applicable in many situations but then again the coach might be foolish to use it. He is the man who must make the decision as to what defense will be used.

1. It demands top condition and stamina. It is not for the weak player who cannot go the whole game.
2. More fouls are made in this type of defense.
3. It is weak against a strong screening game.
4. It requires help from teammates if the offensive man is free and this assistance is not always given.
5. A strong offensive rebounding team is a threat to this defense because of the screening which must be done.

If the man-to-man defense is employed, all of the players must be well versed in the methods and fundamentals which make it function accordingly. It requires individual and team responsibility and team organization.

Coaches like this defense because with simple adjustments they can change to a sagging or pressing type game. It is because of these factors that high school coaches who have feeder systems are using it exclusively in some grade and junior high programs.

Diagram 9–2 shows you our basic man-to-man defense and the positions of each player. It would appear that we have more sagging off by defensive players than ever before in the game. This convergence of men around the basket is especially true of the college game, giving it the appearance of a zone defense.

We like to pressure the ball constantly, never letting the offensive man take his time in passing or shooting. This pressure may come at any point

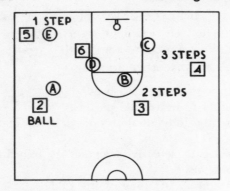

Diagram 9—2. Basic man-to-man defensive positions illustrating steps away from the ball and offensive men.

on the floor and it keeps the offense guessing. This is being done by (A) while (B) has dropped off two steps to the free-throw line. Action of this type makes the weak-side cut by the offensive forward nearly impossible.

The defensive forward (C) drops three steps off his man. His position is straddling the 12-foot lane. He is the last defender should anyone slip through the defense for a lay-up or short shot. Besides this, if the shot is taken, he is the rebounder and fills the triangle's right side.

The defensive center (D) plays on the side of the pivot man discouraging any passes being made to him. The defensive center should have his left arm out in front of the pivot man, ready to knock down any passes. His position also warrants attention. He should be playing his man so he can receive assistance from teammate (E) on feeds to the post. If he does not do this, the pivot man can maneuver to the ball easily.

The other defensive forward (E) is one step away from his offensive man, ready to anticipate a pass, either to his man or the pivot man. He has a difficult task at best so he should be your best anticipator of passes.

OTHER CONSIDERATIONS. Now that the positions have been explained we will add some of the duties the team must perform as a unit.

1. You must have vision on the ball at all times.
2. You should locate the ball without loss of time.
3. Communicate on defense. Let your teammate know what is going on.
4. Break up the dribble as it comes up off the floor.
5. Use the baseline as a helper. The defensive man can shuffle out-of-bounds in defending this area while the offense cannot touch the line.
6. Try to take away the offensive man's pet move by overplaying him.
7. Should you lose track of the ball, you should immediately retreat to the *line of the ball*. Hustle back, even with the ball, and you will be surprised at the number of errant passes you will pick up.
8. Discourage the "star" from getting the ball for any offensive move.
9. The man who has the ball should feel immediate pressure and his passing lanes cut by the other defensive men.
10. Balance, and the use of the slide step, is advised so that you can move quickly in any direction. Never cross your feet!

FORMATION OF A DEFENSE.   It is possible to be blown right off the court by a fast-break team if the defense is slow in returning.

This ability to change instantly from offense to defense is a pattern which must be acquired through drills. If players could have their way, they would rather take their time getting back on defense. With this in mind, the coach must convince them that they can save points by hustling back.

Several years ago, Northwestern had a great fast-breaking team with an excellent center who could get the ball to the outlet man quickly. If the Spartans were to stay in contention we had to get our players back from the offensive end in a hurry. Our practice sessions that week were of primary concern until we hit upon a drill which gave us everything we were looking for to defense the Wildcats. Diagram 9–3 illustrates the drill Coach Anderson found so effective and it still gets maximum work from all our squads.

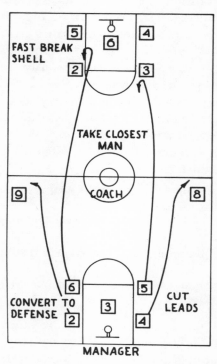

Diagram 9–3. Fast-break defensive drill from fast break shell to encourage offense to convert quickly to defense.

A team of five players is made to run their fast-break shell to the opposite end without a defense. The coach and two other players are positioned on the ten-second line. As the team scores, a manager grabs the ball as it comes out of the net, throws it to either the player (8) or (9) at mid-court or the coach. The offensive men must convert immediately and get back on defense, at the same time delaying the three offensive men who are attempting to get the ball downcourt for the easy shot.

The defense against the fast-break offense is not any different from the regular man-to-man defense. The first man downcourt takes a position around the free-throw line to stop any short shot. The second man goes deep to the basket to protect this area and we now have a tandem defense.

The other three men get back but one will normally pressure the ball to force a delay. Sometimes all three might deploy this tactic. In doing this, they play the man nearest them without regard for any specific defensive assignment.

UNDERSTANDING THE PRINCIPLES. The players must know and understand the defensive principles of forming a defense. No one can neglect his duty in this cause as you are only as strong as your weakest link.

The defense must have vision on the ball and should never run with their backs to it. They run back (not hustle), construct the defense from the basket out, and pressure the offense.

SWITCHING AND SCISSORING. In discussion of scissoring and the switch, it must be noted that both are closely related. Drills should be organized so that both can be practiced at the same time. The players can learn the drawbacks of each and appreciate them.

Offensive teams are attacking defenses more from weak-side plays than ever before. These two-man plays have options which encourage the switch by the defense. The offense then usually has a smaller man guarding a big man who receives the ball and attempts to maneuver against this little man. It is good offensive strategy and the defense must stop the move before it unfolds. We have devised the following rules relative to the switch. These clear-cut regulations give us a basis on which to operate.

1. Be conscious of screens at all times and never switch unless complete necessity demands it.
2. Use the terms "switch" and "switch back" as vocal signals when changing men.
3. The back man will call the switch, jump out, and immediately dominate the play.
4. The key to the switch is that there should be no question on the part of the defense as to who his man is.

The drill, which we think has helped our not having to switch so much in games, is the one in Diagram 9–4. To enact game conditions we put two offensive men against one defensive man and let them have complete freedom in what they can do. We call it "escaping the screen" drill.

The defensive man should break through the screen or learn to avoid it. Apparently some men have a knack for this while others need a great amount of work.

The point of emphasis we stress is that when a screener approaches the defensive man, he should *extend his arm toward the screener*. Almost every time this happens the screener will stop and this extra room will give him space to get through to go with the offensive man.

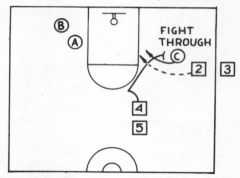

FIGHT THROUGH

Diagram 9–4. Escaping-the-screen drill. Two offensive men against one defensive man.

In scissoring, we want our back man to step back and let the man who is guarding the ball come through. If the man stops behind the screener then we go half-way on him. This means the man guarding him takes one side while the back man protects the other direction. As this occurs, they pinch the cut-away man so he cannot go to the basket.

We ask for help in a scissors situation by telling our teammate to push us through so we can cut off the offensive man. This is not a big shove, causing us to foul the offensive man, but a firm one. With proper drills it is possible to almost eliminate the switch in basketball defense but it is not easy. It cannot be learned in one year!

ZONE DEFENSES

As we organize offensively each year we are faced with many additional defenses, but one which sees more use than any other is the zone defense. It appears that there are as many zones and variations used as there are spectators in the stands.

Coaches have used the zone since the beginning of the game and despite its popularity, it is considered an outlaw. It has been long pointed out that you cannot win consistently, especially the big game, utilizing the zone. At this point, we would like to mention that Wittenberg University and Southwest Texas College have disproved this theory with national championships. Their exclusive use of the zone for an entire season, game after game, has hardly detracted from their success.

PURPOSE OF THE ZONE DEFENSE. Before attempting to place a defense into effect, the coach must give it close investigation. The aim of the zone defense is to concentrate five defensive players into a mass group, cutting down the number of percentage shots the offense can take. It delegates specific areas to be covered rather than assigning men and directs attention toward the ball.

The simplicity of the zone defense is easy to teach the players if they first have an individual defense background. This becomes an actuality when the zone is used with utmost teamwork. This includes mass movement together, assisting one another by talking, and general mental and physical readiness.

ADVANTAGES OF A ZONE. The banning of the use of the zone defense in the professional game is unique. It is the only basketball organization which has done this. It would be our guess that the zone will remain in college and high school games for many years. There are a number of reasons why it will continue, namely:

1. It is fine strategy in changing the tempo of the game. Coaches feel that by shifting from a man-to-man to a zone and then back to the man-to-man it might confuse the opponents.
2. The zone gives a team the better rebounding positions.
3. The zone is easier to fast break out of than any other defense.
4. The number of fouls committed in a zone are usually fewer than in other defenses.
5. A team which has poor outside shooting will find tough sledding against a zone.
6. The zone eliminates the hard driving, cutting and screening game.
7. It is used to advantage on small courts where the width is not regulation size.
8. This defense is the easiest to teach and is learned the most quickly by the players.
9. The zone is equipped to handle one offensive star as easily as any defense.
10. It increases anticipation of passes by players and encourages the interception.

The zone defense is generally accepted in high schools because coaches do not have time to instruct the players in other defenses with completeness. As coaches double-up in other sports it is conceivable that they may have to restrict their team to less than two or three weeks' practice, especially if they are connected with football. In this short time span, some players must shake off their football legs, and they will not have had time for exhaustive instruction and drill in a man-to-man defense.

DISADVANTAGES OF THE ZONE DEFENSE. The zone defense at Northern Michigan and Michigan State is used only as a surprise defense to upset our opponents, and never as the basic defense. The reasons for this include:

1. It offers an excuse for the defensive man, since there is no definite defensive assignment in the zone. It is easier for the players to blame each other for their mistakes.
2. We consistently run into excellent shooting teams who take advantage of the weaker areas.
3. Every team uses the overload principle, wherein the offensive men outnumber the defense and this usually gives them a high-percentage shot.
4. A definite screen can be set against the zone for the offense's better shooters.

5. The zone is never as effective on a regulation floor as on the smaller court.

6. One player not doing his job in the zone makes it susceptible to high-percentage shots.

7. The zone can be forced out of its defense, thus weakening it, by a delay game in the late stages of the game.

8. A passing team can penetrate a zone defense and can gain almost the exact kind of shot they want to take.

9. The zone has its players standing while the offense is usually in motion going to the offensive board after a shot attempt. Zones can be easily out-rebounded!

10. Player attitude in playing the zone must be measured by the coach and a selling job might be necessary.

TYPES OF ZONE DEFENSES

The types of zones we would like to discuss are those which are most commonly used. These are the 2-1-2, 2-3, 1-3-1, 3-2, box-and-one, and 1-2-2 zones. All are as effective as their personnel. The players must realize that as the offense passes the ball they must move in unison and protect another area. They should also adapt themselves to playing the ball and learning to play and cover two offensive men.

It would be impossible to cover in detail every ball situation in relation to the shift of the zone. The many variations and explanations would fill Lake Superior, so for this reason we will include only the basic set-ups.

2-1-2 ZONE. This is one of the most-used zone defenses in basketball. Its celebrated application is most popular in the high schools, although the colleges would not be too far behind in its usage.

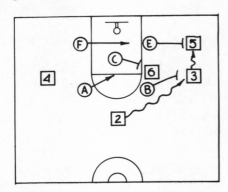

Diagram 9–5. Basic positions of 2-1-2 zone and in relation to the ball (5).

Diagram 9–5 shows you the basic positions of the 2-1-2 zone. Its strength lies in the middle where (C), (E), and (F) form a triangle which gives them an opportune rebounding position. It can also be used against a team that has a good pivot man who must be bottled up. Fast-break opportunities are also enhanced by use of this zone by player position and rebounding strength.

Its major weakness is against a good team which can shoot from the sides, since the zone is open to attack from this area. Depending upon your personnel these two sides of the zone can be handled. If you have two quick men, they can pressure and harass the side shooters into forcing their shots and this is all you can ask of them.

2-3 ZONE. Michigan State has made extensive use of this zone. The Spartans will use this as their basic zone but mainly only as an unexpected defense whereby they hope to surprise the offensive team.

The advantages of the 2-3 zone would be that it presents strong rebounding position, resulting in the cutting down of the number of rebounds the

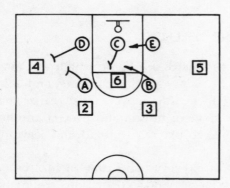

Diagram 9–6. The 2-3 zone and basic positions, with (4) having the ball.

offensive team hopes to get. It is operated very much like the 2-1-2 zone and can be most effective against a club with poor outside shooting.

The disadvantages would include a weakness against the good shooters from the side and middle. The offensive pivot man in the zone can score frequently from this spot while the side shooters can shoot easily from the short 17 area.

Diagram 9–6 illustrates positions of the 2-3 zone in relation to the ball.

1-3-1 ZONE. This is the second best zone defense in which to fast break from. The point man is in excellent position as is the second line of defense. It furnishes exceptional chance for the double-team, with the point man and wing man collaborating in this maneuver.

The 1-3-1 zone will be able to handle the strong pivot attack as well as any defense because of the three men in the second line of defense.

Weaknesses of this zone involve the rebounding positions of the players. They are more widespread than any other zone and jeopardize their strong rebound strength with its use. Another impotency of this zone is in the number of excellent shots you can get out of the corner and off the sides of the point man.

Diagram 9–7 shows you an example of this zone, with a shift being made to ball side and in the deep corner.

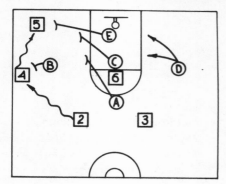

Diagram 9–7. 1-3-1 zone defense alignments with ball in forward position and in deep corner. Note defensive sag by (A) and (C).

3-2 ZONE. When a team has fine outside shooters who can constantly hit the jump shot from 15 to 18 feet, this zone can be a hindrance to their shooting ability. This is also the best zone to fast break from as all three lanes are automatically filled.

The personnel operating this type of zone must have two great rebounders who are agile and quick enough to cover a large area. Diagram 9–8 shows the movement of the zone to the corner.

From the diagram you can see the weakness of this zone. As it is set up mainly for the fast break with its three men up front, there is a definite loss of strength in the corners. Besides this, the middle of the zone is vulnerable to a roll situation by the offensive center. These two elements make the use of this zone infrequent as it does not give a team the necessary protection to stop the offense.

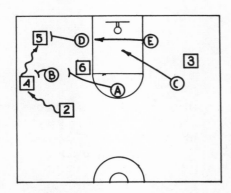

Diagram 9–8. 3-2 zone defense. Seldom used but still the best method of fast breaking from a zone.

1-2-2 ZONE. A team which has many good drivers is a threat to any man-to-man defense. The 1-2-2 zone was designed to levy a stopper to this offensive game (Diag. 9–9). It is durable around the basket and has excellent rebounding position which leads to splendid fast-break opportunities.

The side shots against this zone are very good ones although the side men can make this shot difficult through harassment. On occasion, the pivot area is weak when sharp, crisp passes are made by the offense.

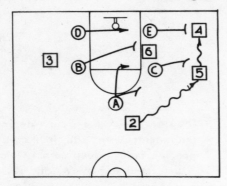

Diagram 9–9. 1-2-2 zone defense. Most popular in high schools. Gives good protection of scoring areas.

BOX-AND-ONE ZONE. This defense enjoys prominence when a team has a super scorer who does not get much assistance from his teammates. It is effective against a team such as this, which expects one man to carry the offensive brunt of their attack.

Diagram 9–10 positions the defense in a box formation along the twelve-foot lane, with one man playing the star a tight man-to-man everywhere he moves. This is an attempt to keep the ball from him, and even when the star does receive it, the harassment continues. If the star does get by his defensive man the other members of the zone are instructed to pick him up immediately.

Do not neglect the other four members of the zone. Insist that they carry out their responsibilities and understand them.

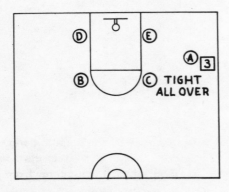

Diagram 9–10. Box-and-one zone defense. (A) is on the star (3) man-to-man, while (B), (C), and (D), and (E) play a zone.

ZONE DEFENSE WRAP-UP. In recent years we have heard the cry by some coaches to "ban the zone defense." We would like to go on record as stating that we are not in favor of legislating against the zone defense. It gives the coach who does not have the "horses" a chance against a team which has better personnel. It is a coach's prerogative to choose the defense which he feels is best suited for his players, and this includes one which he believes will win for him. We would hate to see the zone put out of the game because it belongs in basketball.

10

Pressing Defenses

The pressing defense is just beginning a new, long life in basketball. Although it has seen frequent use down through the years, its presence in the modern-day game is being emphasized more than ever before. It would be our prediction that we will see a greater accent on this defense than any other in years to come. If the defense has been well schooled individually, there is a strong likelihood that it can press effectively. Its increased use has brought many stunning victories and upsets.

Many of your most successful teams are pressing teams. West Virginia, Penn State, Arizona State, St. Louis University, West Virginia Tech, and Loyola University have reputations as pressing teams. These teams employ either the man-to-man or zone-press defense a major portion of the time. It sees so much application that their opponents sometimes believe that they start pressing from the locker-room door!

REASONS FOR THE PRESS. The technical aspect of coaching has augmented the offensive player in many ways. Through encouragement to practice and with more emphasis being placed on shooting, the player has a great advantage over the defense. To compensate for this, coaches have used the press to change the tempo of the game. They believe that through continued harassment this defense will not let the better shooters set. By doing this, the pressing team hopes to reduce the shooters' point production.

The fine screening offenses the game has produced are another reason for the press defense. When given time to set up, the offense of these teams can riddle a defensive club. The press will prevent this by speeding up play and placing pressure on the offense, forcing hurried passes from the poorer ball handlers.

The press fits into the coach's plan when he does not have tall team members. A team which is short and fast can press an opponent and completely alter their offensive play. They can force the better team into bad passes, violations, and hurried shots. This causes total disorganization and multiplies the pressing team's chances of pulling an upset.

Total player development is advanced by the pressing defense. It takes a fine defensive player to perform in this type of defense. A weak player is quickly noticed and can be singled out by the offense. The pressing player must react to ever-changing situations. Other defenses do not warrant these tactics, thus curtailing the individual player in other similar situations.

ADVANTAGES OF THE PRESS. The most significant aspect of the press is in the number of points which can be scored by its effective use. To better illustrate my point, Bradley University in the NIT several years ago pressed their opponent the entire second half of the game, while scoring 72 points. It was an unbelievable sight, as the Braves rolled up 116 points for an NIT record. This is, of course, the exception rather than the rule but the explosiveness of the press cannot be underestimated.

Other advantages would include that it produces:

1. A fine defense against slower opponents.
2. A surprise for opponents who are inexperienced and poor ball handlers.
3. Excellently conditioned teams.
4. Tough defense for pattern teams.
5. Aggressive defense which tends to tire the offense.
6. Easy baskets which demoralize the opponents.
7. Disorganization if the opponents are not properly prepared for the press.
8. Last-ditch effort if your team is behind in the game.
9. All-out effort by the defensive men. They cannot loaf.
10. A psychological advantage for the defense. Players fear being pressed.
11. Enlivened spectator interest.

DISADVANTAGES OF THE PRESS. This defense is demanding and requires individual and team speed. Without speed, a team will not be a serious threat as a pressing club. You will never see a good press without good speed! Speed is the first requirement.

The press finds it essential to take numerous chances in order to get the ball. A team with panic-proof ball handlers can hurt the pressing defense.

Some coaches neglect teaching the individual defensive responsibilities of the player and by doing this, cheat themselves of having a pressing defense. The press is predicated upon defensive footwork and it is more a necessity in this defense than in any other.

Fouls present an enigma for the defense. The pressing team normally will foul more because of this aggressive style of play. For this reason, they must rely upon more men than the ordinary six or seven. This also means that players must spend more time learning this defense and its basic uses. Some coaches insist that a press cannot be taught without benefit of at least four weeks' practice.

Quick, accurate passes coupled with baskets will shake any defensive press, with the players beginning to "psych" themselves out. More important, though, is that it generates optimism on the part of the offense by beating the press.

TIMES TO USE THE PRESS. Most pressing defenses are put into effect after a point has been scored. This may come after a field goal or free throw. Another time would be after your team has lost the ball through a violation or an interception. The pressing team must be trained for each of these situations if it is to meet with success using this defense.

PLAYER REQUIREMENTS. The pressing team counts on every individual. To be effective, a press must be a five-man operation; if one man lets up, its purpose is ineffective.

The player must realize that the press is a gamble and that cheap baskets by the opponents will result on occasion. He should expect to yield one now and then. The player must also be "sold" on the fact that the offensive shooter will take hurried and forced shots resulting from the pressure. He will even miss the unmolested 5-to-15 footer because of this type of defense. The mental attitude with which your team meets the press will bear importantly upon its effectiveness. If the team is not ready to press, this defense will not resemble one which is aggressive, high scoring, and harassing.

Often the offense will stop and set up, even after penetrating the press. When this occurs, the defense has an opportunity to reorganize. Of even greater significance is the fact that the offense has not even tried to score but has expressed satisfaction in just getting the ball safely into the front court.

Finally, the press emphasizes unity. The five players on the floor must understand the principles of the press, be able to adapt without delay to various situations, and carry out the delegation of responsibility as a team.

TYPES OF PRESSES. Basically, there are two types of presses: the man-to-man and the zone-press, both having become important factors in our high schools and colleges throughout the country.

The man-to-man press ordinarily commences when the defensive men pick up the offensive guards inside the free-throw line. The zone-press can be slapped on at full-court, at three-quarters court, or at half-court. It is the more versatile of the two, and is the most popular.

Since every press is in some way connected with the man-to-man, we will cover it before the zone presses.

NORTHERN MICHIGAN MAN-TO-MAN PRESS. Before we attempt to instruct the press, we have three teaching stations in which we give our players a thorough indoctrination of their assignments and responsibilities. This includes a briefing on the blackboard, walking through on the floor in various situations which the defense might expect and, finally, the actual running of an offense against the press. We insist that our man-to-man be played aggressively. The day of the passive defense is gone forever.

The distribution of player responsibility is made by the coach. He makes the assignment of defensive men according to the offensive team but one point should be remembered by all squad members—*try to stop your man from getting the ball.* This is attempted on the in-bounds pass but if unsuccessful we do not concede until we have gained possession. We know that we will have extreme difficulty in accomplishing this feat but we want this pressure on both our players and opponents. In this way, they cannot relax and will know we do not tolerate such a party in the press. They are expected to run and press, then run and press some more. If they are not dedicated to this idea and style of game, it will meet with little if any success.

In Diagrams 10–1a and 10–1b you will see a breakdown of our drills, showing how we pursue the man-to-man press. Again, we start with the player in a single situation because this is the maneuver in which it must be played.

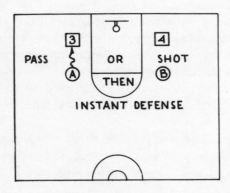

Diagram 10–1a. Northern Michigan man-to-man press drill.

Our first drill can start with the defensive man (A) passing to the guard (3) and then attempting to stop him from bringing the ball upcourt. If the offensive man can bring the ball to mid-court, he gets a point. They then change positions and the same drill is started over at the mid-court line. The first player to score ten points is the winner.

Another method of conducting the drill can be seen. (B) can try a field-goal attempt with (4) rebounding the ball and bringing it up, while the defense plays tough and aggressive. The scoring method is the same in this game, with winners meeting to determine a champion.

This drill has more merit than the obvious conditioning involved. It develops the footwork ability of the defensive player with the sudden re-actions to changes by the offensive man which it demands, and it behooves the coach to constantly check the position of the defense, as this is the key to success for this defense. We want the players to gamble for the interceptions and steals, anticipating the offensive moves. The more situations we can present in practice, the better prepared our press will be.

While our defensive ability is of major magnitude in this drill, we have found that it is also an asset to our ball handlers in facing the opponent's press. They have more confidence in their ability after continued drill against this pressure defense and do not fear its ingredients.

Our second drill is the three-versus-three drill with three offensive and three defensive men. The action commences with (A) throwing the ball to

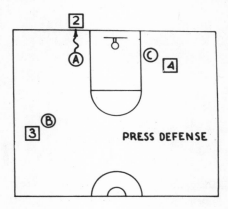

PRESS DEFENSE

Diagram 10–1b. Northern Michigan three-versus-three man-to-man press drill up to half-court.

(2) out-of-bounds. The other offensive men can move to any area they wish but the defense must over-play them to the ball side. We want the man guarding the out-of-bounds man to be as close as the official will permit with hands extended trying to deflect the ball. This is all we ask for; if it is deflected we then have an excellent chance of getting it.

As we have the reputation of a pressing team, our opponents like to throw the ball in quickly before we convert from offense to defense in order to beat our front line of defense. To avert such a situation we assign one of our players to the man out-of-bounds and it is his duty to prevent the quick pass in-bounds. On occasion, and after scouting an opponent, we let the man throw the ball in, but only to a certain offensive player. This man is usually the poorest ball handler of the opposition and we encourage this man to dribble or pass, hoping to force him into a mistake.

Our other defensive men are positioned in front of the offensive men (Diags. 10–2a and 10–2b) which affords them a better chance of intercepting the first pass when it is made. We have done some experimenting with our front-court defensive men recently and have had them guard their offensive men with their backs to the ball. This is not a new method but one which you seldom see employed.

Our players were able to stay with their men better, since they did not concentrate on the ball, and when a lob pass was thrown they threw their arms up to deflect the ball. As yet, we have never used it in a game, but this could be the next step in our pressing defenses.

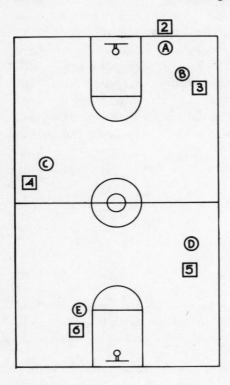

Diagram 10—2a. Man-to-man press positions with defensive men fronting every offensive man.

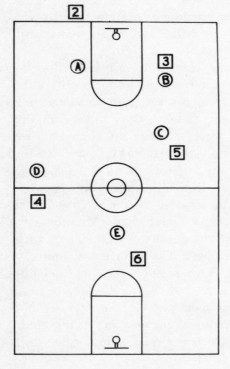

Diagram 10—2b. Man-to-man press with (A) ready to double-team on first pass in. Other defensive men front their opponents.

If an offensive player passes and breaks past our front line of defense for a return pass, he must be picked up immediately by the second line of defense. Should he have the ball, he must be stopped! This obstacle is ever-present in this defense and adjustments by the second-line anticipators will determine to a great extent whether or not you gain possession of the ball.

The back man in your press is burdened with two chores. First, his conversion from offense to defense must be cat-like. He cannot tarry in getting back because a long pass will net an easy basket. Second, he must zone his area to prevent the lay-up shot; but more important, he must play the ball side in anticipation of a possible pass interception.

Another point of the man-to-man press is that all defensive men should converge upon the middle when a deflection is made. This has enabled us to pick up more than our share of loose balls.

Finally, whenever the offense crosses we automatically jump out for the switch and double-team possibility. We play the ball tight and tell the defensive men to raise their hands high to knock down the pass. Rarely do you see a player throw a bounce pass when bottled up by the defense. It is a lob pass in most instances. *We do not want the foul.* In all double-team situations we never go after the ball but trust that the offensive man will panic because of increased pressure.

In explanation of the press, we have broken down the basketball court into four different areas (Diag. 10–3). It has four lines of defense which

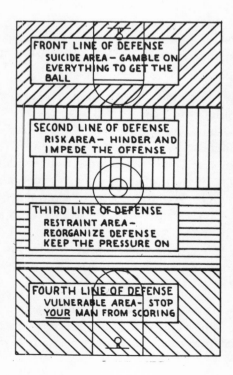

Diagram 10–3. Four areas of the defensive pressing attack.

we feel the defensive team must be informed of and know the rules which govern each. This division of the court tells our players where they are on the floor and the defense they should be playing. In the first three zones they can make mistakes and still retain their assignments. However, the fourth area is the most detrimental to a team and extra caution is needed here. All players should realize this fact and refrain from errors in this section.

MICHIGAN STATE PINCH-PRESS. A zone press for which the Spartans have been known and respected is their pinch-press. It is based on 2-2-1 alignment, with each individual responsible for both an offensive player and an area. As we have explained the theory of the press and why and when it is used, let us now explain the rules of this particular zone press. Diags. 10–4 to 10–12 show an entire sequence of the responsibilities of each man and the complete pinch-press in various strategic play situations.

1. We concede the first pass in to the offensive man. Seldom do we alter this rule unless the game plan calls for a change.
2. We make the offense commit themselves first by encouraging the dribble. We seldom rush the first man until he has done something with the ball.
3. We will always switch in the front line defense on any moves by the offensive men.
4. The side men and center should play their positions.
5. We want all defensive men to force the man with the ball into the middle for a possible double-team situation. *Never do we want the offense to go down the sideline.*
6. As the front-line men make their attack, the second line takes on a zone responsibility, looking for a long or lob pass.
7. Once the ball penetrates into the front court we return to a normal defense.

BASIC POSITIONS. The positions of the defense can be seen in Diagram 10–4. The front-line defensive men usually are the guards who are fast in general but especially quicker with their hands and feet. They are referred to as the left and right front men.

The second line consists of the forwards, called left and right middle men, and their proper place is three feet in front of their offensive men and watching the ball first, their man second. We attempt to discourage the sideline pass upcourt in this manner. At the same time, we invite the man out-of-bounds to throw the long pass over our head.

The center is our back man on the pinch-press and he must really hustle when getting back on defense. He should play in front of his man and just back of the center jump circle facing the ball.

PINCHING THE BALL. Diagram 10–5 shows the first pass being made and the immediate rush after the dribble. The right front man is one full step *outside* of the offensive man (3), which prevents him from going down the

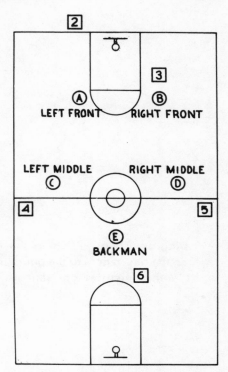

Diagram 10–4. Basic positions of Michigan State pinch press.

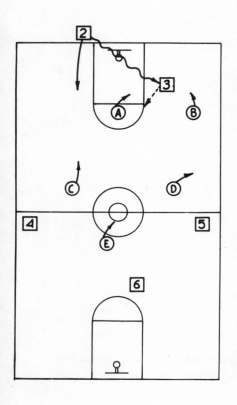

Diagram 10–5. Pinching the ball after first pass inbounds.

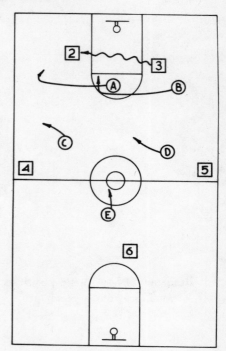

Diagram 10–6. Pinching the ball on the return pass to the guard, and the defensive adjustments.

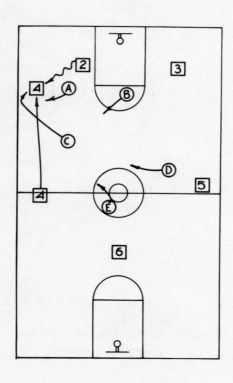

Diagram 10–7. Pinching the ball on the sideline pass to the forward.

sideline. We advise this player to make the man with the ball go to the middle by maintenance of this position. The left front man then "cheats" toward the man receiving the ball.

The second line adjusts to the ball. The right middle man moves to the ball side position to prevent a pass to the offensive man (5). The left middle man moves up expecting a pass to be made to (2) or his own man (4). The back man has the zone responsibility but he moves to the same side the ball is on.

RETURN PASS TO GUARD. In order to give you a complete picture of the pinch-press we have now passed the ball back to the other guard (2) (Diag. 10–6). This is a common maneuver in order to further study the defense and it calls for a quick adjustment to stop this man from passing or dribbling past our front line of defense.

We inform the players that they should disregard their position completely, but they must make (2) consummate his dribble. As we move our front line laterally, it is now the left front man's assignment to protect the outside and force (2) into the pinch.

In pinching the ball, we never attempt the outright steal. This leads to fouling which we want to avoid. We insist that the boys never leave their feet until they see the ball leave the passer's hand. We never encourage contact, but we do demand compelling attention to the hands and arms. Those body parts are to be extended over the head so a high lob, or any other desperate pass, will result.

The second line of defense swings over to ball side. The left middle man plays the path of the pass to (4) to stop this move. The right middle man supports the middle of the court and is ready to pick off any cross-court pass which might be made to (5). Another interception possibility exists should (2) decide to throw back to (3), so the right middle man should be looking for this. The back man again zones his area but returns to ball side looking for any long pass.

SIDELINE PASS TO FORWARD. Let us watch the operation of the press when the pass has been successful to (4). Diagram 10–7 tells you the left middle man in the second line moves quickly to stop the dribble down the sideline. Again, he protects the outside, forcing (4) into a pinch with the left front man who comes up fast from his position.

The right front man moves to the line of the ball, looking for a cross-court pass to (3) or (2), and is prepared to pick up any deflections. The right middle man swings over toward the ball and protects the middle of the court against any men penetrating the area or any passes made into this position.

The back man who is in the center jump circle moves to the ball side and should be expecting a long pass to (6).

CENTER BREAKING UP MIDDLE. This is the most frequent method of breaking up the pinch-pass and it calls for constant practice by the defense. We practice hard to bring this situation under control and have settled for what you see in Diagram 10–8.

With (2) in possession, the offensive center (6) comes high and receives the pass beyond the center jump circle. When this happens, our back man goes up with him and, because of his advanced position, should be able to contest this move. The front men *retreat to the line of the ball* as the right front man pinches with the back man on the ball. The left front man plays between the ball and (4) awaiting a possible pass from the offensive center.

The middle men have a tough job in this situation as the left middle man must retreat a couple of steps back to stop a quick break by (4). The right front man is faced with the same problem and should be ready to fall back or pick off a pass to (3) if it is passed by the center (6).

Should the offensive team hurt us with this play, we have an alternate plan in which the center does not go downcourt with the offensive center. He zones his area just behind the center circle and the pinch is applied by both front men. This gives you better coverage and cuts down the risk involved. The middle men can play their side men or gamble on an interception, with the right middle man having the better opportunity.

DIRECT PASS UP-COURT TO FORWARD. This pass should not be made if the left middle man is carrying out his assignment (Diag. 10–9). However, should it be completed, the defensive man must get to the outside and force the offensive player (4) to the inside of the court. He will get assistance for the pinch from the left front man, who hurries into position. We tell everyone to *retreat to the line of the ball,* which is a fine teaching point for all presses—especially the two front lines.

The right front man hustles back toward the middle and establishes his position for playing the ball. The right middle man shades to the middle and protects against a pass to (5) or plays any cutters in this section. The back man watches for a long pass to (6) and moves to ball side.

DIAGONAL CUT BY FORWARD. This play is recognized as a leader in helping the offense bring the ball upcourt against the zone press. It never ceases to give our team a problem and has caused us trouble. Learning from this situation, we now attack the offense as shown in Diagram 10–10.

The ball is in-bounded by (3) to the other offensive guard (2) and after he commits himself, the pinch is made by the front men. In spite of their efforts, a pass is made to (5) breaking diagonally toward the ball. This sets up a chain reaction by the defense with the right front man rushing the man with the ball. He is helped with the pinch by the middle man on the right side. This defensive player must also be ready to release from the pinch and move across to intercept (3) if he receives a return pass from (5).

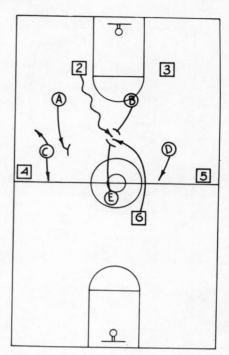

Diagram 10–8. Pinching the ball as the center (6) breaks up the middle to receive the pass.

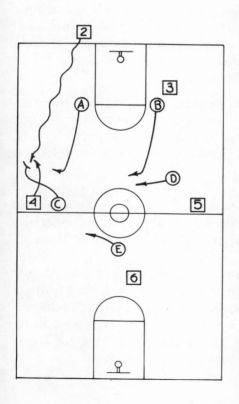

Diagram 10–9. Pinching the direct pass up-court to the forward, and the other defensive reactions.

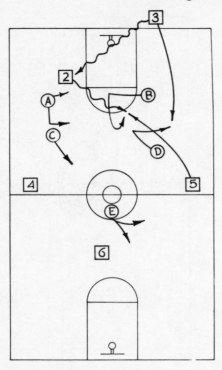

Diagram 10–10. Pinching and combatting the offensive diagonal cut by the forward (5).

The left middle man proceeds to protect the middle and left side against a pass to (4) while the left front man *retreats to the line of the ball* and advances cautiously. The next move of the offense might be a pass back to (2) which the left front man must counter. The back man always moves ball side while zoning the area against long passes.

CENTER TO GUARD COMBINATION. With many teams utilizing the center on the press offense, we have been confronted at times with two quick passes, with the center hitting the guard coming in from out-of-bounds. This maneuver has caused confusion on the defense's part as to individual responsibility.

To clear up this situation, Diagram 10–11 indicates our adaptability to this play. If our personnel is such that our center can move, we have him play the offensive center when he breaks downcourt. This is especially true if our opponents establish a pattern of passing to the center breaking down the middle.

As the pass is made in to (2), he throws a quick pass to (6) before the pinch is applied by the front men. We then regroup immediately for a second pinch as the center handles the ball, with both front men administering the pressure. As the second pinch is made, the back man slides off to pick up the guard (3) who is moving up the sideline looking for a pass from (6).

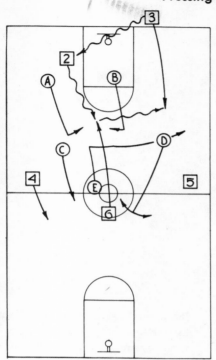

Diagram 10–11. Pinching the ball as the center (6) makes the pass to the guard (3) flying down-court.

The two middle men must protect the backcourt and they fall back with one exception. We frequently let the middle man on the ball side free-lance his area as he can force a pinch in case (3) does receive the ball. In this case, our left middle man has deep responsibility and quickly assumes this position.

GUARD DRIBBLING UP SIDELINE. Spending much time in protecting the outside is essential in this defense but sometimes an offensive player will dribble by the front line. This constitutes a danger to our operation and we attempt to stop him as Diagram 10–12 shows.

The guard (3) has dribbled by our right front man and is headed up-court. When this happens, the front man quickly follows the dribbler and assists in pinching the man with the aid of the right middle man. We tell our middle man to run directly at the dribbler, as he must stop him. This action usually has turned the trick for us and the delay gives the front man an opportunity to catch up for the pinch.

At best, our right middle man is in an awkward position. First, he must stop the dribbler; and should a pass be made to (5) he must drop off and cover it.

The left front man moves back to the line of the ball and looks for any cutter or pass which he might pick off. The left middle man must assume deep responsibility should our back man gamble on picking off a pass to (5)

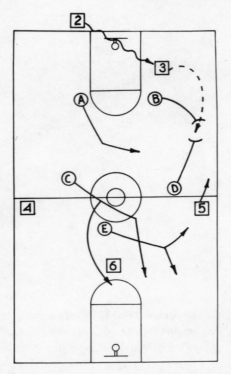

Diagram 10–12. Pinching the ball as the guard (3) dribbles up the sideline, and other defensive adjustments as this happens.

and he normally would tend to retreat, although his vision will tell him what to do.

This has been an attempt by the co-authors to explain in detail our philosophy, rules, player requirement, and coordinated moves in the type of presses we employ. It is not our idea to "sell" you a particular press, but just to give you our opinion on the treatment of two presses.

AUXILIARY ZONE PRESSES

The term "zone press" does not imply one particular press, but rather many types with numerous variations. Coaches have special likes and dislikes concerning the type of zone press they use so we would like to familiarize the readers with other types being used. The main reason for engaging in other presses is simply to make the offense modify and adjust to your defense. We never stay in one press defense, as the offense soon will establish a definite pattern against it.

1-3-1 ZONE PRESS. This press can be sprung on the offense from either a full-court or three-quarter-court position. We will cover the full-court press, as it can be applicable to the other without many adjustments.

We might say that this press is not designed for the gamble. Rather, it is played for pressure purposes in the hope of forcing the offense to com-

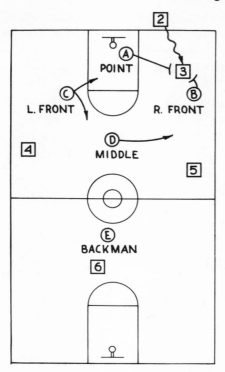

Diagram 10–13. 1-3-1 full court zone press and double-team situation on (3), with other defensive changes.

mit mistakes such as traveling, bad passes, and mental errors—which in turn cause frustration.

Another element in favor of this zone press is that you have better defensive coverage distributed over the court. While you see a lay-up scored on many of the zone presses, it is a rarity when one is scored on this defense. The player requirements are identical with our 2-2-1 pinch press, as are the rules. This has simplified our press defensive code to the point that we are doing the same thing regularly, rather than learning a new code for each press defense. Our nomenclature also remains the same.

In experimenting with this press, we have attempted two different ideas. As you can see in Diagram 10–13, our "point man" plays toward the middle of the court to prevent a close pass in this area. At other times, he may guard the man out-of-bounds. By doing this, he also compels the offense to throw a sideline pass which is favorable for a double-team with one of the front men. Incidentally, these three men up front should be your quickest, while the middle man should be your best anticipator and your back man a solid thinker with good basketball sense.

In our illustration, note the point man encouraging the pass to (3) by his position. If the pass is made to (3), the point men and the right front man pinch the ball quickly, observing all rules relative to pressuring the man with the ball. It is important that he be hurried in order to force a lob pass or another error.

As this action starts, the middle man should move ball side and cover (5) while the left front man slides back to prevent (4) from receiving the ball. This man also must be alert for a return pass to (2), in which case, he also must cover him. Meanwhile, the back man guards against the long pass and zones his area.

It is infrequent when we gamble with this press, and yet, we do not yield to the offense without their being worried by repeated defensive attacks. It can easily be converted into a hazardous press involving risk in securing the ball, so you can see its versatility as a change-of-pace defense.

Diagram 10–14. Three-quarter zone press defense and basic positions, with personnel qualifications.

This zone press can be moved back, as Diagram 10–14 indicates, to give you a three-quarter defense which can be very tough for an offense to crack if they are caught offguard by its use. The same principles and rules govern this press as were given in the full-court defense. The point man can push the dribbler into a side man by actually going behind him and eliminating any other route except this one. This provides an excellent double-team possibility, with the other defensive members adjusting to the ball, and is another advantage of this defense.

THE TRAP PRESS. A team is usually behind in the game when using this type of press. It gives the defense an organized scheme for stealing the ball through group cooperation rather than dependence upon individual abilities as in a tight, man-to-man defense. Its results are far better and more productive than the man-to-man or any defense at this stage of the game. When you are on the "short end" of the score in the closing minutes, this press may be able to "bail you out" of trouble.

It is primarily a short-term press and relies on panic by the opponents in this time span. We do not advise it for continued use throughout the game as it can be solved by the offense. But for brief periods it is excellent.

Diagram 10–15 gives you a conception of this defense and how it works.

The offensive guards are permitted to bring the ball over the ten-second line without pressure. This we do to lull them into a feeling of security so we can then jump them.

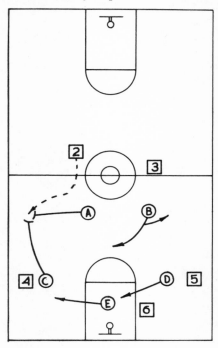

Diagram 10–15. The trap-press operation after the ball is over the mid-court line.

Our left front man waits until (2) has dribbled toward the sideline and then he really pushes him hard into this direction. As this happens, the left middle man times his move with the front man and they pinch (2) on the sideline. By forcing the offensive man to the sideline, he does not have good passing lanes to his teammates and is under direct pressure by the double team. The defensive men keep their hands over their heads, hoping to deflect a possible pass.

We have found through experience that when an offensive man is forced to pass under pressure it is usually to the same side as he is on. Knowing this, we send our back man (who is cheating to ball side) to cover (4). This is the pass we intercept more than any other.

Our right front man drops back to protect the middle but he also must be ready to anticipate a pass back to (3). The right middle man loosens up considerably, and seeing the back man release to play the sideline pass, he assumes the deep responsibility.

On any cross-court passes by the offense, we try to have a pressing man between the ball and playing a possible passing lane. Our right front man is doing this should a pass be attempted from (2) to (5).

Although there are many variations of this zone press, those presented are typical of this defense. They are most advantageous to a team with adequate personnel when utilized and employed frequently and provide basketball with a great "come from behind" device to make the game even more interesting.

11

The High School
Feeder System

As this book is primarily concerned with building better basketball, we would be remiss if we did not talk about the feeder system, which is so important to the coach of basketball. It is a well-known fact that the high school coach depends upon the grade school system to produce his future teams and that the high school coach in turn supplies the college coaches with an abundance of material. The chain continues as the colleges furnish the professional ranks.

One of the best feeder systems in Michigan exists at Escanaba High School. Coach Harold Johnson has described for us how his program functions, and we are indebted to him for his willingness to help the coaching profession with this information.

All coaches with experience know that material comes in cycles. In the small school, the cycle is longer than in the larger schools. Yet, whether small or large and despite such seemingly unavoidable circumstances, some schools continuously dominate league and tournament play while others come into the limelight only as the cycle dictates.

Recognizing the fact that the cycle exists the coach can choose either of two possibilities. One is to trust to luck and be satisfied with an occasional winner. The second is to devise some means of making the "lean years" more productive.

The good businessman will readily admit that the workers who come to him well trained in their task will increase efficiency and production. The high school coach who wishes to have continuous top-notch teams must be a good "businessman."

The best means of increased production in high school basketball is a well-planned, smoothly functioning feeder system, in which basketball players begin learning their lessons in their grade school years.

Before going any farther, the staff at Escanaba High School would like to make it clear that they do not believe winning is everything. They do believe, however, that the game of basketball was, at least in part, designed to be played for fun and that the greatest enjoyment is derived from winning.

Escanaba High School basketball teams have met with fine success during the past years and the boys making up their teams have been excellent players with a sincere desire to excel. The coaches did not acquire these outstanding young men by a sheer stroke of fate. They have been the early products of a feeder system begun six years ago and designed to keep a steady flow of players coming up to the varsity team with the same background and training in their pattern of play.

Their system is neither unique nor fool-proof. Changes and improvements are constantly being made as years pass. The system is designed to fit their particular situation at Escanaba although certainly it could be used, with some modification, in any school regardless of size and location.

Escanaba is a city of 16,000 population containing two Class "B" high schools. Escanaba Senior High School must share many of the city's athletes with Holy Name High School. The elementary and junior high school system is divided into five public and four parochial schools.

The basic difference between the public and parochial system is that the public school system contains a larger junior high school, which consists of seventh, eighth, and ninth grade students. It must be pointed out, however, that some public school students, upon leaving the ninth grade, transfer to Holy Name. The two-school factor is mentioned merely to indicate a problem which required some thought in designing their feeder system.

Working under the theory that "champions are made, not born" has led them to select their boys rather carefully and to prepare them mentally and physically for the tough high school competition they will face.

Each of the five elementary schools has a coach who along with his regular classroom duties also coaches basketball, touch football, and track. These men are not all qualified, well-trained basketball coaches but they do have some fundamental knowledge of the game and enjoy working with boys.

Several meetings are arranged during the season to discuss any problems and necessary changes which they feel will benefit the total program. For example, they are currently considering a suggestion that baskets in the elementary gymnasiums be lowered to the nine-foot height and that a smaller ball be used. They also will help each other by making suggestions and offering constructive criticism.

The first meeting is held two weeks prior to the first scheduled practice session at which time schedules of games, practices, equipment, and what they would like done are gone over thoroughly. Such a planning session is vitally important in order to avoid any haphazardness or misunderstandings. A coach with a plan will do a better job.

On the elementary level they encourage coaches to maintain as large a squad or group of boys as is possible to work with satisfactorily. This is done because they feel it is difficult or virtually impossible to foresee which boys will develop into good basketball players at that age. A second purpose is to keep a large number of boys interested and give many, rather than a few, the opportunity to enjoy the game of basketball.

We might add that they do not attempt to avoid competition in their elementary schools although coaches are told to substitute players freely in order to give all boys a chance to play, even at the possible cost of victory.

During the past two seasons they have had their elementary teams play the preliminary-to-varsity contests to give these youngsters the thrill of playing before a crowd. Great enthusiasm for these preliminaries exists in all the schools.

In looking for high school varsity prospects, the elementary coach usually judges his players by the following checklist:

1. Coordination
2. Attitude
3. Interest
4. Does he accept instruction?
5. Social adjustment
6. Academic background
7. Home background
8. Natural ability
9. Rate of improvement

Their junior high school program is more selective than the elementary program. More extensive training and larger schedules exist here. They have seventh, eighth, and ninth grade teams coached by men who have background and training in basketball.

Each team plays a full interscholastic schedule of games with schools of Escanaba Junior High School's size. Approximately half of the games are played away from home to acquaint players with the problems of playing on different courts and before rival crowds.

Close cooperation between junior high, junior varsity, and varsity coaches is again a distinct necessity. In pre-season meetings, coaches are given a standardized course of instruction designed to acquaint players with the proper method of doing fundamentals and with the various drills that are used by the varsity.

Offensive and defensive patterns are presented only after considerable time has been spent on individual fundamentals. One-on-one, -two, and

BASKETBALL PERSONNEL RECORD

Name _____ Birth Date _____

Height _____ Weight _____ I. Q. _____

Grade School _____ Coach _____

Other Sports Played _____

Parent, Guardian _____ Ht. _____ Wt. _____

Residence _____ Phone _____

Occupation _____ Religion _____

Remarks (6th Grade Coach) _____

_____

_____

_____

_____

_____

_____

_____

Fig. 11–1 (View 1). Basketball Feeder System File Card.

-three man drills are used to stress proper techniques before going into team drills.

All of their teams are well dressed in an effort to create a feeling of pride. Their school budget provides for the purpose of needed equipment, transportation, and meals which are sometimes required when playing away from home.

A recognition banquet, to which parents are invited, is held each year and awards, in the form of certificates, are presented to team members at a special school program after the season ends.

Coaches are asked to look for players who have an ability to remember and carry out assignments. Natural ability, coordination, home background, and scholastic record are the major factors considered. Charts are kept on shooting and on the progress of height and weight for each boy during the course of the season.

Figure 11–1 is a sample of the cumulative card which is used in Escanaba. This card is started on the boy during the sixth grade. All records are strictly confidential and are passed on from coach to coach until they reach the varsity file. The coaches have found them to be exceptionally valuable during the player's school years and as a permanent record after the boy graduates.

The feeder system in smaller schools must be built on a more restricted basis, but certainly no school is too small for an intelligent system of player selection and instruction.

An intramural program is often a valuable aid in discovering players.

7th	8th	9th
I. Q. _____	I. Q. _____	I. Q. _____
Nov. Ht.___Wt.___	Nov. Ht.___Wt.___	Nov. Ht.___Wt.___
Mar. Ht.___Wt.___	Mar. Ht.___Wt.___	Mar. Ht.___Wt.___
Weak Points	Weak Points	Weak Points
Strong Points	Strong Points	Strong Points
Remarks	Remarks	Remarks

Fig. 11–1 (View 2). Basketball Feeder System File Card.

If coaching help is not available it is sometimes possible that someone in the community—a former player, perhaps—will lend assistance if asked.

The test of a feeder system is in the won-lost record of the high school team toward which the system channels its material. Only time will tell how good the plan in Escanaba really is. They are convinced, however, that their system has already paid off in some additional victories.

A good feeder system is not developed overnight. They have made some necessary changes each year and anticipate that this will be a continuous process. The feeder system is certainly not an end in itself but rather is one significant means toward the ultimate end—which is more victories!

12

Improving the Coach's Image

This chapter is concerned with the small details which the coach can take care of to improve the atmosphere of his position outside of the gymnasium. His immediate concern should be his team, but the duties of a coach extend beyond this. The time a coach spends in the office today is just as important as the time spent on the practice floor. Answering mail and telephone calls, attending clinics, and other incidentals must be carried out promptly and efficiently to maintain the coaching image which we desire. In accordance with this image, here are a few ideas which have crossed our desk as ways to improve your stature.

LETTERS TO WRITE

COACH'S LETTER TO FANS. One method of keeping closer contact with season ticket holders, other loyal fans, and prospective followers is through the use of a personal letter. The following could be used as an example:

Dear Fan:

This letter is written to let you know how much I appreciated your support during the past basketball season. Your having faith in what we are trying to do, in no small part, helped us attain any success which we had.

Now another year is coming up and it should be an interesting one. Although we are losing such valuable players as Eddie Jones, Harv Smith, and Jon Kent, we do have Gary Stephen, Roger Kirt, George Rogers, John Doe, and others back to form the nucleus for this year's basketball edition.

Enclosed is a copy of our schedule for the coming season, and you will notice that it is unique in several ways. First, we are having a Christmas Tournament on December 28 and 29 with four power-packed teams which will be the highlight of our non-conference schedule. Second, we have scheduled our first six games at home, which will permit our students to see us in action before the final examination period. Third, our conference schedule will start January 4 with 12 games being played against all of our old rivals. This is what we look forward to, and trust we will be able to advance in the conference standings this year.

So the potential outlook *can* be very good depending upon our getting our share of the breaks. Along with this we must have hard work, effort, and sacrifices on the part of everyone to carry out our plans.

We are conducting a coaching clinic for Michigan high-school coaches and other coaches on November 18 and 19. At this clinic we will explain, demonstrate, and execute our theories of the fundamentals of basketball using the varsity and freshmen teams for demonstration purposes.

The morning of the nineteenth at ten o'clock we will have an intra-squad game. This naturally will be observed by the coaches specifically, but it is open to the public free of charge. You are cordially invited to see this game as sort of a "sneak preview" of what we have to offer for the season.

Once again, my sincere thanks for the splendid support which you have given us and I hope to be seeing you again this year. Our aim is to give the school, community, and our fans a very good basketball season.

Sincerely yours,

Basketball Coach

COURTESY LETTER TO OPPOSING COACH. Such a letter, giving details of the upcoming game, is a small favor coaches do to further and foster relations between coaches and schools. Here is an example:

Dear Coach:

I most certainly hope your visit to East Lansing will be a pleasant one for you and your team as we are looking forward to seeing you.

The game will start at 8:00 P.M. and you may have the floor for practice at 7:30 P.M., with six regulation basketballs (Spalding "Lastbilt") available for you. One of our managers will be at your disposal during the game for anything you may need.

We would appreciate your letting us know how you are arriving in East Lansing so that we can make arrangements to meet you properly. We would also like to know at which hotel you are staying.

Statistics charts will be ready for both halves of the games. If you desire, there will be a copy for the first half before you go to the dressing room. Both copies will be available after the game for you.

Since the fieldhouse schedule is sometimes rather full, we would appreciate it if you would notify us if you wish to work out the day before the game or the morning of the contest. We will do the best we can to accommodate you.

If there is anything more we can do from this end, please let us know at your earliest convenience.

Sincerely yours,

Basketball Coach

COURTESY LETTER TO OPPOSING MANAGER. Just as important as the coach's courtesy letter is one to the opposing manager from your head manager. One of the bigger jobs connected with basketball belongs to the managers, and these unsung heroes never receive the recognition due them. Such a letter might be as follows:

Basketball Manager
Basketball Office
Northern Michigan University
Marquette, Michigan

Dear Manager:

This letter is to introduce myself and offer my assistance at anytime during your coming visit to Michigan State University. My name is Geoff Hamilton, I am the student basketball manager and my telephone number is 355-8902. Please feel free to call me if you need some information or if you run into any problems. If you forget something you need, as I often do, let me know and I am sure we can provide a substitute or work it out.

If you will send me a list of your traveling squad, I will arrange with the Delft Theater to allow you and the team to attend a movie without charge while you are here. This theater is just off campus and within walking distance.

On game night, I will have a freshman manager available to assist you during the evening. He will remain with you throughout the game and I hope you will make full use of him. I realize it is next to impossible to get everything done yourself.

I trust you enjoy your stay at Michigan State and I am looking forward to meeting you and your team either at the airport or at the hotel.

Sincerely yours,

Basketball Manager

COACH'S NEWSLETTER. Nowadays, many departments in high schools and colleges present an annual report summing up their yearly activities. This is then placed in the mail for all interested parties. This same idea has been borrowed in athletics with the use of a newsletter. The following is one which is sent to all of our physical education alumni and coaches in the field.

Hi There:

We are in full swing again after the semester break and the campus is alive with students registering. The familiar groans can be heard about classes closing and the endless writing of your name, address, and telephone number. Our early reports would indicate that another record enrollment is in the making for the university.

Each year our physical education building becomes a little less adequate. However, we hope to remedy that with an addition to our building which will free our present varsity locker rooms for physical education activity classes. This would take care of 1,500 more students and ease the problem. Our new extension would include varsity rooms for all sports, a projection room, coaches' lounge, two small gymnasiums, and a large equipment room.

Our HPER enrollment is currently 150 members, with all of them belonging to the AAHPER and the Michigan HPER—which gives us 100 per cent participation from our group. Quite an interest!

Right beside our fieldhouse, a new two-and-one-half million dollar Fine and Practical Arts Building has been completed. Under construction is a beautiful Science building, so you can see we are undergoing pleasant growing pains.

Congratulations to Fred Boddy, Allan Dighera, and Fritz Wilson, all Northernites who enjoyed unusual success on the hardwoods. Al and Fritz lost state championships by a single point and by the same score—59–58! Fred's championship team claimed the Rudness Trophy, symbolic of basketball supremacy in the Upper Peninsula. Incidentally, in the Class C championship, Houghton lost to New Buffalo whose head coach is also a former Wildcat, Ron Morrison. Also to Gary Silc who is enjoying a fine year with the Allentown, Pennsylvania professional basketball club.

The 14th annual Michigan coaching school is set for August 8, 9, and 10. Headlining the staff will be John Kundla of Minnesota and Doug Weaver of Kansas State. Last year's attendance set a new record and we anticipate even more this year. Make your plans now!

Don't forget our Homecoming on October 27, and all the alumni gatherings which have been slated. Our opponents will be Central Michigan and the Chips are a perennial power on the gridiron.

The Women's Department is busy readying their dance recital and the WRA is sponsoring the event this year. Anybody for a cha-cha or twist contest?

Sincerely,

Basketball Coach

OUTLINE FOR A BASKETBALL DEMONSTRATION. Basketball demonstrations given by the coach, along with his squad, have met with fine approval in many sections of the country. The coach usually invites the public and holds the demonstration at night so that more people will have an opportunity to see it.

The squad runs through offensive and defensive fundamentals, drills, and welds the entire demonstration together with a scrimmage to conclude the session. The following outline may help the first year coach who is thinking of this type of promotion.

Offensive Fundamentals

1. Essential Drills
   (a) Reverses and stops.
   (b) Calisthenics (High jumper, Leg lifts, Fingertip push-ups).
   (c) Related Drills (Bench jumping, backward running, wall-tap drill).
   (d) Use entire squad and have them broken down for group work doing the above drills.
2. Individual Offensive Maneuvers
   (a) Set Shot.
   (b) Fake Shot and Drive.
   (c) Fake Drive and Shot.
   (d) Double Fake.
   (e) Crossover Step.
   (f) Rocker Step.
   (g) Jump Shot off Step.
   (h) Drill—use the best four men, demonstrating one-versus-one.
3. Pattern Shooting
   (a) Inside Screen.

    (b) Outside Screen.

    (c) Man Through.

    (d) Drop Pass.

    (e) Drill—use both ends of the court with squad evenly divided.

4. Offensive Continuity

    (a) 1-2 Cut with weak-side change explained.

    (b) Man-Through offense explained and demonstrated.

    (c) Drill—have two teams execute these moves at both ends of the court.

5. Fast-Break Drills

    (a) Five-Man weave using repeats.

    (b) Fast-Break shells explained and demonstrated.

    (c) Five-on-three fast-break drill.

    (d) Trailer situations explained and demonstrated.

    (e) Scramble drill run 10 minutes for the audience.

    (f) Split squad into groups to handle these various drills.

6. Press Offense

    (a) Explain theory and principles for audience.

    (b) Offense against the man-to-man press.

    (c) Offense against the zone press.

    (d) Alternate two teams using full court for demonstrations.

7. Zone Offense

    (a) Explain theory and principles of your attack.

    (b) Example of 1-3-1 offense against the zone.

    (c) Man-Through offense against the zone.

    (d) Box offense against the zone.

Defensive Fundamentals

1. Individual Fundamentals to Cover (Man-to-Man)

    (a) Stance.

    (b) Shuffle movement.

    (c) Baseline Concept.

    (d) Mass drill by all players (Hands Up).

2. Sliding Through

    (a) Explain workings of sliding-through process.

    (b) Man guarding the ball allows teammate to slide through.

    (c) Slide through aggressively and demonstrate this move.

    (d) Explain the quick adjustment to the ball which must take place.

    (e) Drills—two-versus-two, four-man weave with defense.

3. Defense Against the Inside Screen

    (a) Explain and demonstrate the key points.

    (b) Talk about playing in line with the screener and explain.

    (c) Fight over the top or slide through and show both moves.

    (d) The use of the voice in defense.

    (e) Drill—use four men with two-versus-two, utilizing the above.

4. Defense Against the Fast Break

    (a) Explain to audience the reasoning behind the break and why it must be stopped.

    (b) Demonstrate how to pressure the rebounder.

    (c) Demonstrate how to cut outlet passes.

    (d) Demonstrate defensive balance and the tandem defense to audience.

    (e) Have a five-man team with a defense as the drill to illustrate the above.

5. Zone Defenses

    (a) Explain why teams use the zone.

    (b) Deploy your team in a 1-3-1 zone and explain the advantages and disadvantages of it to the audience.

    (c) Move on to the other zones and do the same with them to enlighten the crowd.

6. Rebounding

    (a) Discuss the importance of the rebound.

    (b) Screening-out procedures clarified for the audience.

    (c) Jumping ability as related to rebounding.

    (d) Position and the role it has in rebounding.

    (e) Drills—four-versus-four, one-versus-one, and two-versus-two.

7. Conduct a Scrimmage Between Two Equally Divided Teams

    (a) Have registered officials for this contest.

    (b) Conduct it as a regular game.

If the coach is going to attempt this schedule, or a similar one, it will take approximately one hour and forty-five minutes to two hours. The key is to organize and run through this practice schedule prior to the scheduled night. You will have time to "iron out" any difficulties and you can orient your players on what they are to do. This can be a welcome addition to your basketball program and we are sure it will be met with enthusiasm should you attempt it.

HOW TO SURVIVE A BAD YEAR. All coaches hope that this will not be such a year for them, but this is often difficult to predict. As long as we have a winner in the game there will also be a loser, and losing, for some coaches, is very difficult. Should you have a poor won-lost record, it might be wise to do a little soul-searching.

An interesting clinic talk was recently presented by Bob Davis, Basketball Coach, at Georgetown College in Kentucky on this particular subject. Here is an outline of his talk:

1. Use valid tests to locate the reasons for the bad year. Don't guess. You should test for the following possible weaknesses:

    (a) Poor shooting

    (b) Poor rebounding

    (c) Poor ball-handling

    (d) Inadequate defense

    (e) Inexperience

    (f) Lack of effort

    (g) Lack of physical ability (height, weight, and agility)

    (h) You should question the use of the run-and-shoot offense, or the freedom offense.

2. Keep extremely accurate statistics and utilize their findings in organizing your master practice schedule.

3. Encourage each boy to improve in his specific area of strength. This is not a time to be a jack-of-all-trades player.

4. The practice schedule must double. *Hard work* is the only substitute for talent.

5. When talent is not available a team must play aggressive, rough-and-tumble basketball and not allow their opponents to play as they wish.

6. Give an award to the boys who do the following things most often in a game:

    (a) Hit the floor in an effort to recover a loose ball.

    (b) Draw the most step-in-front fouls.

7. Study game films with the squad members. Give elaborate hint sheets, scouting reports, articles concerning basketball, weight work, and chalk talks.

8. Have the squad members carry a basketball to class until they reach some goal that the coach has established for them. This is just another way to create interest in the game.

HOW TO ORGANIZE A HIGH SCHOOL AND COLLEGE TOURNAMENT. This phase of the game is included here because of the number of new members in the field each year who must hold a district, regional, sectional, or college tournament in their gymnasium and who have no idea of the work involved. The discussion is intended merely as a guidesheet on which coaches might expand, and is not intended to be meant for anything else. The type of tournament you run will reflect back in many ways, and the coach will thus want to do the best possible job.

Your first duty after knowing the teams which will participate in your tourney is to have several forms made up to answer many questions a tournament manager and coaches might have. One such form could be an information sheet for advance publicity and programs. This would include the name of the school, head coach, assistant coach, superintendent, principal, athletic director, managers, conference newspapers that cover the team, radio and television outlets, record of the team to date, school colors, school and coach's telephone numbers, and the school nickname. It is also advisable to include a section in which the team personnel can be listed as well as their numbers on both home and away game uniforms. It is always nice to acknowledge the cheerleaders in such a project, so don't neglect them. Advise the people competing that you must have this material returned promptly to necessitate meeting deadlines of your own.

Tournament Drawing. If you are sponsoring the tourney for the state high school association there are certain rules and regulations which must be observed. The tournament manager must accept these responsibilities when conducting such a tournament.

All participating teams should be invited to the drawing, or pre-game meeting, and they should be encouraged to send a representative if this is feasible. The time and place should be made known one week in advance by all competing teams. The meeting should always be conducted by the tournament manager so that he can tackle any problems which come up, such as practice schedules for the teams entered in the tournament.

Rules which might be decided upon after discussion at the drawing include:

1. The state tournament committee has stated that no noise-makers, pep bands, or derogatory signs are to be permitted at the tourney. Signs are welcome if put up with masking tape and removed after the contest.
2. The team on top of the pairing will wear the light jersey and will shoot at the West basket in the first half.
3. Practice schedules will be prepared by the tournament manager.
4. Remind the coaches when they are not participating that a reserved section has been set aside for them and they are to use these seats.
5. Free admittance to all games will be for coaches and participants only. This will include the cheerleaders—in uniform and numbering six only.
6. Parking space will be available in Lot A in front of the gymnasium for school cars and busses.
7. Assignment of locker rooms and a team host will be available to all teams the night they are to play.
8. All teams' expenses will be paid after completion of the tourney.
9. Equal distribution of tickets will be made to all schools. Please return to the main office all tickets which have not been sold one hour prior to your game.
10. After your game each coach should do one of the following:
    (a) Sign an expense voucher if you lost the game.
    (b) Pick up your tickets for the next contest.
11. On Saturday night at the conclusion of the tourney, the winners should remain on the floor for a short trophy presentation.
12. In the case of a high school tourney be sure to pick up your regional application as these forms must be in the mail Sunday morning.

Personnel and Instructions. This is the test of the tournament manager and the organization of his tournament. Knowing this we have set down the responsibilities of many of the people who will be helping run off this event. A clear-cut policy should involve all personnel, and a meeting with all the helpers before the tournament takes place is mandatory for complete success. The personnel should be aware of their assignment and made to recognize the importance of it.

Ticket Sellers—Manager: Sheree Lynn

DUTIES:

1. Pick up change and tickets from the main office an hour and a half prior to the first game. Change should include thirty dollars in half-dollars, twenty dollars in quarters, fifteen dollars in dimes, and ten dollars in nickels.
2. Record ticket numbers at the start of sale so that a proper checkout can be made.
3. Sell until the end of the first half of the second game.
4. Complete your game ticket report immediately following your checkout time.
5. Check out your report in its entirety with the principal.
6. Ticket booths will open as follows:

Wednesday, March 8	6:45 P.M.
Thursday, March 9	5:45 P.M.
Friday, March 10	5:45 P.M.
Saturday, March 11	5:45 P.M.

7. Ticket prices:

Students	40 cents
Adults	75 cents

Ticket Takers: Mr. Maki and Mr. Koskimaki

DUTIES:

1. Collect the entire ticket and see that assistant marks the hand of each spectator upon entering the gymnasium.
2. Be on duty at the following times and collect as long as the ticket office is open:

Wednesday	6:45 P.M.
Thursday	5:45 P.M.
Friday	5:45 P.M.
Saturday	5:45 P.M.

Ticket Takers—Student Assistants: Dunk Powell and Ralph Wagner

DUTIES:

1. Mark each spectator with a Cado marker as he enters the gymnasium.
2. Double-check the starting times to avoid being late.
3. Use of the marker will be as follows:

Wednesday—green Cado marker
Thursday—red Cado marker
Friday—blue Cado marker
Saturday—black Cado marker.

Players Entrance: Don Butcher

DUTIES:

1. Determine who is to be given complimentary admission.

2. Direct players and coaches to proper locker rooms.

3. Direct outside ticket men to Mr. Peters for ticket checkout.

Student Hosts: Merle Reel and Bill Laycock

DUTIES:

1. To assist Mr. Butcher in greeting players and coaches and see to their needs in the locker room and on the bench.

2. Check out towels for managers of these teams.

Outside Ticket Manager: Tom Peters

DUTIES:

1. Meet with visiting school representatives and check tickets and money they turn in.

2. Complete ticket report using the faculty lounge as your base of operation.

3. Turn in money, tickets, and report to the principal.

Official Announcer: Ron Brown

DUTIES:

1. Make pre-game announcements informing spectators that there is no smoking in the building.

2. Inform spectators that they must have a pass-out check if they plan to leave the building and return.

3. Inform spectators that there is to be no confetti thrown during any part of the game.

4. Make any emergency announcements.

5. Announce the lineups of both teams.

6. Following the game, call collect to the wire services for release of the scores.

7. On Saturday night, ask the winning coach and team to remain on the floor for the trophy presentation.

Official Scorer: Roy Bullock

DUTIES:

1. Keep an accurate and official scorebook.

2. The state will supply the scorebook and it is to be returned to the tournament manager after the last game.

3. Check scorebook with the opposing teams.

4. Assist Mr. Brown in calling in the results of the game. They might want information found only in the scorebook.

Student Ushers and Rope Men: Lowell Meier, Rod Fosdick, Darrell Wagner, and Neil Nystrom

DUTIES:

1. Help spectators find their seats.

2. Have the rope ready before halftime to keep people off the floor.

3. Maintain same procedure at the end of the game.

Parking and Security: Duane Stambaugh

   DUTIES:

     1. Keep available space for school buses and official cars.
     2. Maintain maximum inside control.
     3. Cooperate with the civil defense, who can be expected to assist us.

Programs: Max Seibel

   DUTIES:

     1. Hand out programs.
     2. Be on duty at the same time as the ticket takers.
     3. Assist in seating of spectators.

Custodians: Joe Kind and Ed Parent

   DUTIES:

     1. Have the clock set up and ready to go. (Conduct prior check.)
     2. Team signs should be taped to the clock.
     3. All bleachers pulled out and cleaned off.
     4. Scorers table set up.
     5. Rubber mats placed on the sides of the floor.
     6. All baskets raised.
     7. Railings placed on the end bleachers.
     8. Clean and recheck the rest rooms.
     9. Microphone set up and checked prior to the game.
    10. Thermostat set at 60 degrees for all games.
    11. Make sure the visiting locker rooms are open and clean.
    12. Sweep the gymnasium floor between halves of each game, as well as at the end of each game.
    13. Check all ceiling lights over the floor and replace if needed.
    14. Snow removal from entrance ways and walks if necessary.
    15. All outside lights and exit lights should be turned on.
    16. Glass backboards cleaned and the nets checked.
    17. Hall gates closed and locked.

Tournament Manager: Les Epperson

   DUTIES:

     1. Check all final preparations.
     2. Pay the officials after each game.
     3. Have losing coaches sign expense vouchers after the game.
     4. See that all results are called in to publicity media.
     5. Issue necessary number of tickets to the winners for next game.
     6. Wire regional managers of winners Saturday night.
     7. Give appropriate blanks to the winners.
     8. Assist in checkout of ticket money.
     9. Present the trophies and medals to the respective teams.
    10. Trouble-shoot during the game.

Tournament Manager—Student Assistant: John Mann

DUTIES:

1. Handle emergency errands for the manager.
2. Stay with the tournament manager at all times.

General Information:

1. The first-aid room will be set up in Classroom #3 and staffed with a doctor and two registered nurses.
2. The officials will use the physical education staff office as their headquarters.
3. A press room has been established in the school library for newspaper, radio, and television people. The coaches may also use this room. Cokes courtesy of Jones Bottling Company.
4. The participating teams will be:

Class C	Chenoa
	Pontiac
	Weston
	Ballard
Class D	Fairbury
	Cropsey
	Roanoke
	Flanagan
	Lexington

Assignment of Officials:

DATE	GAME TIME	CLASS	OFFICIALS	ADDRESS
3/8	7:30 P.M.	D	Duane Kennedy	517 E. Livingston
			George Mital	515 E. Livingston
3/9	7:00 P.M.	C	Mike Jackson	1303 N. 8th St.
			Sam Mindel	1301 N. 8th St.
	8:30 P.M.	C	Cecil Fosdick	203 Henry St.
			Gil Canale	97 Northrup St.
3/10	7:00 P.M.	D	Dave Blomquist	23 Stonegate Rd.
			Jay Downes	161 Pine St.
	8:30 P.M.	D	Roger Ehrhardt	905 Cedar St.
			Tony Couri	1980 Spruce St.
3/11	7:00 P.M.	D	Anthony Bell	999 Lincoln St.
			Jerry Jenkins	888 Jackson St.
	8:30 P.M.	C	Hudon Hudson	109 4th St.
			Georgie Gripper	1798 Park St.

This will, in part, give the reader some idea of what an organizational job lies ahead of him in undertaking the sponsorship of any type of tourney. This program is not complete by any means, but it is discussed because of the number of excellent tournaments we have witnessed in past years and is a tribute to these tournament managers throughout the country.

College Basketball Tournament. Although conducted in a similar manner, a college tournament will vary from a high school tournament. The differences being mainly the services provided and the financial arrangement involved.

For instance, the host school may provide transportation from the airport to the hotel, likewise to the gymnasium and fieldhouse prior to and following the game for any group requiring such service. The college teams might have their meals furnished by the host team and these arrangements must be considered. A coaches room with fruit and soft drinks is also provided by many schools.

A press party and banquet prior to the opening day is another feature many colleges arrange for their guests. This fosters a closer relationship between coaches, players, and officials for the ensuing tourney play.

The teams frequently are treated to sight-seeing tours, entertainment, and other courtesies extended by the host officials. This develops geographical knowledge of the area and is educationally enlightening for the visiting players and coaches.

Most college tournaments offer a guarantee to the teams entered to help defray their expenses. This might range from a flat guarantee to a proration of the gate receipts. An example of a financially successful college tournament is the University of Kentucky Invitation. It is possible for the participating teams to realize approximately $10,000 to $12,000 for their appearance in the two-day classic.

Index

253